W9-DFE-602

Keeping Literary Company

Keeping Literary Company

Working with Writers since the Sixties

Jerome Klinkowitz

State University of New York Press

Published by
State University of New York Press, Albany

For information, address State University of New York Press,
State University Plaza, Albany, N.Y. 12246

Production by M. R. Mulholland
Marketing by Dana E. Yanulavich

Library of Congress Cataloging-in-Publication Data

Klinkowitz, Jerome.
    Keeping literary company : working with writers since the sixties
/ Jerry Klinkowitz.
        p.   cm.
    Includes bibliographical references (p.   ) and index.
    ISBN 0-7914-3723-X (hc : alk. paper).

    1. Klinkowitz, Jerome—Friends and associates. 2. American
literature—20th century—History and criticism—Theory, etc.
3. Authors and readers—United States—History—20th century.
4. United States—Intellectual life—20th century. 5. Authors,
American—20th century—Biography. 6. Postmodernism (Literature)-
-United States. 7. Critics—United States—Biography. I. Title.
PS3561.L515Z469 1998
813'.5409—dc21   97-24765
                                                                              CIP

10 9 8 7 6 5 4 3 2 1

Contents

Preface

Can it be an accident that the literary disruptions so characteristic of American fiction during the 1960s and 1970s coincided with radical transitions and disruptions within the country's larger culture as well? That the two are connected has been suggested from the very start, in studies of Kurt Vonnegut, Jerzy Kosinski, Donald Barthelme, and others that were published scarcely before the ink of their own work was dry. Now, a generation later, it becomes clear that critics of the contemporary were responding no less to their own involvement in those changing times, with fiction itself being just one index to the turbulence being perceived on all fronts. If Heisenberg's Law, which cautions that the observer's presence is implicated in the results of whatever is being observed, can be said to pertain to literary studies at all, it is in scholarship of the contemporary that its results are most clear.

Keeping Literary Company is dedicated to exploring the literary history of such figures as Vonnegut, Kosinski, and Barthelme with these personal factors in mind. My own interest in contemporary American fiction began with the chance discovery of Kurt Vonnegut's work in 1966 as a welcome diversion from the traditional canon I was supposed to be studying as a graduate student. By 1970 I was teaching his fiction because its departure from that tradition corresponded with other departures so obvious around me: my first such class was conducted on a campus occupied by the Illinois National Guard and threatening to go the way of Kent State a few days before. By then our culture had taken a turn that merited the prefix "counter," and Kurt Vonnegut's work no longer seemed strange or so apart from the styles of academic life—for I was an academic myself, with my own life and the lives of those around me changing pell-mell. Back in 1962, in my first undergraduate literature course, I'd been taught that the world was best of all like a novel by Henry James or Robert Penn Warren, and for a while that image was sustained. But now it all seemed more like *Cat's Cradle*. Around me colleagues my own age were flying over the cuckoo's nest in order not to be caught in the catch-22 of conventional life; we read Kurt Vonnegut, taught him, and lived him, just as professors of our grandparents' and parents' generations had done with James and Warren. Making Vonnegut the subject of my own scholarship became a logical next step.

Teaching a living contemporary made for differences in such work. There were no previous studies, bibliographies, or biographies—all had to be done from scratch. Which was a good thing, because it bred a familiarity and confidence with all aspects of the subject: *Slaughterhouse-Five* made more sense after one had dug out all those short stories and transient reviews the author had done during his twenty-year apprenticeship to this first widely noticed novel.

But matters could be much more personal than this, as my students from a subsequent class taught me in 1971. That year we studied James Simon Kunen's *The Strawberry Statement*, an account of the Columbia University student disruptions whose New Journalism format shared many features with the fiction of Vonnegut. Kunen's book touched my students' lives personally—so personally that they asked one day if he could come to class. They had found him listed in the New York phone book and given him a call; then, using student government funds provided for a lecture series, they had booked him for an appearance at our school. Two weeks later I was picking him up at O'Hare and driving out to DeKalb with a James Taylor tape playing along the way. He mentioned that as teenagers he and Taylor had been friends when their parents summered on Cape Cod; another friend from those days was Mark Vonnegut, whose father wrote *Cat's Cradle* and *Slaughterhouse-Five*. A fourth friend, John Short, had written one of the first essays on Mark's old man in the Harvard *Crimson*. By the visit's end Kunen had agreed to write the foreword to the anthology I'd co-edit next year for Dell, *Innovative Fiction*. And so another involvement was underway.

My students' contact with Kunen prompted me to try the same approach with other writers, and soon I was in touch with a wide range of figures. What those authors did, within my scope of observation, is the subject of *Keeping Literary Company*. There would be formal interviews, but also informal correspondence and many meetings. I felt close to their work, seeing it evolve from year to year, often reading drafts. I would introduce one writer to another, and interesting exchanges would result; projects would develop, others would abort. Their literary lives evolved before me, and it is that aspect, the literary, I cover here. It did strike me how much literary capital they drew from their lives. For example, I could only wonder about Michael Stephens's personal struggles when reading his first novel, *Season at Coole* (1972); but almost twenty years later I could sympathize when he wrote a brilliant essay, virtually to order for my class that had been studying him, on his former days of alcoholism and family mayhem, a piece that appears in my anthology *Writing Baseball* (1991) under the typically contrary title, "Why I Hate Baseball." Between the two I had seen a literary life evolve, as I had for Vonnegut, Barthelme, Kosinski, and the others as well; and it is to these literary qualities that *Keeping Literary Company* is addressed.

For twenty-five years I have taught at the University of Northern Iowa, which has been the sole support for all my work, including a Professional Development Leave that made this book possible. Nearly all the writers discussed were visitors to Cedar Falls, where several made their own friends and developed their own reasons for returning. Heisenberg to the contrary, being part of the experiment has been, I hope, mutually profitable, for *Keeping Literary Company* is by that same law much more their story than mine.

1

Kurt Vonnegut

The first word of something new came from outside, well beyond the English major curriculum that had me fully occupied as a student. At Marquette I'd completed all my undergraduate work and had begun an M.A. as a teaching assistant. Having graduated in January, a semester early, I found myself in the odd circumstance of teaching quiz sections of the literature course some of my classmates in other majors had put off until the end, in a few cases making them my students, while among my colleagues were grad students as far along as their doctoral dissertations.

Thus empowered, I felt like quite an authority and was ready to field all questions. In class and out, literature in English was something I felt I could command. Yet one of the first collegial queries, from a TA in philosophy, had me stumped, even as I'd plunged halfway into a brashly confident answer.

"Who are some good contemporary writers?" my friend had asked, and as I began running down the list my training had provided I suddenly felt superannuated at the age of twenty-two.

"F. Scott Fitzgerald" was the first name I'd suggested, followed by Hemingway and Faulkner and a few words about T. S. Eliot's poetry. It was 1966, and Eliot had been dead less than a year, while Hemingway and Faulkner were still alive when I'd read them in high school. But the works I had in mind were from the 1920s—hardly contemporary, more than forty years later—and I could see my friend's face falling as I ticked off *The Sound and the Fury*, *In Our Time*, and other works I suddenly realized were the most recent books I knew.

Today I know that Fitzgerald, Hemingway, and Faulkner were the era's great canonical writers, those whose reputations were so soundly made that there could be no doubt but that *The Great Gatsby*, *The Sun Also Rises*, and *Absalom, Absalom!* would not be out of place in the same student bookcase as works by Dickens and Hardy or even Shakespeare and Milton. Yet to leave no room for literature in progress, for works created in and out of our own day, suddenly seemed a disappointment, if only because of the embarrassment felt at being unable to recommend a current book. But at least the reason why was clear.

That well-ordered bookcase from which I'd drawn my sadly outdated examples owed its existence not to any effort at dealing with our present moment but to having the bookcase itself neatly filled. Leaving room for contemporary authors would mess things up, with acknowledged classics falling out of line as they tumbled into the gaps left for newer works. This would devalue the system itself, a system meant to guarantee authenticity rather than spark speculation. Its beauty fit right into the mannered world of Marquette's English department, from chairman Jerome Archer, who dressed in Harris tweeds and walked a matched pair of Borzoi hounds across campus, to the distinguished scholar John Pick, appointed even more debonairly, changing his watchband each day to match his bow tie. Each month there would be a department meeting to which we TAs were invited; after a perfunctory half hour of business the faculty would adjourn to the lounge, where several bottles of sherry set the tone for a most civilized social gathering. Like the canonical bookcase, all was orderly and fine, a rewardingly livable system into which one could buy at the cost of letting one's interest close with a generation of writers flourishing nearly half a century before.

Thus the news of current fiction was from another quarter altogether, outside the English department and beyond the style of careerist respectability that characterized the university at large. The news was "Kurt Vonnegut," and word came from a philosophy TA: Bob Tatalovich, who was presently distinguishing himself from the modes of acceptable behavior by satirically deriding everything about his graduate student's life.

"Fools and incompetents!" he would rage, in easy earshot of the professors who controlled his fate. "Utterly ridiculous!" he'd exclaim when reviewing some new requirement. Needless to say, his status in the graduate program was uncertain, while any future in the profession would depend more upon luck and his own talents than any blessing he'd be taking with him from Marquette. Yet unlike his colleagues in English, Bob was up on current writers, and when he recommended Vonnegut as the best of them it was hard not to listen.

Would this new writer's attitude be like Bob's own? He promised that I'd find Kurt Vonnegut funny—also irreverent and disarmingly brash. He ran some scenes from *The Sirens of Titan* past me, such as the series of messages the Tralfamadorians spell out on Earth so that their stranded flying saucer pilot looking on from a moon of Saturn will know help is coming. The first message this pilot reads is that a replacement part is on its way; the text itself is conveyed in the form of Stonehenge. Four subsequent communiqués are eventually written out: that the pilot should be patient, he hasn't been forgotten (the Great Wall of China); that the supply depot is doing the best it can (the Golden House of the Emperor Nero); that he will be on his way before he knows it (the first walls of the Moscow Kremlin); and the advice to pack up and be ready to leave on a moment's notice (the Palace of the League of Nations). Bob's roisterous laughter at these lines was in the manner of what he presumed to be their sick humor. For him, Vonnegut was a kindred soul to be deriding the foolishness and incompetency of human effort, and was uncommonly successful at deflating all pretensions to both authority and seriousness. Consider the canonical importance of those weighty human artifacts, their monumental stature in the history of our civilization—and then see how those pitifully banal statements that follow not only destroy their seriousness but deconstruct their purpose. Take Lincoln's "Gettysburg Address" and read it in the speaking voice of Donald Duck, or give the job of announcing the most solemn pronouncements from Moses or Zarathustra to Laurel and Hardy. Bob Tatalovich would laugh just as hard, making apparent what type of canon he had in mind for the enshrinement of Kurt Vonnegut's work.

As I followed Bob's advice and sought out Vonnegut on the paperback racks, the writing I found confirmed my suspicions that here would be found healthy doses of irony and irreverence. The first novel I read was *Mother Night* in the library's new hardcover edition, prefaced by Vonnegut from the University of Iowa, and it took great delight in spoofing canonical texts, much as I had imagined. Here "The Gettysburg Address" is read not by Donald Duck but by Adolf Hitler, another cartoon character from our storehouse of anxieties, who is brought to tears by Lincoln's sentiments. Are those sentiments then to be mistrusted? No more than Hitler is to be trusted for loving them. Rather, both are now seen in a new light, from a fresh angle that by its startling defamiliarity sharpens our attention all the more.

But what an angle to be coming from, an angle sufficiently oblique to make for great comic interest by itself. It was in this spirit that I read all the Vonnegut I could find, including the dark sarcasm of *God Bless You, Mr. Rosewater* and the teleological slapstick of *Cat's Cradle*. Both were relatively recent works. It was still early in 1966, and there was as yet no *Slaughterhouse-Five* to anchor all these sentiments and techniques. Nor was there the overwhelming cultural disruption and transformation that was to characterize the much hotter years with which the decade made its explosive conclusion, years that would find *Slaughterhouse-Five* such a necessary work but also cast its author as a more serious figure.

What made Kurt Vonnegut so appealing in 1966 was his brilliance at surviving and even flourishing at the margins—at making that marginality the substance of his work and the essence of his vision. Unlike the professor-poets and philosopher-novelists my teachers at Marquette espoused, Vonnegut was not part of the academic crowd. We'd recently hosted readings by W. H. Auden and Saul Bellow, but here was an author who, if he had to list influences, would not count off generations of writers but the great radio and film comedians of the 1930s. And unlike Bellow, who'd published fiction in *Partisan Review*, Vonnegut's short stories were placed no higher than in such popular family magazines as *Collier's* and *The Saturday Evening Post*.

Which was fitting, as his fiction was made from just such materials. Looking back on those years, Vonnegut now recalls that his role as a short-story writer for these journals had much in common with that of the cartoonists whose work also appeared there: he was constantly on the lookout for generative ideas, and those ideas would come from the same popular culture these magazines served. In the 1950s it seemed an ideal system, a perpetual motion machine that alternately fed on material from its own pop context and codified that culture in return. For my part, I loved it, because it was the world in which I'd grown up, seeing these magazines on my parents' coffee table and watching the whole style unfold around me on television and in the daily adventures that formed our middle-class lifestyle, all of which seemed a planet apart from the concerns of the English department at Marquette.

Vonnegut's career made for a virtual checklist of noncanonicity. He'd been a science student, learning how to write not from his English teachers but by being managing editor of both his high-school and college newspapers while working part time writing ad copy for prep clothing at the local department store. Afterwards, he'd put off university teaching until age forty-four, having written his first five novels and almost all his short stories while living as a fellow citizen among the business- and tradespersons of small town Massachusetts. Several of these novels had been paperback originals and were marketed within the decidedly nonacademic subgenres of science fiction and intrigue, while Vonnegut's magazine sales were to that equally lowbrow market called "the slicks." Even when he did resort to teaching—after the family weeklies died and the monthlies had ceased publishing much fiction—it was teaching on the margins: not in the English department but on that fringe known as creative writing, where the degree involved was not the standard M.A. or Ph.D. but the still questionable Master of Fine Arts, the M.F.A. diploma that found its only recognition back on the same margins of university life, for teaching creative writing to future M.F.A. graduates. Plus Vonnegut's writing lacked the ponderous probity of canonical literature, its wisecracks and irreverencies shaped within the minimalistic abruptness of pop humor.

At Marquette, the only person likely to appreciate Kurt Vonnegut's work was Bob Tatalovich, and in Bob's case it was because of Vonnegut's superficially black humor and wickedly funny iconoclasm. But the farther away from school I carried these novels, the more receptive I found people to be towards them. At the time, I was earning extra cash playing baritone sax in a rhythm and blues band. Junior & the Classics was a group of young but solid professionals who'd chosen work over college, though all the guys were thoughtful and intelligent. From his keyboard where he also sang and directed the band, Junior Brantley would call out our parts in proper musical terminology, instantly transposing keys for Kent Ivey's tenor sax and my bari. Kent was an Army vet with some junior college, while drummer Victor Pitts was the son of a prominent black businessman who owned a chain of car washes around town. Because I'd bring along books to read during breaks, Junior and the other musicians would be asking me about them. Over the year they found T. S. Eliot "obscure" and Ezra Pound "crazy," but a chapter from *Cat's Cradle* would have them in stitches.

The realization that Vonnegut's appeal might well be universal came during a break when one of our employers paused to sample my reading. Most of our gigs were at downtown clubs owned by a reputed gangster who had his henchman "Little Frankie" ride herd on us. I'd suffered silently through his patriotic speech about avoiding appeasement in Vietnam after he'd seen me reading A. J. P. Taylor's *The Origins of the Second World War*, but was able to laugh happily along as he chuckled through Vonnegut's description of the weasel-like attorney Norman Mushari in *God Bless You, Mr. Rosewater*. Little Frankie kept remarking what a bitterly accurate characterization it was of the profession, and when he got to Vonnegut's admission that Mushari "had an enormous ass, which was luminous when bare," Frankie laughed so hard as to dislodge the revolver from his shoulder holster which thankfully didn't fire as it clattered to the floor.

At school I was making my way dutifully through seminars on Chaucer, Shakespeare, and Milton, with other courses on Victorian prose writers, modern British poets, and the like. Not until my last semester did I add a couple classes in American literature, and then turned back to British poetry for an M.A. paper on Wilfred Owen. The twentieth-century novel course I took ended with Hemingway from the 1920s and works by Faulkner and Fitzgerald from the 1930s. That I stayed with Vonnegut through all this showed both that I could read out of class and that novels like *Player Piano*, *The Sirens of Titan*, and *Cat's Cradle*, which I bought as they came back into print, were a world apart from what Marquette taught me was the tradition.

At Wisconsin, where I began doctoral work in 1967, Vonnegut was even more out of the question. The department did venture much farther into the contemporary than Marquette ever dared, but in a direction I found decidedly unappealing. In my undergraduate and master's courses on the modernists I'd been dismayed at their willful obscurantism; and now, in the current writers the profs at Madison favored, I was even more put off by the eggheaded density and humorless pedantry of those for whom one needed specialized training to appreciate. Taking a look at John Barth, in print and in person, I could not share the delight in his fabulative mythology; and reading Thomas Pynchon, the other great Wisconsin favorite, left me soundly resentful. And so, while the English department and its journal, *Contemporary Literature*, pursued a style of literature consonant with the heady theorism of Pound, I read a few more books by writers I guessed to be in Vonnegut's style: Terry Southern, Bruce Jay Friedman, and Hughes

Rudd. In the meantime, Southern had turned to the movies while Rudd became a newsman and raconteur for CBS Television, and it was in this popular realm, rather than in the ethereal atmosphere of the university, that I continued to place Vonnegut.

Yet by the time I finished my doctorate—in record time, just two years later—Vonnegut and the others had been almost forgotten. I do recall seeing the hardcover of *Welcome to the Monkey House* in a bookstore and felt happy that Vonnegut might be making his way back into commercial respectability (after all those brilliantly written but shabbily packaged paperbacks), but in the meantime I'd been seduced by the classic beauty of nineteenth-century American literature, especially by the writers of that golden age known as the American Renaissance. Here was order and clarity with no need for philosophic intricacies and intellectual pyrotechnics. Hawthorne could be dark and even ambiguous, but never obscure. And as taught by Harry Hayden Clark, that kindly and elegant gentleman who had helped found the field over forty years ago, works like *The House of the Seven Gables* and *Twice-Told Tales* stayed ripe for analysis and appreciation even in the disturbed new world of 1968 and 1969.

With a dissertation on the problematic ending to *The House of the Seven Gables* I took a job as assistant professor at Northern Illinois University, where a rapidly expanding program in English on all three degree levels put no less than two dozen of us freshly hired Ph.D.'s to work in advanced courses. I taught two sections of a course on realism and naturalism that fall, and was anticipating a spring seminar on Hawthorne and Melville when an enrollment crush in the twentieth-century American novel course caused me, as the most junior Americanist on the faculty, to be drafted into teaching it, even though it fell outside my specialization and was the area I'd failed first time on my doctoral comprehensives.

Putting together the first three-quarters of the course was no problem, but in resolving not to replicate Marquette's practice at closing off consideration at nearly half a century, I found myself in a dilemma: the only current academically serious novelists I knew were those so highly touted at Wisconsin, those geniuses of obfuscation and soul-killing technicalism that I swore I'd never force upon students as representing the literature of their time. That last summer in Madison I'd audited John Lyons's course on contemporary fiction and had filled a big gap by reading Updike, Bellow, and

Malamud—a book or two by them would take me a couple decades beyond Fitzgerald, Hemingway, and Faulkner (with whom I would begin rather than end). But what of the 1960s? What were the students themselves reading?

Less than six months ago *I'd* been a student, and only a few years before had been enjoying Kurt Vonnegut's novels. His work was still current, for I'd seen *Welcome to the Monkey House* on the shelves back in Madison. But imagine my surprise when I asked around and learned that his string of paperback reprints, the beginning of which I'd navigated back in 1966, had now swelled to include all his novels and a book of short stories as well, and that both college students and the counterculture at large had claimed him as their own. Plus Vonnegut's fame was advancing on a second front, among the middle-class readers whose purchases made their mark on the national bestseller lists. Here his latest novel, *Slaughterhouse-Five*, had made its impact last spring (when I'd been failing my comps!). Vonnegut himself was everywhere, as a lead news item in *Time* for his campus speeches, as an outspoken essayist in magazines from *Life* to *Esquire*, and as the most frequently and extensively interviewed novelist since Hemingway. Here was the author to conclude my course on just the level of currency and pertinence I found so lacking at both Marquette and Wisconsin. Plus there was the added benefit that I'd loved reading him myself and could, with quick and happy trips through *Welcome to the Monkey House* and *Slaughterhouse-Five*, know that I'd covered his full range of work so far.

But, beyond all of this, what a time to be teaching Vonnegut! Getting the assignment in fall of 1969 and fulfilling it in spring 1970 made for unique intersections with both literary and social history. True, Vonnegut was now a world-famous author; but I had known his work beforehand, and was one of a relatively few other critics who'd been able to read *Mother Night, Cat's Cradle*, and the other early novels completely innocent of knowledge of what *Slaughterhouse-Five* would bring to the structure of his career. It is now a critical commonplace that Vonnegut's writing of this novel was the culmination of previous themes and techniques, specifically the destruction of Dresden and the ability to articulate it in print, which in this case meant talking candidly about his own difficulties with the project and how it eclipsed the limits of both memory and voice. Thus all his other novels could now be read—could not really escape being read—as thematic feints at the topic of unimaginable destruction, with subthemes regarding technique as well as experimentation with different modes of narrative expression. Little by little he'd been incorporating himself as a factor in the text, from the tombstone meant to bear his own family name in *Cat's Cradle* and the abundance of back-home Indiana lore in *God Bless You, Mr. Rosewater* to the personally implicating preface to *Mother Night* signed from Iowa City. Now with *Slaughterhouse-Five* Vonnegut had finally perfected each stream, finding a repetitive, cross-narrational device to handle the temporal and spatial difficulties in acknowledging overwhelmingly rampant death, plus making himself and his act of writing part of the narrative action in those remarkable opening and closing chapters. From here his art would grow in scope and technical daring, as with successive works the real Kurt Vonnegut would take on increasing prominence both in his fictive narratives and public commentaries on issues of the day. Thus as a critic I was in just the right place at the right time, renewing my acquaintance with Vonnegut's works to see how they had grown to this key point and to appreciate the technical logic in all that would follow.

Yet there was even more, for as a college teacher at the end of the American 1960s, when the protest of a war half a world away brought military violence and eventually death to the campuses themselves, I could see Vonnegut's special readership facing not just the fulfillment of his vision in *Slaughterhouse-Five* but the confirmation of their own view in both his account of Dresden and their experience of Kent State. We would read Vonnegut's Dresden story with the knowledge of what he'd said about the bombing in the preface to the second edition of *Mother Night* written on a university campus not that far from ours, and which was now experiencing its own violence. Will his texts ever be studied again while soldiers in battle gear occupy schools and fight a style of antiguerrilla warfare with tear gas and bullets? One hopes not, just as Vonnegut hoped never to see another firebombing. That "only" four died in Ohio is not the issue, any more than the Dresden story depends on casualty counts of 250,000 (the highest estimate) as opposed to 75,000 (the lowest figure considered). Nor is the issue simply death. Rather, what's shocking is death where it is least expected.

Despite having this focus, I still found myself in Vonnegut's own position when poised to explain the meaning of Dresden:

speechless. *Mother Night* just didn't conform to the patterns established in the novels we'd studied previously. There was always something in Updike's work, for example, that I could relate back to Fitzgerald's, such as their common mannerist techniques, and philosophically Bellow could be talked about in some of the terms we'd used for Faulkner. But what was there to say of the vision and technique of *Mother Night*? I could see now why Marquette had closed things down as early as they did, and why the profs at Wisconsin welcomed only writers conversant in the lofty tones of high modernism.

Because Vonnegut's works followed none of these models, not even to revolt against them, a new style of discourse would be needed on the critical side of this dialogue as well. Late into the night before class I still could not find a handle on the book other than such aleatory expedients as having each student pick a line from the novel and read it in unison, hoping that some order might be fortuitously revealed.

It was this thought that made me suspect Vonnegut was doing something of the same in *Mother Night*: giving up on rational explanations for the world Dresden had provided and taking random, seemingly unconnected little shots at it instead. By allowing them to be apparently diverse, however, he was giving his shots a chance to hit targets beyond the range of reason's inhibitions. Now that they had been taken, however, was there a new structure to be revealed? There was, and to my great delight it was a pattern not indicative of a hidden rationality but of something new altogether, something that deconstructed naturalized assumptions in order to create a radically new understanding of what our age had become.

Consider the conventional approach to what *Mother Night*'s preface calls "the Nazi monkey business." It follows neither the weighty seriousness of William L. Shirer's *The Rise and Fall of the Third Reich* or the cartoonlike reductionism of so many popular accounts of German atrocities, but rather pictures Hitler and his colleagues in a way we've never seen them, yet in a way they most surely were: at work and at play in the normal business of quotidian life. In a day when the Adolf Eichmann trial was exposing the banality of evil, Vonnegut went much farther capturing such top Nazis as Goebbels and Heydrich at humdrum pursuits including theatergoing and an intramural ping-pong tournament. Even in the aftermath of evil, Eichmann turns his own banality into a revealing style of commentary, finding his prisonmate deficient in murdering enough of the six million and offering to lend him "a few hundred thousand" to enhance his stature.

Throughout the novel are other such surprising touches: Goebbels admiring the propaganda artistry of Lincoln's "Gettysburg Address," a former colleague turning up in Ireland as a gardener, and an Israeli prison guard boasting "what a fine Nazi" he made as a spy. Yet as wickedly funny as these jokes were, they served as more than one-liners peppered through the narrative for shock effect. That was the style of Terry Southern and others whose effect was more strictly limited to "black humor," a category once thought to contain Kurt Vonnegut. What made the little twists and turns in *Mother Night* significant was that they formed a pattern—not a glaringly obvious one, and even working subliminally at times—that subtly dismantled our previous assumptions about everyone's role in World War II.

Consider the joke about "The Gettysburg Address." It is ironic that Goebbels admires its genius as propaganda. But it is disconcerting when it makes a second appearance as the speech whose emotive powers bring Adolf Hitler to tears. Yet even here Vonnegut is not done, for only half of our most trusted assumptions—those about the Nazis—have been deconstructed. What about the American side, the home of Lincoln's hallowed sentiments? Here we find Franklin D. Roosevelt, Lincoln's successor and the spokesman of morally enabling sentiments himself, laughing with glee over Howard Campbell's grossly anti-Semitic broadcasts—indeed, qualifying as their greatest fan, just as Lincoln's greatest fan is Hitler. There is a reversal at work here, of course. But beyond the conventional structure of comedy is the fact that Vonnegut has set the tension for these punchlines with a third element: Goebbels's first appreciation of the great president's most famous speech, the irony of which has defamiliarized it and roused the reader's attention for the more transformative surprises that follow.

Such disruptions happen frequently enough to provide a structure for the novel, a series of triplets whose 1-2-3 punch keeps the reader continually off balance as anything likely to be taken for granted quickly changes form. Is it cruel that Campbell steals his friend's motorcycle to escape Berlin? No, because the friend escapes the war himself to become a gardener in Ireland. But even here there is a third surprising stage that takes us back to the beginning for a complete restructuring, for as the action concludes it turns out that the friend has been an anti-German agent all along and is now ready to help indict Campbell for his war crimes. Hardly any person, place, or thing escapes this rebounding confusion of identities and values. Even the judgmental noose with which Campbell is confronted serves secondary and tertiary purposes: discarded, it is taken by a garbageman who hangs himself, despondent not for any usual reason but because his cure for cancer has gone unheeded.

All of this restructuring serves a purpose, convincing both Howard Campbell and the reader that Campbell may well be falsely accused but that he is not ultimately innocent. Thus his death at the novel's conclusion is not at the hands of the Israeli court for crimes against humanity, but by his own hand for crimes against himself. Like the world around him, he has let his own identity—and his integrity—be corrupted by the convenient schizophrenia that lets people do as they please while feeling secure that a very good self remains hidden inside. "We are that we pretend to be," Campbell has learned, and finding a structure for resolving that pretense after systematically deconstructing the assumptions allowing such fakery to pass as fact has been Vonnegut's main achievement in *Mother Night*.

Teaching *Mother Night* in the context of Kent State and our own disruptions was an adventure. Trigger-happy Illinois National Guardsmen were on campus, and each night state police in tactical gear patrolled the streets, inhibiting any student violence but menacing passersby as well. From one class to the next we wondered if any of us might fall to clubs as had happened at Wisconsin or to bullets as in Ohio. Neither happened—there was a sit-in on the bridge where traffic was blocked on US 30, the Lincoln Highway of folksong fame; but the school's president defused tensions on both sides by joining the demonstration, and DeKalb escaped the semester without serious troubles.

Yet students across the country had seen values restructured, and they formed a natural, understanding readership for Kurt Vonnegut's novels. There they found not meaninglessness, and not the nihilism or even bitter self-destructive irony older critics feared. *Mother Night*, *Cat's Cradle*, and his other works did not destroy but rather deconstructed, with an emphasis not on obliteration but on revealing the nature of the structure that was there. And even that act of deconstruction was just a phase, a needed preliminary to the reconstruction of a world undertaken this time with a clear view of the artifice and imaginative empowering underway.

Having deconstructed, with my students, some of the assumptions that had built the American literary canon, it seemed appropriate to undertake a similar task with regard to the profession of such works. Thanks to its recent mass hirings of radical young Ph.D.'s and its recruitment of an equally young group of instructors, M.A. graduates from around the country who could teach the huge numbers of general education students while dabbling in Northern Illinois's doctoral program (which hoped to seduce them as eventual grad students and turn them back into TAs), the department was alive with dialogue and debate, especially among this younger crowd who felt so excluded and estranged from the fat-cat professorate that by virtue of their seniority ran the place. As opposed to these elders, whose taste was settled and whose curriculum was virtually petrified, we assistant professors and instructors were not only reading new works but were struggling to incorporate them in both our value system and our teaching. Bookshelves in our offices and at home would be speckled with the same colors, including the blue Dell paperback of Heller's *Catch-22*, the orange of *Cat's Cradle*, and the wild heliotrope of Ken Kesey's *One Flew Over the Cuckoo's Nest*. These works were taught as well, which meant taking a chance, for there were few critical resources from which we could draw ideas or to which we could direct students. Therefore, as eager to publish as we were, the idea occurred to leave off from rehashing our dissertations or old seminar papers into submittable essays (with which I'd scored already on Hawthorne, Howells, and Faulkner) and undertake some criticism and scholarship on these new writers for whom the field was almost completely open.

It was this aim that brought me to John Somer, one of the still young but more experienced instructors who'd published four introductory textbooks on fiction, poetry, drama, and composition. John was on his way toward opting for a doctorate, with which he'd return to Emporia State and a professor's career. Now, however, he was exuberantly aswim in the lively currents of freshman lit and the joys of campus life. With his wife and daughter he shared a pleasant house near school, large enough for parties where the instructors, grad students, and new assistant profs could band together as a nation apart from the older folks who still seemed like *our* professors back in our undergrad and graduate programs. Any sense of exclusion from the grown-ups' world was more than compensated for by the camaraderie we shared. The most important quality of this kinship was not just that it derived from tastes in literature and styles of teaching but that it extended right in line to values of lifestyle. We not only read and taught Vonnegut but lived him, and what a difference that made! Leaving one of the stuffily awkward receptions hosted by a senior prof, one had the clear impression that the time had been spent among readers of Philip Wylie and Robert Penn Warren. Dropping by John's house, where at midnight the party was just approaching a full tilt that would careen on 'til three or four in the morning, it felt like walking into Vonnegut's text, for here all the rigid pretentions and outdated professorial styles were kept far away by the cheap wine and rock and roll.

It was from this atmosphere that our first idea for publishing something derived. It was just before Christmas break, and everyone was feeling especially loose and free. The senior professors let their liberated fancies take wing in a night of carolling and eggnog at one of their homes where those younger colleagues privileged with an invitation roasted in their mandatory tweed jackets and wool ties and yet were chilled by the fear of placing a drink where it didn't belong (and nobody seemed to be having more than one). My wife and I managed to escape this torture by eleven, and after stopping home to check with the baby sitter and her boyfriend, who'd made the funkier atmosphere of our house a natural place for their evening of candles, incense, and some of our rock music on the stereo—I think it was Paul Butterfield's rendition of "One More Heartache" blasting away while our little son and daughter slept upstairs that made me so grateful for having escaped the phony seasonality of those awkward songs at the reception—we headed over to the friendly ambience at John Somer's. Here similar music was in the air, an air filled with immensely more animation than where we'd been forced to spend the evening's first hours. I poured myself what seemed to be a canning jar of Chianti, and while my wife sought out some friends I fell into talk with the host himself.

At the time, I didn't think much of it, because John and I would get into conversations like this almost anywhere and at any time. Our topic was a common, workmanlike one, mere shoptalk between two toilers in the world of innovative fiction: how one of the newest writers we'd happened on, Ronald Sukenick, was more complicated and at times much harder to read than was Vonnegut, but that if one had spent some time playing with Vonnegut's devices in *Mother Night* and *Cat's Cradle* a novel such as Sukenick's *Up* could be seen to follow naturally (if a bit more deeply). If a course could start, rather than end, with Vonnegut, we decided, a writer like Sukenick would become a lot more accessible.

But for there to be a course, I argued, there'd have to be critical materials and a text. With my last words John cracked a smile, and I realized we were in business. As a veteran of the process, he'd lead us through. A student would be teaching a professor, but that fit the style of inversion and disruption we were seeing in everything else regarding this new field. The plan would be a simple one, reflecting our own necessarily inductive method in encountering this strange new literature and exploring our way through it. The easiest and most appealing fiction had been the comic variety—indeed, the initial promptings for fracturing so many old conventions had been for the sake of humor, and John agreed that the most promising way to approach both naive students and skeptical professors would be with a laugh rather than a challenge.

Our own laughter filled the rest of that night, during which I assumed the plans for a critical anthology were being set aside. But next morning at ten John was on the phone, asking if I could pick some stories, assemble some notes for an introduction, and meet him that afternoon to put our thoughts together.

The stories were no problem, and from their range came both the table of contents and a rationale for introducing it. As agreed at the party, we'd begin simply and with humor, and from there proceed to more complex effects. Vonnegut would be at the start, followed by a similar story by Hughes Rudd, "Miss Euayla is the Sweetest *Thang!*" which set the terms for this new style of fiction: vocal, dramatic, and disruptive of both the usual expectations and the conventions that expressed them. Vonnegut's "The Hyannis Port Story" would establish a mode of fabulative critique by means of self-conscious signs, semiotically (we'd learn much later) systematic enough to satisfy the most committed deconstructionist, yet sufficiently obvious to appear as a billboard (an actual billboard, the strobe-lit display of Barry Goldwater's face that glares across the property line into the Kennedy compound). Then Hughes Rudd would unleash the comedy of a benighted character living his entire life within just such a self-generated semiosis. From there we'd move on to more complicated effects, but the tone of humorous disruption would underlie it all.

John and I met that afternoon with a pile of books and played with various ways of stacking them until we had a satisfactory structure for our table of contents balanced on his study desk. Then we decided what needed to be said in an introduction and divided it between us, starting from Ronald Sukenick's requiem for traditional fiction that begins, in mock-critical fashion, his aptly titled novella, "The Death of the Novel." That evening we worked separately for a couple hours each, producing a total of twenty pages that after another few hours the next morning melded together quite easily. With the title *Innovative Fiction: Stories for the Seventies*, we sent it off to Sukenick's editor at Dell, who accepted it on what must have been the same day it arrived.

By the time our book appeared, I'd left DeKalb for the University of Northern Iowa in Cedar Falls, but there were still two projects to be done in the interim. Flushed with our luck at selling *Innovative Fiction*, John and I—a few parties later—struck on the idea of doing something on Kurt Vonnegut. Again the book was born of give and take, drawing its power from the exchanges between us and then amplified by the roles we shared with several contributors.

As a critical subject, Vonnegut's work was just too new, too diverse, and too unorganized to allow any single critic's view to function comprehensively. His antecedents and place in the tradition were not yet clear. Indeed, from a political point of view, he was being claimed by both the radical left and the extreme right, as the story "Harrison Bergeron," crafted for the 1950s science fiction movement, became a favorite of the earth-shoes and granola set even as it was reprinted in William F. Buckley's conservative journal, *National Review*. Was the author a sassy black-humorist like Terry Southern, a comic fabulator in the manner of John Hawkes, a cynical commentator along the lines of J. P. Donleavy, or even a SF specialist sharing company with Theodore Sturgeon and Harlan Ellison? With only the slightest critical attention, Vonnegut's reputation could be taken in just about any direction, and the few critics who had treated his work—Conrad Knickerbocker, Robert

Scholes, C. D. B. Bryan, and Leslie Fiedler—seemed willing to lead Vonnegut down one path only and among the exclusive company of its particular travelers. For the body of work John and I had in mind, we'd need a broader view, studying not just individual facets and dispositions but considering what such features shared in common. Plus there was the background work in bibliography, literary history, and the context of popular culture. And so we divided the work among a dozen contributors, including ourselves and even, by means of an interview done by Bob Scholes, Kurt Vonnegut himself.

We had science-fiction buffs, popular-culture authorities, bibliographers, literary critics adept in everything from mythology to social manners, and folks who'd known Vonnegut as a mentor and colleague. As we wrote, we avoided temptations to overstress our own lines by exchanging views among ourselves. As editors, John and I followed clues in Vonnegut's work itself, finding out about his association with Bob Scholes from the preface to *Welcome to the Monkey House* and learning from his review of *Going All the Way* that novelist Dan Wakefield would be a pretty good source for understanding how important was the Indiana background and all those commercial sales throughout the 1950s, a region and period Dan was treating in his own fiction. Getting Wakefield in the group proved the key to publication, for he suggested his own and Vonnegut's publisher, Seymour Lawrence, who had a line with Delacorte Press. As Ron Sukenick had provided an entry point with Richard Huett at Dell, now Dan's name served as an attention-getting opener in our letter to Seymour Lawrence, who accepted the book as a hardcover and arranged for simultaneous issue as a Delta paperback. Received more as cultural anthropology than as scholarship, *The Vonnegut Statement* won good prepublication reviews in the trade journals and was covered by *Time*, *The New York Review of Books*, and even the *Times Literary Supplement* in London. Extra printings were ordered and the initial royalty check was as good as a half year's assistant-professor salary. But by then I was an associate professor—at the University of Northern Iowa—and enjoying a new style of life, not the least of which would include friendship with the man himself, Kurt Vonnegut.

Cedar Falls, it turned out, was part of Vonnegut's fanciful back yard. His two years in Iowa City had been a happy time, more rewarding than the years immediately previous when he'd struggled with a deteriorating magazine market and seen his novels virtually ignored. At the University of Iowa he had a steady paycheck for the first time in fifteen years, and was introduced to the company of others as committed to writing as he was. The state's generosity in supporting such arts encouraged and charmed him. His students were eager and bright, and among them he found some friends for life. One of them graduated with her M.F.A. degree and took a job at the University of Northern Iowa, where in 1972 I moved into the office next door.

Loree Rackstraw had taken Kurt's fiction-writing course in 1965–1966. While he remained in Iowa City for a second year, Loree's professorship at the University of Northern Iowa just one hundred miles away let them keep in touch. In spring of 1967 he visited UNI, speaking to a tiny but interested audience in one of the English department's classrooms; ten years later he'd return to address a standing-room-only crowd of two thousand packed into the same building's auditorium. By 1977, of course, he was the world-famous author of *Slaughterhouse-Five* and several other best sellers, but even then he felt a special fondness for this state that had not only made him happy and secure but had served as the turning point in his career—he had rolled into town broke, dejected, and with few prospects of continuing a self-supported writer's career, but had left with a Guggenheim grant and a contract to write *Slaughterhouse-Five*.

As with Bob Tatalovich at Marquette and John Somer at Northern Illinois, Loree Rackstraw confirmed that I was being blessed with a succession of resourceful and generous colleagues. We shared more than just Vonnegut's books in common, for we'd each begun reading them in 1966—years before the fame and notoriety and other distractions. To me, Vonnegut had felt as natural and familiar as a good buddy, so unlike the strict formality of Marquette and its canon. Loree, however, had the man himself as a teacher, mentor, and then friend, and who now—at the height of his fame and presumed inaccessibility, as legions of guru-seekers sought his presence—was one of the few Vonnegut fans who had his number in her pocket and would be hearing from him by phone and letter.

Loree's view of Vonnegut was a unique one. Like the photo she'd taken of Kurt in his office—barely recognizable with short hair, no mustache, wearing the wash pants and v-neck sweater in which he'd dressed himself for years as a private writer about the house, and posed in a old chair from which the springs and stuffing were bursting, part of the casual accommodations the Writers Workshop enjoyed in its quonset-hut offices—her vision of Kurt from these years was quite different from the larger-than-life impression he was making in the media those days. Yet beneath it all was an understanding, obvious to her even back in 1966, that his work was something special. His was a special sensibility, liable to turn up in unusual ways. One night, for example, with a group of workshop students Kurt and Loree had found themselves in a bar featuring the unlikely entertainment of female impersonators. While the others mocked the occasion, Loree recalled that Vonnegut was deeply touched by the art these performers brought to their work even as the audience turned their efforts into gross comedy. Another time, while walking to class through the student union, the two found guest-instructor Nelson Algren passed out in the lounge, sleeping through his own scheduled class meeting while he snored off a hangover, oblivious to the bustle around him. Algren had been no great ally in the faculty politics that end up ruining every academic program, yet Kurt was so moved by this great writer's innocent vulnerability that he told Loree in all seriousness that universities should in conscience support and protect such damaged geniuses in recompense for all they'd contributed to art.

Now, in the fall of 1972, as *The Vonnegut Statement* went through production, Loree told me that Vonnegut had been touched by all my efforts and wanted to say thanks. A few days later a letter from him arrived, confessing that my interest in his work had been useful and had cheered him up. As a gift in celebration of my book's coming publication, he promised to send something "only a college professor could love": the original typescripts of three false starts, dating back to 1957, of the novel he'd just finished, *Breakfast of Champions*. A few weeks later the package arrived, and there they were, about forty pages comprising three distinct beginnings, including one in verse, of a novel called *Upstairs and Downstairs*. Set in the Depression, it featured a character who'd have a role in *Breakfast of Champions*, Fred Barry, only here telling the roots of Barry's wealth during those transformative economic times. Meanwhile, Kurt had begun sending the signed and dated typescripts of his current work—mostly essays, prefaces, and speeches—to Loree as he finished seeing them through the press. This meant the world's best Vonnegut archive was now taking shape in two offices at UNI's Baker Hall.

As the years passed, I dug deeper into Vonnegut's work, historically and bibliographically. John Somer and I kept in touch, finishing another party project—an anthology of stories from the Vietnam War called *Writing Under Fire*—and drew on our research for a proposed volume of Vonnegut's own essays and uncollected stories. *Welcome to the Monkey House*, it turned out, had gathered only half of Kurt's short fiction from the 1950s and early 1960s. Missing was a rare early attempt to deal with World War II, "Souvenir"; also passed over were such middle-class comedies as "Any Reasonable Offer" and "Poor Little Rich Town," pieces I'd found indicative of Vonnegut's roots in the most quotidian familiarity of American life. True, some of these works were crudely vernacular, but no worse than the already collected "All the King's Horses" with its simplistically propagandistic portrayal of our North Korean and Chinese Communist enemies. But the story's mood spoke directly of popular American feelings of that era as expressed in media from comic books to television dramas. We were just finding out that Kurt had written scripts for *Philco Playhouse* and other such shows; at one point he'd collaborated with a TV writer on the adaptation of his story "D. P." for *General Electric Theater*, where it starred Sammy Davis, Jr. in his first dramatic role, and was introduced by host Ronald Reagan. From 1957 to the present Vonnegut, Davis, and Reagan had emerged into much more significant fame, but the fact that the roots of their work could be found in such common, popular soil might provide a clue for understanding who and what they were now. Plus from 1964 on Vonnegut had begun expressing ideas akin to those of his fiction (and often in a similar manner) in essays and reviews for a wide range of journals. His gentle deflation of the Maharishi for *Esquire*, "Yes, We Have No Nirvanas," was as funny and as insightful as his comic critique of religion in *Cat's Cradle*, and offered a good handle on that at times ambiguous novel. *McCall's* had sent Vonnegut to cover the fall of Biafra, and seeing this veteran of the destruction of Dresden witnessing a postmodern version of inhumane horror made for significant work.

John and I had probed junk shops and rummage sales for copies of the magazines that libraries don't keep—*Argosy, Venture, Worlds of If*—and had tracked down all the fugitive stories. We'd begged book-review editors to comb their indexes to see if Vonnegut had taken assignments from them. Then, with an introduction placing this work in perspective, we bundled it together as *Rare Vonnegut: Uncollected Stories and Essays* and shipped it off to Seymour Lawrence, who had been finding ready markets for anything associated with Vonnegut, including his Broadway play, *Happy Birthday, Wanda June*, a quiltwork public-television production called *Between Time and Timbuktu*, and of course our own *Vonnegut Statement*. Not surprisingly, he accepted the work, promising us standard royalties after a permissions payment to Vonnegut. We felt we'd just made our fourth and by far biggest sale to Dell.

And then Vonnegut got cold feet. At first it was just with the title. "*Rare Vonnegut* sounds so utterly posthumous," he complained to Lawrence, who in turn assured us that Kurt was good with titles and could certainly think up something appropriate and catchy. For a while the working title became, at Vonnegut's request, *Canary in a Cat House*, which he'd used in 1961 for his first collection of stories (all but one of which was repeated in *Welcome to the Monkey House*). Then that one was rejected as potentially confusing. Finally Vonnegut sat down, read the manuscript through, and became even more disenchanted. He recalled rejecting this batch of stories twice before, in 1961 for *Canary in a Cat House* and again in 1968 for his larger collection with Seymour Lawrence. He preferred they be kept uncollected, and asked that we not publish the book.

Of course, we agreed. As far as these stories' role in clarifying Vonnegut's roots in the popular culture, we could make that point in critical essays; indeed, a few years later I'd write up a piece as a "do-it-yourself Kurt Vonnegut anthology" so readers could go to the library and photocopy the bulk of them that was available in magazines that libraries did keep, such as *Cosmopolitan*, *Collier's*, and *The Saturday Evening Post*. But John and I felt disappointed that readers would miss the impact of Vonnegut's essays being collected. His voice as a commentator and spokesman on public issues was both an entertaining and morally commanding one, and we made this argument to Lawrence: forget the short stories, but please encourage Vonnegut himself to publish the essays as a book.

Lawrence did, Vonnegut agreed, and the second half of *Rare Vonnegut* appeared with just the style of title everyone knew its author could concoct: *Wampeters, Foma, and Granfalloons*. As labels for what Kurt called his "opinions," these quasi-religious terms from *Cat's Cradle* seemed appropriate for the sentiments in these essays that spanned the American social construct of the 1960s and 1970s, from moon landings to Moonies and from nuclear nightmares to the politics of Richard Nixon. Lawrence offered to pay for our work, a total of $500 for researching and collecting these essays (Vonnegut admitted that he'd "saved nothing"), and said Kurt would give us credit in the book's preface. When it appeared under the Delacorte Press/Seymour Lawrence imprint in 1974, we found that not only had Vonnegut kept his word but had revealed even more about his attitude toward his work. Describing John and myself as "Two nice young college professors," he acknowledged our research but also confessed that despite our knowing "where almost all the bodies were hidden" we'd missed three or four of his early, fugitive stories and essays. Would he tell us what they were? "Not even the ordeal of the *veglia*, said to be the most excruciating torture ever devised by Earthlings, could compel me to reveal where those three or four were published—and when" (xviii–xix). Why not? Because they were too unabashedly cloying. Yet several of the essays he'd let stand in this volume were sentimental, and before the preface concluded he described one of those hidden items and the role it played in his larger work:

> One of the lost pieces of mine which I hope Professors Klinkowitz and Somer will never find has to do with my debt to a black cook my family had when I was a child. Her name was Ida Young, and I probably spent more time with her than I did with anybody—until I got married, of course. She knew the *Bible* by heart, and she found plenty of wisdom and comfort in there. She knew a lot of American history, too—things she and other black people had seen and marveled at, and remembered and still talked about, in Indiana and Illinois and Ohio—and Kentucky and Tennessee. She would read to me, too, from an anthology of sentimental poetry about love which would not die, about faithful dogs and humble cottages where happiness was, about people growing old, about visits to cemeteries, about babies who died. I remember the name of the book, and I wish I had a copy, since it has so much to do with what I am.
>
> The name of the book was *More Heart Throbs*; and it was an easy jump from that to *The Spoon River Anthology*, by Edgar

Lee Masters, to *Main Street*, by Sinclair Lewis, to *U.S.A.*, by John Dos Passos, to my thinking now. There is an almost intolerable sentimentality beneath everything I write. British critics complain about it. And Robert Scholes, the American critic, once said I put bitter coatings on sugar pills.

It's too late to change now. At least I am aware of my origins—in a big, brick dreamhouse designed by my architect father, where nobody was home for long periods of time, except for me and Ida Young. (xxiv–xxv)

Though no one had expected *Wampeters* to be a bestseller, it got feature-review coverage, went through several hardcover and then quality paperback printings, was picked up by Vonnegut's major foreign publishers, and remains a strong-selling Dell edition today. More importantly, it set a precedent for subsequent essay collections, including *Palm Sunday* (1981) and *Fates Worse than Death* (1991). As Kurt admitted, having so much ancient material unearthed got him thinking about his origins, admitting his sentimentality, but also to start considering himself a serious public spokesman. He'd soon begin combining sentiment and message by giving self-styled "sermons" in the country's major churches. Such developments were quite natural, for since 1966, when introduced to the candidly professional treatment of literature in Iowa City, he'd been beginning each new or reissued book with an autobiographical preface, and had made that autobiography part of *Slaughterhouse-Five*'s first and last chapters. *Breakfast of Champions*, *Slapstick*, and most subsequent novels would feature such prefatory material, serving to make Vonnegut as person and as author an integral part of the fiction to follow.

The phenomenon of developing from metaphor to discourse has been evident in the careers of many writers who attain major recognition only after several works—you can see it in the Hemingway of *Across the River and into the Trees*, in Faulkner's *A Fable*, and elsewhere. In Vonnegut's case, it pointed back to a seriousness now more evident in such early works as *The Sirens of Titan* and *Mother Night*. That, after all, was the most impressive thing Loree Rackstraw had told me about her years as a student and then friend of the almost totally unknown writer: even then, when his writing was earning him virtually nothing and he had to be happy with a measly $6,800 annual salary from the University of Iowa, Vonnegut was convinced that he had something crucially important to say.

Kurt's admission that there were three or four small pieces of his work we'd yet to find served as a tease and temptation. With Asa Pieratt, acquisitions librarian at the University of Delaware, I'd begun work on what I hoped to be the definitive bibliography, and with the help of other bibliographers we eventually did locate one of them: an innocuous little story titled "The Cruise of the Jolly Roger" which Kurt had written in 1953 shortly after having moved from his job as a publicist for General Electric in Schenectady to the more bohemian environs of Cape Cod. Yet even here Vonnegut settled not in the artists' colony at Provincetown but in the decidedly middle-class village of West Barnstable, which is where this story appeared, in a local magazine advertising the area in a chamber-of-commerce way. When Asa's and my bibliography appeared in December 1974, we felt we'd won a move in the friendly chess game that was developing between this alternately secretive and candid writer and the eager young "archaeologists" (as he'd described us in the preface to *Wampeters*).

With our first copies of the volume at hand during the Modern Language Association meeting, which was held that year in New York, Asa and I wondered if we could summon enough nerve to deliver Vonnegut's copy in person. He lived, after all, just six or seven blocks from the convention hotel. We'd written him, he'd written us, and so we wouldn't feel like strangers. But there was still a great sense of intimidation, for here was not only a major writer whom we'd admired greatly but a figure whose fame made him larger than life—and who, as an essentially private person, had been grievously put-upon by the raging popularity and even notoriety achieved since *Slaughterhouse-Five*.

For all three days of the convention Asa and I debated back and forth the possibilities of going over to visit him. It finally took the encouragement of another friend, novelist Susan Quist, to give me sufficient backbone to walk up and ring Kurt's doorbell. Susan had been a help throughout the week, and knowing her turned out to be almost as good as having an affiliation with Vonnegut. We'd met for drinks the first afternoon, an hour in the hotel's lounge that produced a parade of magazine editors dropping by to say hello to Susan, whose novel *Indecent Exposure* had made an impact in such circles. The next afternoon we wandered the exhibit floor, and I joined the line where Erica Jong was signing the new paperback copies of *Fear of Flying*. For a moment I was given the spotlight, as Jong complimented me on the interview I'd done with Jerzy Kosinski (implying I should do a similar one with her) and confiding that I'd been dealt a shabby hand on *Wampeters* (having learned I'd been paid just a $250 share for producing a book grossing millions for Dell). All this of course went to my head, until I noticed that there was now a longer line than for Erica Jong, as a crowd of professors and graduate students gathered around Susan.

Now it was Sunday afternoon, the convention was ending, and we had less than half a day in which to see Vonnegut. Asa, Susan, and I checked out, left our bags with the bellhop, and crossed Sixth Avenue to the Stage Delicatessen, determined to do at least something famous before leaving the city, if only eating a corned-beef sandwich on rye at this landmark restaurant. We chased the food with drinks, and I was still kid enough to be ordering rum and Cokes. I'll never forget the waiter's response, entoned in a somber accent that only halfway through could I place within history and politics. "Yes, rum and Coke," he repeated, and then continued. "Once we said 'Cuba Libre'; but now there is no more Cuba Libre, and so we say 'rum and Coke.'" I looked up to see an elegant gentleman whose waiter's tuxedo echoed the formal attire he doubtless wore on occasion in his former life in Batista's Cuba. Susan and Asa covered my immature hickishness by ordering the same, and we settled down to our seemingly eternal topic: getting up the guts to see Kurt Vonnegut. Tired of it to boredom, Susan resolved things by looking at me squarely, saying I was a big boy now, and after all this fussing had damn well better go see Vonnegut.

Thus emboldened, Asa and I walked down Sixth Avenue to the Forties, turned east, and a few minutes later found ourselves in Vonnegut's neighborhood of townhouses.

Kurt has written about the area, looking into its history and taking a certain amount of pride in being a homeowner in this part of town known as Turtle Bay. The area was laid out by German builders in the 1840s and most of the residences were put up as three-story townhouses over tall street-level basements. It was on this lowest floor that photographer Jill Krementz, Vonnegut's companion since the early 1970s and later to be his wife, set up her office and lab; Kurt and Jill lived on the next two stories, and up top was the writer's study. Its midblock location made it as quiet as any small town street, and Kurt had commented about the neighborly environs, with editor Robert Gottlieb living across the street, his own publishers' offices just around the corner, and a streetlife on the busier avenues where, with so many editors, publishers, and major bookstores around, he was likely to bump into fellow writers.

Now Asa and I were walking up the steps to Vonnegut's front door. I rang the bell, and in a moment saw through the heavy glass that someone was coming down the hall to answer. It was Kurt himself, tall and almost gawkishly awkward—"this tall, shambling bear of a man," as more than one early interviewer had put it—who pulled the door open, peered out at us, and seemed confused as I stuttered out my silly line, "Delivery boys from Dell Publishing!" When I quickly identified ourselves he smiled and said, "So this is what you look like," and stood for a moment measuring us up, as if the purpose of the visit had been to show him what we were like rather than vice versa. In the background we could hear a football game on TV, probably the same Minnesota Vikings playoff that had been tuned in at the Stage's bar; and so when Kurt broke the ice by asking us if we'd like to come in, we said only if we could watch the game, which pleased him.

The hallway turned into an open corridor, taking us past a front parlor to a kitchen and dining room where it seemed Kurt and Jill spent a lot of their time. It was an odd mix of a formal dining room table surrounded by director's chairs, a few of which were turned toward a portable TV on the sideboard. Kurt introduced us to Jill, whose first impression seemed a bit skeptical (later, after leaving a phone message with Ron Sukenick's wife, I was told by Ron that she'd been so surprised to talk with me—as involved with his fiction as I was, she'd thought he'd invented me, and perhaps this was how Jill felt as we came in out of the blue). We sat down and as promised concentrated on the game, leaving small talk for between plays.

And so my first hour or so with Kurt Vonnegut was spent in the shared presence of America's most popular culture of the moment, a highly touted football game on TV with the season's most expensive commercials washing over us every ten or twelve minutes. This was the Vikings of Fran Tarkenton, and his scrambling style made for an interesting and less-conventional game. Kurt was interested in the quarterback's techniques, but saved most of his comments for the camera work. "They've been doing this all day," he observed after a particularly hard hit. The safeties blitzing? we asked. "No, a close shot of the player's face right after he's been flattened," Kurt explained, and added that of all the networks CBS seemed most obvious at playing up football's violence. Watching the show from this angle we noticed what Vonnegut had been seeing all along: how after a particularly vicious sack there'd often be a time-out, letting the screen change from the close-up to an exuberant beer commercial; routine pauses in play, following no especially jarring action, would be saved for more sedate ads for batteries or tires. It was interesting to see Kurt both within his culture and rising above it to make structural comments on how it worked. Here was the writer of all those stories for *Collier's* and the *Post*, plus we were seeing the graduate-trained anthropologist watching humankind at play and the scientist, adept at chemistry, biology, and mechanical engineering, fascinated with the tinkering behind how things worked.

The game finished with a Minnesota win, cheering Kurt, who'd remained the supportive Midwesterner instead of pulling for the rival Giants, the team representing his new home. Asa and I said we should be off, but were countered by Jill arranging place mats at the table and inviting us to stay for a sandwich and another beer to follow the several we'd enjoyed during the game. And so our hour in the quiet East Forties turned into nearly half the day. After the meal Jill brought out her cameras for some photographs, which further lightened the mood as she joked about the odd twists to this shoot: having to frame us vertically as Kurt and I, each well over six feet tall, stood, and laughing at how a horizontal shot of the three of us was a "mustache picture," both Asa and I favoring the same droopy style that Kurt had made famous. She got serious when remarking how Kurt's rarest book, the old paperback collection *Canary in a Cat House,* had been stolen back when he'd held his City University of New York seminar in the front parlor, but Asa cheered her up by promising to send her (and not Kurt) an extra copy of his own. Vonnegut joined the potlatch by pulling down copies of *Wampeters, Foma, and Granfalloons,* at the time his current book, and signing one each for Asa and myself. Then he reached into some papers on the sideboard and handed us two each, "for your archives." They were the beginning for an essay he'd decided not to write, about a West Point cadet who'd challenged the academy's strict honor code. He'd come to Vonnegut, claiming he was accused unjustly, and asking for support. After looking into the case, Kurt decided not to pursue it. Why not? "Because he wouldn't say he wasn't guilty," Vonnegut shrugged.

Now time was really running short, as I had a flight leaving LaGuardia in less than an hour. But Kurt was still pulling things off shelves, this time a fine bottle of French wine "for Loree," and with our arms full Asa and I said our goodbyes and dashed over to Third Avenue and hailed a cab. Asa had time to spare, but I asked the driver to wait while I grabbed my bags at the hotel desk and then urged him to hurry to the airport. What time was my flight? In about half an hour, I exclaimed. That was plenty of time, the cabbie assured me. "But it always takes that long to get to LaGuardia, and what if there's traffic?" I complained, and with fatherly patience the driver calmed me down by saying there were "other ways."

There surely were, for by cutting under bridges and through side streets we made it from Seventh Avenue to the main terminal in about twelve minutes, at a pace leisurely enough to chat about the day's news event, the death of comedian Jack Benny. "Benny was always one of the nicer comics," the cabbie remarked, and I agreed, remembering that any cruelty in his humor was always at his own expense instead of others'. Assuring me that there had been nothing to worry about and to enjoy my flight home, the driver sent me off charmed by New York, a mood I never thought I'd share.

Kurt's generosity that day continued through coming years. He always seemed amused that such leavings as false starts on novels and abandoned essays could be of any possible interest. That Asa and I made a living from studying such documents amazed him, and from time to time he'd play little games with our vocation, such as one day mailing Asa an envelope filled with "junk" cleaned out of his wallet, including outdated membership cards, ticket stubs, receipts, and the like. "I herewith send you the contents of my wallet on October 17, 1982," Kurt wrote in a cover letter, "minus only my cash, credit cards, and current driver's license." Asa predictably had the letter and contents mounted in a custom-made leather folder, the results looking like an assemblage by Kurt Schwitters or a Joseph Cornell box. Kurt would send me odds and ends he thought might be of interest: a German genealogy chart taking his father's line back to the 1500s, letting me see that his great-grandfather was a tax collector in the same region of Germany, northeast of Cologne, where my great-grandmother's people had been woodcutters and cigar makers. Then some declassified pages from the U.S. Bombing Survey covering the destruction of Dresden, plus copies of recent letters to him from some old P.O.W. buddies and from Gerhard Müller, the Dresden taxi-driver in *Slaughterhouse-Five* who'd just left East Germany for West Berlin. Loree, of course, was still on the truck for deliveries of all Kurt's current work, from galleys of his novels to typescripts of speeches, essays, prefaces, and reviews. Without this we, and consequently literary history, would have missed many pieces. Some were significant, such as two new prefaces to *Mother Night*, one for an American-based Russian-language edition, the other for an underground Polish edition; each added new clarifications in his relation to the text, a posture Vonnegut had begun to refine in the 1966 Iowa City introduction.

Knowing Kurt's wish for privacy—for simple peace and quiet, really—I tried to keep from bothering him. Yet a couple times each year there would be a need to exchange letters, all of which he answered promptly and helpfully. One occasion proved especially apt, when in April of 1976 I was asked to consider teaching at the State University of New York in Albany, where the English department would lose its doctoral program if it didn't recruit an actively publishing group of new faculty members. During my campus visit I slipped away and sought out Bernard Vonnegut, Kurt's older brother and a renowned atmospheric physicist (he'd invented cloud seeding for rain), who after a brilliant career at the General Electric Research Laboratory was now a distinguished professor at SUNY-Albany. I found him in the department office, introduced myself, and was invited to his combination office and lab.

Bernard Vonnegut's nine-year seniority on his brother made for subtle differences, principally a courtly style of polite formality that seemed of an earlier generation, yet the family similarities were obvious. Even more apparent was the kinship Bernard shared with Dr. Felix Hoenikker, the brilliant but erratically attentive physicist of *Cat's Cradle* who is distracted from inventing the atomic bomb by playing with dime-store turtles, and who on the morning he takes off for Sweden to receive the Nobel Prize absent-mindedly leaves his wife a tip beneath the breakfast dishes. Bernard's office was truly the model for Hoenikker's, as equipment, gadgets, and junk littered every surface, including the chairs. Warning me not to touch anything dangerous (and everything looked dangerous), he found a place for me to sit by clearing away the remnants of his fast-food lunch. Then he spent a patient hour answering my questions about the school and chatting informally about Kurt. I'll never forget the quaintness of his response to my identifying comment that I'd done scholarly work on his brother: "Our family is honored," he said, with a nod of his head that could have been a slight bow.

Before my trip I'd written Kurt for his opinion, asking how serious were the rumors that the state might be going broke. His reply was waiting for me at home, and was abundantly helpful. He opened by saying that he'd called his brother for some inside information and learned I'd been there just an hour before—so now I already knew more than he did. He agreed that New York was in terrible financial trouble, but that even in good times the Albany-Schenectady-Troy area was not that interesting. He'd been there for three years when working for GE and recalled that the only nice thing about it was being able to live next door to his brother.

If I moved East, he counseled, I'd become a floater, detached from any sense of place—at his present age of fifty-three he admitted to being almost pure helium, having cut loose from his Midwestern moorings almost thirty years before. He insisted that I was doing good work and was surely needed where I was now, and felt that must be a nourishing situation. He remarked on what he understood to be my sense of style, driving an old Mercedes sports car and playing with a blues band on weekends. Then came his conclusion, stated flat out. Given that it was foolish to ask his opinion but that I had anyway, here was the most stylish and useful thing to do: stay where I was, because Iowa was a better place than New York. And so I did.

That next fall I was in New York again, in the city, doing my purportedly useful work as an Iowa professor, researching another book on Kurt Vonnegut. It was another collaborative project, *Vonnegut in America*, this time coauthored with Donald L. Lawler, whom I'd helped with an MLA session the year before. I was in town to see Kurt, but only partly for professional reasons. One of my own chapters, from which the volume took its title, would be a critical biography, reading Vonnegut's fiction as a structural response to American life prompted by the major events in his life, from the joys of growing up in a big family, seeing that family happiness and security disrupted by the Great Depression, and finding the ability to fashion an extended artificial family while away at college, to military service in World War II, postwar work for a big corporation, and eventually establishing his own small business manufacturing and selling short stories for the family weeklies with the workmanlike ethic of the honest tradesperson. In each case the operative factor—the flexible artifice of extended families, the arbitrary nature of reality changeable at any time by economic fortune, and so forth—provided Vonnegut with the materials to shape an accommodating vision. Because these same materials were shared as the collective autobiography of his generation, Kurt Vonnegut had become one of the age's most popular and representative writers.

And so I wanted to run down this biographical checklist with Kurt himself, making sure I'd covered the essentials and hopefully prompting some revealing comments. But I had a personal motive behind this meeting as well. In the process of moving from one marriage to another, I was bringing my fiancée to New York, introducing her to the writers I was working on and appreciating their responses to my happiness. All of them, from Donald Barthelme and Jerzy Kosinski to Thomas Glynn and the crowd for his publication party at the Gotham Book Mart, seemed to approve, and I was anxious to show off a bit in front of Kurt. Julie was just twenty, yet mature and capable to the point of helping care for my children and being willing to raise them. It was her response to the writers that proved most insightful. Barthelme she thought oddly funny, like an overgrown troll. Kosinski she sensed was not being entirely candid—hers were the first hints I received about his tendencies toward equivocation and deception. Tom Glynn's party had been a merry adventure, from watching him go nuts trying to host the Gotham affair to rollicking down Broadway in a taxi, six of us crammed in illegally with Tom hiding on the floor, to find a new Lebanese restaurant in Chelsea that promised at least a few more good meals before being discovered.

It was Vonnegut, however, who proved Julie's favorite. Plans called for us to meet at his home, then proceed to lunch nearby. At the door this time was Jill's assistant, a polite but firm young woman who seemed accustomed to having to turn away many

Vonnegut-seekers—thankfully Asa and I had crashed the gate on a Sunday, or our afternoon with Kurt might never have happened. She was questioning Julie and myself about our business when Kurt walked down the stairs behind her and said it was ok, we were expected. Jill joined us in the hall, and we walked a few blocks to the Mona Lisa Restaurant where Kurt had booked a table.

Lunch was pleasant. Jill at first seemed even less comfortable than during our previous meeting, but as Julie drew her out on her work, which included some recent shootings of a Bob Dylan concert, she grew more personable. It was because Jill was so much younger and less famous, Julie later guessed, that she froze up. I hadn't noticed until then that Kurt and I were in a similar position, each living with a younger woman who was not yet officially (but soon would be) a second wife. As it was, Jill seemed happiest talking to Julie, their generational styles and interests giving them much in common. Yet Julie got enough attention from Kurt to be utterly delighted with him. He signed her copy of *Cat's Cradle* "To my pal, Julie Huffman," and took note of what she had to say. That night she confided that of all the folks we'd met, she liked him the best. "Because he twinkles," she explained—not just his eyes, but everything about him.

Kurt's business with me was more serious. After our meal and over coffee we ran down my checklist. He agreed about the structuring effect of those key experiences I was naming, particularly that of the Great Depression, which he said was a more difficult and upsetting period for most Americans than even World War II, affecting the most personal aspects of their lives and fortunes as it did. Comedy had helped, he remarked, and ran through some Depression-era jokes whose bitter coating had a sweetly humorous center, such as the exchange that begins "Do you know that cat who inherited a million dollars?" and ends with the news that "It died last week. Left its money to another cat."

Much of what I mentioned drew some type of ironic response, with Kurt laughing at his own humor. I noted that his first agent was Kenneth Littauer, and Vonnegut told me he was a veteran of the World War I Lafayette Escadrille—and added, with a chuckle, that Littauer could boast another first, being the first pilot to strafe a trench. His laugh rumbled, then stuttered into a cough, after which he paused for the next question—but alert, I sensed, for any possible humor in it.

When we got to the matter of Dresden, I had the diffidence to presume Vonnegut had nothing to add. He agreed, recalling the raid's futility. A quarter of a million people had died there, most of them very young, very old, or infirm, as the city was considered a safe haven for those unable to survive the war elsewhere. And for all of that, what was the result? "Bombing Dresden didn't end the war one day earlier," Kurt stated. "It didn't advance the Russians one mile, didn't save one American soldier's life, didn't rescue one prisoner from a concentration camp." He stopped to light a cigarette. "Absolutely no one benefited," he concluded, "except one person." Kurt let me wonder who for a moment and then gave the answer. "Me. I got three dollars for every man, woman, and child killed."

I was stunned into silence, the same silence that serves such eloquent purpose in the novel that earned him that fortune, *Slaughterhouse-Five*. Our lunchtime conversation had been orchestrated much like a piece of Vonnegut's fiction, commencing with a bit of common wisdom, softening up his audience with a few jokes, asking a question that implies there is no reasonable answer, and then answering with a punch line that upsets even the firmest assumptions. Like Jack Benny's humor, whatever sting it had turned not on the listener but on the speaker himself. Even as a successful artist, Kurt Vonnegut was feeling the horror of Dresden again.

After lunch Kurt and Jill left to meet Alan Arkin for some business about film rights the actor wished to purchase. Kurt sold the rights (in this case to *Player Piano*) but no movie resulted, a common fate shared among the options to his other novels purchased but never developed by groups from Hollywood producers to The Grateful Dead. Which is a shame, as it kept an important writer's work off the screen and therefore out of the minds of a large proportion of the culture. Until *Mother Night* became a movie in 1996, what did get filmed was flawed—*Happy Birthday, Wanda June*, because Kurt wrote the script himself without allowing sufficiently for the difference between stage and screen; *Slapstick*, thanks to the unsupervised indulgences of producer-director-star Steven Paul; and *Slaughterhouse-Five*, because despite the film's overall excellence it remains one character short: Kurt Vonnegut himself, who for the novel to work has to be there clarifying his problematic role in its creation and saying "So it goes" every time somebody or something dies.

Yet writers had reached the great general public without movies—certainly before movies, as Mark Twain had carried his ideas and values to a world a hundred years ago from the lecture stage. Vonnegut would choose the same medium now, and as inappropriate as was the screen for the nature of his work, so much better would the podium serve his purpose.

It was as a public speaker that Vonnegut next touched bases with me. Less than five months later, in March of 1977, he had been invited back to the University of Iowa for some talks with the new generation of workshop students and a string of parties with his old friends. At the end of that week our own university, just one hundred miles north, was having its annual "Student as Critic" conference, for which Kurt would make an ideal speaker. Many years later, when I'd begin another book by citing Granville Hicks's report of being impressed with Vonnegut's speech at Notre Dame, Kurt would write to say that it seemed to make a big difference in people's opinions of his work if they'd heard him speak. Indeed, in Cedar Falls that evening I saw how so many otherwise radical features of his writing come across quite naturally in the circumstances of a public lecture. There's a colloquial tone and vernacular style of expression to Kurt's fiction, an approach that with its short sentences and timed effect works much like direct address. It all demands a sense of the author's presence and invites interaction with the reader, much as Kurt would question his audience and make their reactions part of his ongoing presentation, just like he did with me after lunch at the Mona Lisa.

Kurt arrived from Iowa City a bit bleary-eyed; he'd been lionized down there for a week, and was ready for a couple days of welcome sobriety and peace. At each meal I'd see him reach across the place setting and quietly turn his wine glass upside down. Though Kurt was interested and engaging during the day, each evening one could see his energy level plummet. My friend Gordy Menninga, a former UNI student finishing an M.F.A. at Iowa, told me how one of the parties down there had gone. Like most Iowa City events, it had been a heavy drinking affair, and toward the end Vonnegut was seen sitting by himself and not looking well. Was there anything Gordy could do for him? Kurt had given him a tired, almost helpless look, and began to mutter, "I want . . . I want. . . ." "This was *Kurt Vonnegut*," Gordy exclaimed to me. "Anybody there would have done anything they could for him. So

I kept asking what he wanted, but couldn't get him beyond those first words."

"Did you ever figure out what he wanted?" I asked.

"He finally got the sentence out," Gordy replied, looking as if he'd just lost his best friend.

What had Kurt wanted?

"He said he wanted to be dead," Gordy shrugged, and I saw him stunned by the same silence, the same inability to answer that had transfixed me that day at lunch when a sober, alert, but still emotionally depleted Kurt Vonnegut had taken me through those questions and answers on the destruction of Dresden.

This news from Iowa City confirmed my dislike for the place, which was obviously big-time but bore little relation to the people and styles of Iowa. It had great bookstores, but so did New York, and in New York you didn't have to elbow your way through aisles of browsers all wearing serapes and none of them likely to spend money on a book. Wealthy out-of-state students panhandled to be trendy, and the workshop's writers, faculty and students alike, spent lots of time talking about the great books they'd write but precious little time doing it. Kurt himself once recalled that the town's best business was done by its pinball machines, which seemed an apt metaphor for what most folks, from bookstore browsers and panhandling students to the crowd from the workshop, were doing with their lives.

When a genuine success like Vonnegut visited town, it would be an occasion for one great pinball game, with Kurt as the ball. I'd seen it happen with other writers' visits—Robert Coover, Walter Abish, John Irving—where the guest would suffer through endless displays of pinball wizardry by countless partygoers, each one insisting that the writer share a drink while being expected to marvel at the fancy talk.

When Kurt came up to Cedar Falls, I was proud that my own colleagues and students were more interested in his well-being than in showing themselves off. People respected his privacy and always apologized when approaching him with a request, and when I broke this code by hauling out a stack of first editions for him to sign before dinner at our house Loree Rackstraw was furious. Yet Kurt waved Loree off and signed them, happy enough that he was in a quiet home and about to share a peaceful dinner with friends. We'd kept the faculty away and included just one student and my children, who helped serve. Thirteen years later in Chicago, with no meetings in between, my daughter Nina would see Kurt at a book signing and be remembered as the six-year-old who'd ladled him a second helping of onion soup—"And how's dear Dad?" he asked her in amusement.

That Kurt enjoyed the company of everyday people more than critics and professors was obvious, the explanation being that he'd spent immensely more of his life out in the normal world than up in the ivory tower of academe or even among others in the writing business. I saw evidence of this one day at lunch, when Loree and I had taken him down to a restaurant on Main Street, away from campus in the city's business section. We'd hoped not to be bothered, and when the waitress interrupted with a request for a gentleman across the room for Kurt's autograph Loree was ready to shoot another icy stare. But I saw that the fan was neither a professor or a student and told Kurt, knowing he'd be pleased.

"That's Dick Witham," I said, identifying him as the local Ford dealer.

"I used to sell cars," Kurt perked up. "Ran the second Saab dealership in the country, called it Saab Cape Cod." I'd known this, and was delighted to see Vonnegut's pleasure in knowing he was read by someone who had a lot more in common with him than the English professors surrounding him during such visits. After signing Kurt stayed with us, of course, but I knew his heart was with Dick Witham; I should have insisted Kurt move over to Dick's table, where talk of inventories and factory discounts would surely be more interesting and relevant.

Kurt's speech was set for Friday night, in any other case a hopelessly dead time for a university event. But he filled the hall and more, drawing over two thousand students to the quaintly turn-of-the-century auditorium down the hall from the classroom where, as an author known only to his former students Loree Rackstraw and Robley Wilson, he'd spoken to a handful of people back in 1967. This was the first time I'd see or hear him speak—tapes of earlier lectures would only turn up later—and I was pleased to learn that he approached his audience in the same manner as with an individual over lunch.

Like so many of his presentations—public, private, or in print—this one began with a question. And not just a normal question, but one which built on the nature of the occasion and the audience's presumptions in order to deconstruct both.

"How many of you believe that the great Eastern religions, with their marvelous depths of profound meditation," Vonnegut asked, "are superior to our Western styles of faith?" Hands shot up throughout the auditorium; everyone, it seemed, was eager to show this great iconoclastic writer, this legendary hero of the psychedelic sixties, that they shared his enthusiasm for such exotic things.

"Well, you're all full of crap!" Kurt snorted in reply, deflating his listeners for just a half-second while their lungs emptied with a collective gasp, then refilled with laughter as they realized the joke that had been played on them. As the laughing subsided he explained why he felt getting lost in meditation was less valuable than interacting imaginatively with one's world, and the audience duly took note. But their willingness to accept what Kurt was now saying had been orchestrated by the interactive routine he'd played: opening up their minds by blowing away one of their most smugly held assumptions, yet in such a common, familiar way that reminded them how much happier they were with vernacular American attitudes than with the esoterics of Eastern mysticism.

After expanding on his theme by making a similar comparison between the programmed imaginations in subservience to film and the more creative minds encouraged by literature, and noting the crushingly collective economics of filmmaking as opposed to the cost of writing a novel (which can be as cheap as a ream of paper and a typewriter ribbon), Kurt announced that he'd like to move on to something else, an interview done for *The Paris Review*, the literary quarterly that had made such probing dialogues with writers a tradition since starting off with Faulkner, Hemingway, and E. M. Forster back in the early 1950s. The formality of such occasions seemed contrary to Kurt's style, but here again he startled and then pleased his listeners by dismantling the interview form and recasting it for his particular purpose. Instead of submitting to the ponderous questions of George Plimpton or some other critic, Vonnegut had interviewed himself. And now for his speech at UNI he'd read through several portions of it, using different voices for questions and answers respectively.

"I'll ask the questions in the tone of voice I've been using so far tonight," he advised, "which is not my normal tone of voice at all." He let his audience ponder this for a moment, then chimed back in with a choked, squeaky falsetto, revealing that "My real voice actually sounds like this!" At once the inhibiting seriousness of the interview and the awkwardness of having the author interview himself were dismantled and set aside, and both speaker and audience were free to enjoy the occasion for what it was: a master of Socratic interrogation using his best strategies on himself.

Ending the speech, which ran close to two hours, were some pages from Kurt's novel in progress, the initial scene of what would become *Jailbird* but which was now being called *Mary Kathleen O'Looney; Or, Unacceptable Air*. For all this time there had never been a dull moment for either speaker or audience, and when we met Kurt backstage his first question was an eager inquiry as to how we thought he'd gone over. But as he settled in the passenger seat of my car for the ride back to his hotel, he fell silent, lit a cigarette, and had one of the greatest energy sags I'd ever witnessed. The speech and all his antics necessary to convey it had wrung him dry, and whatever life he was going to have for the next hour would have to be dragged out of that cigarette.

Yet next morning Kurt was back for more, a press-conference style session with about one hundred students. Then lunch in the student union before Loree would drive him to the airport; he'd changed his flight, heading not home to New York but directly to Boston where his first grandchild had been born the day before. I remember how awkward I felt standing there outside the union, unsure of the polite way to say thanks and goodbye. I stammered something about "not seeing you again" simply as a way of covering my exit, but as I should have expected Kurt turned it into a prank. Feigning an expression of great concern he paused to look at me mournfully and ask "Is it really that bad?" as if I'd implied I was about to kill myself. In truth, I was suffering my own energy drop just then; Kurt sensed it and made this little joke to cheer me up and most thoughtfully provide a crest of laughter on which to make my way from this stage I'd been privileged to share for half a week.

After that my work with Vonnegut's writing slacked off. Much of it had been motivated by the joy of discovery, the thrill of getting involved with something totally new and virtually unknown to the rest of the profession. Kurt Vonnegut, of course, had been no secret to the middle-class readers of *The Saturday Evening Post* and all those drugstore paperbacks, but the level of culture that got its literature off newsstands was news to the academic world, and part of the fun of working on Vonnegut was bringing this whole new world of both author and readership into play. Now similar work was waiting with Donald Barthelme, who'd begun his career reviewing variety shows and Abbott and Costello movies (traces of which, unintelligible to most academic critics, made his fiction seem immensely more exotic than it was), and Jerzy Kosinski, who'd left a midden heap of early sociological work that promised to clarify the otherwise unspeakable nature of his terrifying fiction. Yet my early interest in Kurt had linked my name with his, and others would call from time to time with a project that brought me back into involvement.

First it was Michael Dirda from *The Washington Post Book World*, for whom I'd done a few reviews. In the summer of 1979 as Kurt's new novel, *Jailbird*, became available for prepublication coverage, Dirda asked me if I'd be talking with Vonnegut soon. Assured that the *Post* would give my efforts feature space, I wrote Kurt to ask if he'd be willing to let me visit and talk with him about the book. Of course—never yet had he ever refused a request for any type of help whatsoever. And so I made plans for a few days in New York, one afternoon of which would be spent discussing *Jailbird*.

Since the early 1970s I'd stayed at an inexpensive midtown hotel, the Royalton, which Dan Wakefield had recommended for several reasons, including price, location, decency, and the fact that throughout the 1950s and 1960s it had been where Vonnegut himself stayed when coming down from West Barnstable. Kurt had not forgotten it; Billy Pilgrim books a room there in *Slaughterhouse-Five* the night he appears on the radio talk show, and in *Jailbird* it would be the Royalton's coffee shop that Walter Starbuck discovers as a haven of care and compassion. The hotel was famous for many reasons, such as the 1920s residence of drama critic George Jean Nathan (a bellman once showed me what had been his suite), and it was still the place Jacques Cousteau favored when visiting New York. For the most part, however, its large, clean, yet inexpensive rooms were chosen by literary folks on low budgets; it was directly across the street from the Algonquin, where contacts could be met at the bar or in the lobby without the high expense of one of that hotel's rooms.

Until its renovation in the 1980s, when a French firm turned it into luxury affair (with corresponding prices), the Royalton had been a quaintly stable hotel, the same staff serving the same set of guests from year to year and from decade to decade. On this visit I mentioned to a bellman that Kurt Vonnegut used to be a customer, and he at once remembered Kurt, happy with the thought. Then his face fell a bit as he confided, "You know, he doesn't stay here any-more . . ." I felt glad that I could clear up this concern by explaining that Vonnegut moved to Manhattan in 1970 and now lived just a half dozen blocks away. The bellman brightened at once, and exclaimed with relief, "Oh, he doesn't *need* to stay here any more!"

My afternoon with Kurt was unexceptional. What struck me most were his working conditions: I'd been up in the Dell Publishing offices the day before, and from my editor's window could see into Vonnegut's back yard just half a block away. Now from Kurt's room I could look back up at Dell, and wondered at the sense of intimidation he might feel as an author, so long used to working in obscurity, who now not only knew that virtually any and every word he'd write would be published and read, but that the very skyscraper from which these words would issue was towering right up above him like a broadcast station to the world. I knew there were peculiar features to this arrangement. Earlier he'd told me the story of how Dell was rushing *Breakfast of Champions* through the editorial process even as he wrote it. A messenger would pick up sections of novel once Kurt thought they were ready, hurrying to the sixth floor offices down the block and around the corner. Just when Kurt thought the book was finished, however, the messenger returned. He'd been reading the pages as they came along, and felt the ending was inconclusive.

"I knew exactly what he meant," Kurt agreed. "It's like I learned in combat training for the infantry, the need to 'close with the enemy' in order to succeed. There were elements in the book that I was unconsciously avoiding, and the messenger could sense that." And so the original ending of *Breakfast of Champions*, which had Dwayne Hoover indulging his madness in an insane asylum, was rewritten to have Vonnegut himself hearing Kilgore Trout, in the voice of Kurt's father, crying out to "Make me young, make me young, make me young."

Did Kurt feel the presence of Dell Publishing so nearby? Only as part of the community in which he now lived, a neighborhood that also included the style of urban architecture his father had taught him to perceive and to appreciate. There was also an "angry energy" to the city that he could sense and feed from, a far different situation from when he would visit New York regularly but "never had a place to sit down." Yet this energy also served up plenty of interruptions: the phone would ring at least once every half hour, and each call was important, from *People* magazine requesting an interview (he declined) to the folks producing a musical version of *God Bless You, Mr. Rosewater* in a theater downtown.

The second instigation to do more work on Vonnegut came in a cutely roundabout way. The year before I'd begun spending time in Paris, where Julie and I had spent much of our month's honeymoon. Thereafter I'd make sure to return for a few weeks each October and April, the city's two most charming seasons. The reasons for these trips were several: my introduction to Paris coincided with the happiness of our new marriage, and spending time in a different culture, geography, and language went right along with this stage in life; I was beginning to savor the new style of Parisian writing, by Roland Barthes especially but also by Peter Handke, who'd shifted his residence from Austria and West Germany; and most of all I loved the pleasant routine of living for two or three weeks in a small hotel where no English was spoken, yet where a neighboring concierge still remembered Ernest Hemingway living across the street. Sometimes I'd come alone, but whenever possible brought along Julie, one of our children, or—for her seventieth birthday—my mother. Ihab Hassan helped me make contact with his old friend André LeVot, a Sorbonne professor who directed a center for the study of contemporary American fiction. André arranged invitations to speak at his campus, Paris-III (where the English department's offices occupied the house where actress Sarah Bernhardt was born, and where the principal lecture hall was built before 1600 as the amphitheater for the medical college's anatomy classes), and soon I'd met the whole crowd of young Americanist professors, all of them André's doctoral graduates serving their first appointments at universities around the country yet still commuting to their jobs from Paris, the inexorable center of everything important in France.

A Vonnegut project developed from one of these Paris encounters during April 1980. André LeVot had organized a conference at the Sorbonne—not the American-style mass-meeting of hundreds or even thousands, but rather a dozen specialists from three or four countries who'd spend a few mornings and after-noons sitting around a large table in the department's conference room (Sarah Bernhardt's dining room, perhaps?) while fifteen or twenty graduate students sat back along the walls and listened in on the exchange of ideas. From the University of East Anglia came Chris Bigsby and Malcolm Bradbury, who were planning a new critical series on contemporary writers with Methuen. My own closest friends at the conference were among the French—Marc Chénetier and Régis Durand—and most of my free time was spent with them. But for this trip I had my son Jonathan along. He was eleven at the time, about the same age as Malcolm's son, and before long Jonathan (bored by the conference proceedings) and Malcolm (who'd been traveling the world and seemed lonesome for his family at home) hit it off and became the best of friends, chatting away in the background about science-fiction plots, favorite films, and so forth.

Jonathan himself had been writing a SF novel about a society of rocks that organizes its own culture along geological principles. Malcolm was intrigued, and more than just flattering the kid's interest seemed anxious to hear how the plot would develop. When Jonathan asked what Malcolm was writing, his new friend described his editorial plans for the series, saying there was one science-fiction writer to be covered: Kurt Vonnegut. "My Dad's done work on him," Jonathan explained, and during the lunch between sessions that second day actually arranged the deal that brought me a contract with a thousand pound advance. Honest to God, that's how it happened. A year later I tried on my own to sell Malcolm and Chris a similar book on Peter Handke and botched the deal completely.

There were plenty of events from those weeks in Paris, including the night the Sorbonne's rector took the conferees out to dinner at a fancy restaurant on the Boulevard St. Germain where Malcolm helped Jonathan with the menu and coaxed him into ordering something only a child could have gotten away with in those circumstances: a Lobster Thermidor that cost the Sorbonne nearly three hundred dollars. But there was serious business, too, and in the end *Kurt Vonnegut* (London: Methuen, 1982) was the result. Not expecting to write again about Kurt's career, or at least so soon, I was surprised that I could devise something new: analysis of progress in his work from metaphor to discourse that began with formal experiments with various subgenres (dystopian narrative, science fiction, a spy thriller, the novel of apocalypse, and a run through a prince and the pauper story) and developed into an even more self-apparently technical manner of expression by first prefacing his works autobiographically and then incorporating his own authorship as a narrative component.

The book came easily, its concisely direct one hundred pages taking less than a month to write. But then I sat, stalled for six weeks with the conclusion. With Kurt still so obviously in mid-career there seemed no logical way to end the book; who knew if he'd continue in this personal vein of autobibliography or would move on to something else? Would he write two more novels or two dozen? Every few days I'd reread my hundred pages, think I had the momentum to crash through to the end, and then pull up short before the empty page. A critic's block more than a writer's block, it suddenly impressed me as being a problem of thinking too hard, of trying to be too smart. And so one evening, when I never write anyway, I poured an extra three or four pints of Guinness and let myself get a bit tipsy, then floated into the study to bang out what immediately (and again the next morning) seemed a satisfactory conclusion:

> From his family-magazine entertainments of the 1950s to his Nativity story reshaped for the American 1980s [*Sun-Moon-Star*], Kurt Vonnegut has been a writer simultaneously at the heart of his popular culture and in the forefront of the literary avant-garde. His work for *Collier's* and *The Saturday Evening Post* exploited structures sophisticated enough for a master's thesis in anthropology, yet effective among the country's least pretentious readers. Thematically his novels have challenged traditional American assumptions of hard work in the service of God-given destiny—yet they have been cheerfully accepted by a middle-class readership only tardily acknowledging such suspicions themselves. Kurt Vonnegut's fiction is a precursor of the great turnabout that American culture experienced during the late 1960s and early 1970s, an unsettling time in which age-old stereotypes of race, sex, and national character were challenged and in part overturned; from *Player Piano* through *Jailbird* Vonnegut progressively anticipates and evaluates the substance of these changes.

Structurally, such works as *Cat's Cradle* and *Slaughterhouse-Five* rank as major achievements in the novel's progress toward abstractly expressive, self-apparently honest writing: a fiction that does not demand a willing suspension of disbelief but instead respects the reader's creative intelligence and incorporates it in the making of literary art.

Kurt Vonnegut's harshest critics have accused him of being unable to end his stories and make conclusive decisions about the rightness or wrongness of his characters' beliefs. Too often, they say, his narratives close with an "et cetera," an "and so on," a "so it goes." But Vonnegut's genius is to tell the whole truth without fabricating a phony ending. The only real conclusion, he knows, is when one's own life ends, at which point everything quite simply stops. The child of a suicide, he has lived with that option since 1944, even before the great public trauma of his life, the needless destruction of Dresden. Phony endings ruin life: this was the message of *Breakfast of Champions*, where life imitated art in all the wrong ways. The true ending, the only conclusion with legitimate hope for man, is that life goes on. In Vonnegut's works there are no heroes, no villains; the best and the worst turn out to be pretty much the same. "This intolerable balancing of characters and arguments," Vonnegut admits in the headnote to *Happy Birthday, Wanda June*, "reflected my true feelings. I felt and still feel that everybody is right, no matter what he says." How thorough is that belief? We can only trust Kurt Vonnegut, that ultimately reliable Dutch uncle from the heartland of America:

> I had, in fact, written a book about everybody's being right all the time, *The Sirens of Titan*. And I gave a name in that book to a mathematical point where all opinions, no matter how contradictory, harmonized. I called it a *chronosynclastic infundibulum*.
> I live in one. (p. 90)

That conclusion is repeated here because I trust Kurt would like it to be. Shortly after the book appeared his wife, Jill Krementz, phoned me. She was putting together a privately printed book of comments on Kurt and his work to celebrate his upcoming sixtieth birthday, and she wanted permission to reprint my book's conclusion in hers. Why these pages? Because Kurt had told her they were the most truthful words anyone had ever written about him and his fiction.

What had those pints of Guinness liberated? The lines about "abstractly expressive, honestly self-apparent writing" were the nascent thesis of a study I'd write two years later, *The Self-Apparent Word: Fiction as Language/Language as Fiction* (Carbondale: Southern Illinois University Press, 1984). And the thoughts about life going on even while the artwork's conclusion hung in suspension came from Michael Stephens's novella, *Still Life* (New York: Kroesen Books, 1977), a work whose lyric equilibrium had given me a motto for living: that a *still* life is still *life*. It was the only time I used inebriation to get some writing out. As Vonnegut himself has remarked, drinking doesn't help your writing, just your *thinking* that you're getting something done—and then only for a half hour. But thirty minutes was all I'd needed for those pages, and they came out clear of any typos. The beer hadn't made me smarter, just dumber; but a certain amount of stupidity had been needed to cloud over that search for a rational conclusion that by definition would remain elusive.

Kurt Vonnegut, I thought, would be my last work on Kurt Vonnegut for some time. But in the hopscotch way that life proceeds, Kurt's pleasure with the book led to another project: helping producer Bob Weide prepare a television film on Kurt and his importance to the comic vein in American writing. When Bob called and introduced himself, the first thing he had to say was that Vonnegut had given him a copy of my book as the most reliable accounting of his work. Did I want to help write a documentary for public television on Kurt?

I was not enthusiastic. Following the Paris craze and my seduction by the writings of Roland Barthes and Peter Handke, still newer interests were developing. With the closing of our Paris hotel, Julie and I had started spending Octobers in England, on the wilds of Dartmoor; as a kid I'd read book after book about the RAF in World War II and its Spitfire bases out in such countryside, and my immediate plans went no further than rereading as many of these old flying narratives as I could before planning our next trip back. As for summer, that had become baseball time as I got involved with the local minor league club. Still, Bob Weide was emphatic that a Vonnegut documentary be made and that he *and*

Kurt—that was the clincher—felt it was imperative I be involved.

Could Bob come to visit us—to see my Vonnegut archive and sketch out some ideas for a treatment? He suggested a date a few months hence that had us back in England. I thought this would end the deal, but he said he could change his own plans to await our return. And so I dutifully arranged to host Bob for a few days at the end of October 1986.

The person who arrived just a week after we got home was no image of a Hollywood producer. I knew he was young, still in his mid-twenties, having begun his career at the age of nineteen after being rejected for college in USC's film program. He'd gone to work for an agency in Los Angeles that managed the film careers of several comics, the most famous of them Woody Allen, and in these circumstances of self-education and plentiful contacts Bob had risen to become a producer himself, winning a public TV award for *The Marx Brothers in a Nutshell* and an Emmy for his show on W. C. Fields. He was planning a documentary on Mort Sahl, hoped some day to do a similar program on Lenny Bruce, and was a great fan of that mid-range of 1950s TV comedians he'd seen only on kinescopes but whom I'd watched as a child. Like several other million seventeen-year-olds in the late 1960s, he'd read Vonnegut in high school and gone nuts over his style and humor. His enthusiasm for Kurt's work reminded me of mine, especially as it showed itself at a similar stage; how could I deny this kid a chance to produce a testament to his idol?

And a kid is surely what Bob was. He settled in for three days' stay with the enthusiasm our own son would show just a year later when coming home from his first semester in college: chowing down on home cooking, loading up huge cereal bowls with ice cream, and chattering away about everything from literary interests to current girlfriends at the same level of excitement. Thankfully Jonathan, a high-school senior, was still at home, and so our refrigerator was suitably stocked. As it was, having the two of them at our table made it seem less like we were hosting a Hollywood producer than one of Jonathan's friends. In coming years a visit from Bob meant we'd have to make the same grocery list as for spring break or weeks in the summer when Jonathan came back.

Working with Bob Weide brought me back into Vonnegut's immediate orbit. Kurt liked him a great deal, to the extent of calling him by a nickname, "Whyaduck," the formal name of Bob's production company borrowed from a bit of Marx Brothers patter about an ethnic pronunciation of the word "viaduct": "Why a duck?" Our working arrangement had begun with me giving Bob advice and photocopying things from my files, but soon he was mailing me copies of letters, typescripts, and other odds and ends Kurt was sending him. Sometimes the results were hilarious and quaintly insightful, such as when Kurt copied a letter to Bob that began with the salutation, "Dear Beaver . . ." Beaver, it turned out, was the childhood nickname of Dr. Bernard Vonnegut, the distinguished atmospheric physicist; but as Kurt worked on Bob's plans for some filming in upstate New York where Bernard still lived, we were all suddenly transported back over half a century to a little brother addressing his older sibling.

Kurt's appreciation was based on Bob's knowledge of and love for the fine old routines of classic American comedy. In the correspondence they exchanged I'd see frequent references to the comics of this era and their techniques. But what prompted Kurt to really open up was his knowledge that Bob could be counted on to get his joke and appreciate the subtle art of it. Soon I could expect a phone call every few weeks with Bob laughing over something Kurt had just written. These calls, by the way, would always come at three or four minutes before seven, Iowa time. I finally asked Bob why, and he explained that his budget was run on a shoestring and that he was waiting for the phone rates to change at five in LA. "Bob," I reminded him, "don't you set your watch five minutes fast?" and he confirmed it, saying it made him never late for an appointment. "That means it's not five o'clock yet," I chided him, and he broke out laughing. "Why didn't you tell me this years ago?" he complained. "You could have saved the company!" Yet his thoughts, as ever, were on our friend in New York. "Wait 'til Kurt hears why I've always been calling him at five minutes to eight!"

For his part, Vonnegut was doing all he could to facilitate Bob's plans. PBS had come through with $50,000 of start money towards a show for the "American Masters" series, and Bob had elected to shoot as much film as he could in New York. But there already was a documentary filled with scenes of Kurt walking around the East 40s in New York and talking about things from the couch in his and Jill's townhouse. In a month he'd be traveling to Buffalo where the symphony and chorus would premier his

Requiem, a magnificently serious work with a disarming title, *The Hocus Pocus Laundromat* (Kurt's reminder that requiems should not be *too* inhibiting). The folks in Buffalo were seeking ways to raise funds for this production, and Kurt had volunteered to speak the night before so donations could be taken at the door. Perhaps Bob could do some filming here.

Film, of course, is vision in motion, and Bob's cinematic imagination at once conceived a vehicle of expression: putting Kurt on a train from Grand Central to Buffalo and filming him along the way, responding to topics Bob would suggest from off camera. In Albany the train would pick up Bernard, and the two brothers could reminisce for the rest of the way to Buffalo. Amtrak volunteered a private car, and Bob was set for several hours of filming.

There are over three hours of raw film from this train ride, and it constitutes a remarkable treasury of Vonnegut in action. Between New York and Albany Bob fed Kurt questions, and also chocolate chip cookies as insurance against the inevitable energy drops. There is a moment where Kurt finds himself talking about Dresden in mid-cookie, and has to lick some messily melted chocolate off his fingers while describing the physical details of being a "corpse miner" after the firestorm. After Bernard boards the train in Albany, the talk becomes a genuine dialogue—not between a world-famous novelist and an equally renowned physicist, but between two old company men sharing shop talk as the train rolls by the General Electric plant outside Schenectady.

The Requiem itself makes for a typical Kurt Vonnegut story. Attending the premier of Andrew Lloyd Webber's Requiem, Kurt found himself reading the English translation of the old Council of Trent document that formed its text. "I was absolutely flabbergasted by its grisly details and overall theme of suffering and damnation," Kurt remarks. "What terrible sentiments to hold when being sent to the grave!" And so he decided to write his own Requiem, a gentler work that promised an afterlife not of agony and torture but of lovely, peaceful sleep. On jury duty, he found himself serving with a composer, who set his words to music— words that had been translated into Latin by another fortuitous acquaintance. As performed by the Buffalo Symphony and a massed church choir, Vonnegut's Requiem would be the centerpiece of his visit and the climax to Bob's film.

But first there was the business of Kurt's lecture the night before. It was his standard stump speech, "How to Get a Job Like Mine," which I'd hear in person a year later during Kurt's third visit to Cedar Falls. Bob was along for that trip too, and so he remains wedded to Kurt in my appreciation of this perhaps most classic Vonnegut performance. On both occasions Vonnegut had been spending so much time with Weide—not just for the filming, but because he genuinely enjoyed Bob's presence—that "Whya-duck" seems a personification of the audience for whom Kurt performs.

If in 1977 Vonnegut had profited by playing with his audience's notion of him as an exotic guru (and then revealing just how avuncular and vernacularly American he really was), the late 1980s found him approaching his listeners as a wise but unprepossessing elder who had some helpful wisdom the young folks might wish to share—as a grandfather, in other words, which is what he had become during his last Cedar Falls visit, leaving for Boston for his introduction to such status and duties.

Both speeches began with a reference to the weather. It was March in Buffalo and early April in Cedar Falls, but complaints about the climate are a common-enough topic to work with any time and any place, and it is to this reality that Vonnegut draws his audience's attention. As always, his method is that of asking questions for which the presumed answer is not only incorrect but which prompts the listeners to deconstruct the problem so that it can be seen clearly—at which point the speaker takes advantage of the cleared ground to make his point.

Why are we always so unhappy about the weather? Kurt's initial question presumes a broad base of agreement—everyone is always ready to find some complaint about it—but then goes on to show how the roots of this dissatisfaction are in one's most basic presumptions. How many seasons are there, he asks: four? No, that's wrong, because there are actually *six*! Summer, fall, winter, and spring fail to allow for those two in-between seasons: the "unlocking" of March and April, when the joy of spring is not yet here (even when we expect it to be), and the "locking" period of November and December when nature begins to shut down in preparation for the deep freeze of true winter. It is a piece of wisdom Kurt himself picked up nearly forty years before from a friend when living in Schenectady, and which has made him happier about the weather ever since. As for his audiences in Buffalo and

Cedar Falls, his words were equally hopeful and assuring: "I think you'll be a lot more comfortable on this planet now that I've told you that."

Having set the tone for his speech and indicated its structure of friendly advice, Kurt proceeded to acknowledge his own somewhat fallen status (at least in terms of being an almost universally praised author). To make the point, and also to comment wryly on its silliness, he faced his audience each time and apologized. For what? For nothing in particular—just to make fun of the traditional rule in public speaking that warns the speaker never to begin by appearing apologetic. "I'm terribly sorry," he told us, and then ran through a litany of apologies, saying he felt absolutely terrible about it, that it would never happen again, and so forth for a full minute. His tenor and demeanor were sincere; indeed, he projected the essence of apology, even as we noted that there was nothing whatsoever that he was apologizing *for*. Like his story about the weather, the item brought to the audience's attention was textual and deconstructive: a rule for public speaking, itself detached from any topic, was here turned inside out, again without any reference to a subject. The listeners were left with just Kurt Vonnegut himself, apologizing for being Kurt Vonnegut, who in breaking this rule was setting the stage for other traditions his speech would question, and making himself utterly loveable in the process.

Both items were generated by an interaction between Kurt and his listeners, and these points of interaction followed what he had described in *Palm Sunday* as the classic joke structure favored in his fiction: asking a question, prompting an answer, and then revealing that the response is off the mark thanks to either the humor or corrective information being supplied. The pages of Vonnegut's novels, written and then rewritten to satisfaction just one page at a time, are a series of just such settings and releasings of energy, kinetic in the sense that they incorporate the reader's movement as part of the story's larger process. Just as the reader is asked to take a step and is then pushed off balance and sent in a different direction by Vonnegut's fictive texts, here in his lecture he was citing a text, requesting the audience's attitude toward it, and then gently deconstructing that attitude by showing how the simple facts of the matter lead elsewhere.

"How to Get a Job Like Mine" followed this practice with any number of other texts, some of which Kurt asked his audience to help him rewrite: the Requiem Mass of the sixteenth century (which his own version transforms from one of hideous judgmentality to one of beautitude and rest), the Bible (which he replaces with the Free Thought corrections from his grandfather Clemens Vonnegut's pamphlet, *An Instruction in Morals from the Standpoint of a Free Thinker*), and his listener's own attempts at writing novels or short stories. Then came a set of positive citations, from Nietzsche, Marx, and Eugene V. Debs, all of which indicate that true liberty is just now being born in America (a country that didn't free slaves or enfranchise women until the second century of its existence, with much progress still to be made). Along the way there are rudely funny stories, such as Thomas Jefferson being unable to free his slaves not because of any philosophical or moral reasons but because they were mortgaged.

Both lectures concluded with Vonnegut's story-line chalk talk, an item in his repertoire since the 1960s (and drawing on late 1940s material from his studies in anthropology at the University of Chicago). But now in the context of both Vonnegut's canon of works and his posture as a spokesman on public issues it was used for a different purpose. The first half of it revealed the common rise-and-fall structure to narratives that readers so delight in. For the second half of his chalk talk, however, Kurt contrasted such patterns to the essentially flat nature of primitive tales, in which there are no perceptible highs or lows, just simply level progress. Against what appears to be the flat-line boredom of Native American (and other primitive) narratives Vonnegut displayed with great panache the roller-coaster fortunes of Cinderella and other beloved protagonists. But can truly great literature be simplified along such structures, systematic enough to be generated by computers (which earlier in his talk Vonnegut had rejected as an evil of modern life)? As a test, he subjects Shakespeare's *Hamlet* to such analysis, finding out—to the audience's amazement—that its trajectory is just as flat as any primitive tale. There are no great rises or falls to Hamlet's fortune, no way of telling whether one incident or another is "good news" or "bad news."

Does this mean, Vonnegut asked with the same disarming simplicity that characterized his other deconstructive questions, "that Shakespeare couldn't write any better than an Indian?" Not exactly, for the genius of both the greatest writer in the English language and of the anonymous authors of culturally central tales preserved by primitive societies is that each recognizes that the truth about life is that it does appear flat to us, because we really don't know what is the good news and what is the bad. Yet for our interest and entertainment we tell ourselves that we do, and such pretense yields enjoyable tales like "Cinderella" and countless other civilized narratives existing as novels, short stories, films, and television shows.

Could there be a danger in such practice? Here is where Vonnegut swung toward his point: that we become bored not just with level stories but with our lives themselves when they lack the delightful but ultimately mischievous variances of entertainment. It is a fallibility that reaches from family life to national policy, including the current administration that gets the country into a little trouble (Grenada, Panama) and then gets it out again, making for a manageable roller-coaster ride when in fact the duty of government should be to keep things stable and level.

Ending as he did on the topic of how poorly our government was serving us underscored Kurt's commitment to public issues. Two years later, during the Gulf War, Dan Wakefield would tell me how Kurt had been using whatever forum was available in New York to speak out against President Bush's administration of the affair and was calling for the president's impeachment, something none of us had ever seen Kurt do, even during the most disgraceful final days of Richard Nixon. "I've never seen him so mad," Dan remarked. Would Kurt's passion have any effect on events—would it save one soldier's or civilian's life, would it end the war one day or even one minute earlier? That was not the point. I recalled what Vonnegut had told interviewers over two decades before, when *Slaughterhouse-Five* and his earlier novels were being embraced by a new generation. If you can influence how young people form and hold their values, he advised, there would be a chance for a better future when these readers would have grown into positions of power and leadership. Such was the power of Kurt's words from the podium that night in Cedar Falls: not that President Bush would desist from military adventures, or even that the citizenry would rise up and stop him; but that the future citizenry of America would, having learned by this example, prevent anything so horrible from happening again.

Kurt's visit in April of 1989 was less involved and engaging than in 1977. Loree was determined not to exhaust him, and so there were no fancy meals and certainly no parties. Kurt did want to make himself available to the students, however, and so the afternoon before his speech he took his place on the demonstration stage of the university's largest science auditorium where, flanked by Loree and myself, he answered our questions for a while and then others from the audience. Literary queries bored him, but when I remembered Bob Weide's success at getting Kurt and Bernard to talk about the old days at GE I was able to spark his interest by asking about the publicity material he wrote when working for the Research Lab and then later for a Boston agency. Shop talk! And not about the lit business, but real life! For about twenty minutes Kurt went on about how he'd been privileged to learn about industries famous for their engineering in cement, for the amazing sturdiness of their castings. Had we taken him over to talk with the engineers and development workers at the John Deere Research facility on the other side of town, he could not have been happier.

Kurt had ducked the conference banquet in favor of a quiet dinner with Loree, and so he was fresh for his speech. But addressing over a thousand people—especially when the key to one's approach is personal interaction with the audience—is physically and emotionally draining, and so we all knew well enough not to schedule anything else for Kurt that night. Loree said he'd feel most comfortable if he could unwind afterwards with "his friends," and so an intimate group of us gathered for a few hours on the cozily furnished sunporch of Loree's home just a minute's walk from campus: Kurt, Loree, Loree's adopted daughter Dede (now twenty-one but in Kurt's mind still a toddler), myself and Julie, and Bob Weide (who'd been along for the whole week in Iowa and whom Kurt adored).

For awhile Kurt and Bob bounced jokes off each other. Kurt's material was classic, spanning styles from Laurel and Hardy to Bob and Ray. Bob was of course more current: he'd been working on comedy specials for HBO, was an analyst of all the new comics, and had been associated with Billy Crystal. Yet Kurt and Bob's interplay proved that there is a timeless vein to American comedy, shaped as it is by both vernacular speech and attitudes and glorying in the delights of deft timing. Above all, it capitalizes for effect on making the speaker rather than the listener seem silly. Not just because he'd known most of us so long but because he'd first met Dede as a baby, Kurt was laughing at himself for being caught up in the pose of being grandfatherly. As always, the key was to turn the situation's humor back on himself, as he did when one of us made a slightly off-color remark; everyone suddenly realized that Dede was so much younger than the rest, and a moment's silence intervened. Comedy to the rescue, with a combination of timing, vernacular speech, and a line whose language deconstructs the situation: "Oh my God," Kurt gasped in mock horror, "don't say *fuck* in front of the B-A-B-Y!"

It has been through Bob Weide's ongoing work that I've kept involved with Kurt Vonnegut on a personal level. Things will pop up in the mail from Los Angeles, and from Kurt in New York because he knows I'm engaged in plans for Bob's show. The good that this has done for Kurt is obvious. His worst fears have been that both scholars and taste-makers would consign his work to the dim past of the 1960s, writing off his importance with the same gesture that reduces passing trends to oblivion. Which is vexingly unfair, because Vonnegut was expressing his ideas in a unique literary style almost two full decades before the hullabaloo of 1967–69, and has continued doing so well after the trend-followers have wandered off in search of other fascinations. With Bob Weide as his ideal audience, Kurt feels understood and appreciated. And as I watched the two of them interacting that night at Loree's, it was evident that Bob was one instance of Kurt having attained his goal from twenty years before: reaching the young and "poisoning their minds with humanity," so that this new generation's own work would be more beneficial to mankind. Back then, Bob had been a high-school kid reading *Cat's Cradle*, and if Vonnegut's influence on him was even a fraction of what Bob recalls, it must have contributed to his developing genius and ambitions that took him into film work and award-winning documentaries on America's great comedians. Now, as one of the brightest and most successful producers in his field, he was not only doing the definitive treatment of Kurt and his work but had won the old man's confidence to the extent of getting option rights to *Mother Night* with plans for translating the essence of Vonnegut's art to the screen. Through two decades of obscurity, another of unwanted frenetic fame, and now in a third career as a somewhat elder spokesman for moral and cultural values, Vonnegut was witnessing the payoff: a kid whose mind had been suitably infected with all the best of American art and who was now producing art of his own.

In several contexts Kurt has written about "the vast polymer of existence," something his training as a biochemist made evident in theory and that his life experiences have confirmed. Connections are everywhere, and they are endless; when asked about "influence" he laughs, because they are so infinite as to defy articulation or even comprehension. Trying to expound on them, he knows, leads to great silliness, for in our limited state we never get the idea quite right. In *Cat's Cradle* he calls such essentially pointless projections of organized meaning, such as national states and institutionalized religions, "granfalloons"; the significant connections are always indecipherable, and they're referred to as being in a "karass."

Needless to say, everyone who truly likes Kurt Vonnegut's works, let alone those who are lucky enough to know him, prefer to think that they are members of his karass, and vice versa. As a critic I would not make such a claim, for karass-membership is surely limited to such truly magical people as Loree Rackstraw and Bob Weide. But elsewhere in Vonnegut's canon of beliefs is the feeling that the best one can do in life is to be "of use" to someone else. And that was the phrase he employed when thanking me for my critical work and later advising me to keep teaching in Iowa: both activities were *of use*. I accepted his thanks, and kept on writing, and then later took his advice and stayed in Cedar Falls. Those are the ways knowing Kurt Vonnegut has been of use to me.

2

Jerzy Kosinski

With Kurt Vonnegut, I had always been reserved and respectful. He was, of course, the most important writer I'd work with, and I had been reading his books as a student beforehand. The key inhibiting factor, however, was generational: he was about my father's age, and his eldest son was not much younger than myself. In my dealings with Jerzy Kosinski, all this got turned around. Although still a young assistant professor when meeting him, I'd already had one book (*Innovative Fiction*) accepted for publication and was beginning to get in touch with a wide range of authors. Kosinski was only ten years older than myself—about the age of my uncle, with whom I was prone to kid around. That whole generation of writers born between 1931 and 1934 would seem like older brothers and sisters, and because a number of my adolescent interests looked back to the history, popular culture, and music of their own era I sensed a comfortable kinship.

Consequently, I felt a lot more relaxed with Jerzy, and almost from the start treated my acquaintance with him in a much more casual manner. I should have realized that Vonnegut could give me advice: "Those are always the ones," he'd say about anything one was taking for granted, "that blow up right in your face." My working relationship with Jerzy certainly did. Another contrast with Vonnegut should have made it even more obvious, for even as Kurt was dissuading me from taking the SUNY-Albany job and urging me to consider how much more wholesome and worthwhile my life would be in Iowa, Kosinski was proclaiming, in his manner that was at once shrilly imperative and smugly self-aggrandizing, "Why not to try? As one who has failed many times, I still advise the life of risk!"

Yet there remains a curious influence, The Kosinski Effect, that I cannot efface even as my contact with him vanished and his writing has ceased to be part of my own scholarly work. His counsel "to risk, to try" was given in 1976, four years after I'd taken the job at Northern Iowa that seemed to materialize out of nowhere. I'd been hired in my first position just before that disastrous 1968 MLA Convention in Denver when the profession was amazed by a simultaneous glut of graduating Ph.D.'s and a dearth of new positions, and as I struggled through three unhappy years at Northern Illinois University there seemed no exit. Then in November 1971, I met Jerzy Kosinski; on his desk was a letter from Daniel J. Cahill, department head at the University of Northern Iowa, who had been researching Kosinski's work for some time. Did I know "this Cahill," Jerzy asked. If not, I certainly should, and he promised to put us in touch. He did, and a half year later I had a sparkling new job at a higher rank and half again the salary, with convenient teaching and research benefits galore.

Was Jerzy responsible? The Kosinski Effect is such that one never knows. It's unlikely, given the complications of university hiring, but the point of Jerzy's manner was to make one suspect that he was involved, in some way controlling things. *Control*, I found, was the key element in his fictive vision as well, a vision that became indistinguishable from his personal life. And control for his own and not anybody else's benefit. Although Vonnegut knew that my job in Iowa was a blessing, Kosinski's motive for getting me there translated as clear self-interest: having time and money and a senior position from which to do my research on him, and doing it under the supervision of a Kosinski friend and specialist, could only benefit Jerzy's reputation.

Until 1970 I'd never heard of him. But as with Vonnegut, word of Kosinski's work came from a friend. Mike Krasny, who'd been with me at Madison, wrote regularly from California, where he was teaching African American lit at San Francisco State, and one letter commented on how bizarre he found contemporary American fiction. "I've read *The Painted Bird* and all those Vonnegut and Brautigan novels," Mike complained, "and it still doesn't make sense." What, I pondered, was *The Painted Bird*? Within a week I'd read it, *Steps*, and some essays by this new writer named Jerzy Kosinski. A dust-jacket biography said he'd written two books on collective behavior under the pseudonym "Joseph Novak," so I sought out those as well. Then came another piece of fascinating information: he taught at Yale, and had a third novel, *Being There*, soon to be published. One final note from his bio clinched it: as a student in postwar Poland, he'd attended the national film school in Łodz with a close friend, Roman Polanski. It struck me as obvious that there were tonal similarities between Polanski's sometimes horrific films and the macabre aspects of *The Painted Bird*, especially in the way both artists managed to contain and control their effects short of falling into what would otherwise be titillating or ridiculous. As with Vonnegut's work, here was a trail to be followed of early efforts and influential associations. Kurt had left tracks in all those essays and popular magazine stories; perhaps in Jerzy's sociological writings and experiences (artistic and otherwise) from Eastern Europe could be found a key to understanding not just *The Painted Bird* but much else in contemporary American fiction that was puzzling Mike Krasny and perplexing me as I tried to prepare my courses and get to work on the era's scholarship.

And so I wrote Kosinski at Yale, describing my interest in his work and asking if there might be a time when I could meet him for an interview. This was in fall of 1971 when, heady with my sense of discovery of contemporary American fiction, I was getting involved with projects all over, including the collaborative books with John Somer and explorations of experimental fiction by African American writers with another doctoral student and part-time instructor, John O'Brien. I'd written Donald Barthelme and received a polite reply indicating that an interview by mail was possible. Ronald Sukenick wrote back with details of his just-completed novel, *Out*, and how I might meet him later on when he'd be speaking at the University of Chicago. Similar contacts were made with Steve Katz, Clarence Major, Jonathan Baumbach, and Gilbert Sorrentino. There was a formality to these approaches, and quite often the writer's response was guarded, worried that I might be overstressing certain aspects of my research (Katz, for example, assured me that it was no use trying to find any copies of his M.A. thesis on Coleridge, as he'd burned them all.) Thus I expected somewhat of the same from Kosinski, who might not be too happy with my plans for digging up influential elements from his sociological work and experiences in Poland.

Hence the surprise when my letter to him was answered not in kind but with a phone call. Yes, he was very interested in meeting me for an interview, and hoped I could come to New Haven before the end of semester (when he'd be leaving for a skiing trip in Europe). Had I seen the pamphlets he'd written offering commentary on his first two novels? He'd "rush" copies of them to me that day. His voice was emphatic, sharpened by an Eastern European accent that made his words hurry forward like bullets to a target, each sentence cresting at midpoint like a siren being cranked and then winding down with its own momentum. The atmosphere was one of *film noir*, a black and white cinematography capturing the shadows of Iron Curtain intrigue, with Kosinski's presence as a startling flash of energy amid the murkiness of narrow, winding streets, and foreign-looking fixtures.

Soon afterwards a good-sized package arrived, festooned with multicolored stamps and stickers advising that everything was RUSH, PRIORITY, EXTREMELY URGENT, and even a few odd references to FRAGILE and HANDLE WITH CARE, although the reinforced mailer was solid as a rock. None of these imperatives had anything to do with postal rates or regulations; the postage added up to the tariff for simple first-class surface mail. Yet Kosinski's purpose had been achieved, as his package reached me in one day, thrice as fast as mailings from the east coast usually took.

If his phone call had impressed me and his stamps and stickers had intimidated the mail carriers, the materials he sent were not only pertinent to my research but overwhelming. There were the two neatly printed booklets, the first discussing the roles of memory and the imagination in *The Painted Bird*, the second discoursing in apparently random manner (like the novel itself) on issues associated with the writing of *Steps*. Then some offprints from *The American Scholar* and a raft of interviews and reviews from all over. He'd taken great care with these clips, using a photocopier's enlarger where the original print was small, screening out extraneous material, and employing a clever system of colored stickers and highlighting to draw attention to each piece's salient point. Often there would be typed responses in the margin, replete with underscoring, caps, and exclamation marks, as if Kosinski were undertaking a dialogue with every utterance about him and his work. Had I wished, I could have completed my research and published my conclusions right there. Indeed, the contents resembled nothing less than a publicist's package. I noted that the sticker bearing Kosinski's return address was headed "Scientia-Factum, Inc.," and that this logo appeared on many of the enclosures (as well as being the purported publisher of the two booklets, *Notes of the Author* and *The Art of the Self*). Yet everything written by Kosinski himself bore his signature and a lavish inscription, and I had the feeling that he'd be more than willing to write up my research for me.

With plans set to meet Kosinski in late November, I went about learning whatever I could. *Being There* was now published, and I read it with great pleasure, delighted at the way its author could play out the simplest of practical jokes into a sustained narrative. I looked into the sociological climate of the late 1950s and early 1960s in which Kosinski's doctoral work and early research had been pursued—it was an era, just then ending, in which such studies (as those by Vance Packard and William H. Whyte) could be bestsellers and even (in the case of books by C. Wright Mills) crafted with a lyricism appropriate to the finest novel of manners. Mills had taught at Columbia, where Kosinski had worked toward a doctorate, and so that was one more connection to be explored.

But first there was the business with Roman Polanski. I'd known about the filmmaker long before the novelist, and had been fascinated with how his Polish film-school education, a distillation of everything I'd admired in European art films, somehow equipped him to become a quintessential director of British and American films in the 1960s. Could there be a parallel track in Kosinski's development as he brought similar nuances of the Continental novel into the current stream of American innovative fiction? Then, too, Polanski and Kosinski had endured similar childhoods, separated from their families and terrorized as orphans by some of the most grisly aspects of the war. Each had learned self-reliance, and each now flaunted a highly idiosyncratic style of independence. To learn about Kosinski I would certainly have to become even more familiar with Polanski's life and work.

On my own campus the university film series was screening *Repulsion*, appropriately enough on Halloween. I'm no fan of horror movies, but knew how obvious it was that I should see this one, Polanski's first film after leaving Poland (and his success with *Knife in the Water*) for the West. So I dutifully showed up and let myself be wrung through the mangle of devices that made this film such a classic of terror.

Like Kosinski's fiction, Polanski's cinematic art depends upon subtlety of control. Horrific works in both media often rush into extravagant display, giving readers and audiences the orgy of violence they've come to expect. *Repulsion*, however, takes these expectations and, for at least the first half hour, disappoints them. As the camera follows Catherine Deneuve home from work, passing through a neighborhood pub (where she is good-naturedly teased by male colleagues) and back to the flat she shares with her sister and her sister's boyfriend (whose ambiance seems one of constant lovemaking), one is struck by nothing more apparent than the young woman's beauty and shyness; at the very most, she is discomforted by the atmosphere of sex that surrounds her, and the only caution a viewer might sense is the unspecified fear Deneuve's eyes seem to be expressing. When the first turn of plot reveals only that the sister and boyfriend will be away for the weekend, leaving Catherine Deneuve alone, one feels that the major threat to the protagonist's composure is being removed and that everything will be all right.

Which is just when everything begins to go wrong. In the couple's absence, the bright and cheerful flat becomes dark and foreboding. The hallway especially seems long and shadowy, and in her discomfort Deneuve begins noticing odd details, such as a crack beside the light switch. As viewers, we note this crack because its presence is montaged with the actress's worried glance. A bit later, we see her worried glance again, but now know why: she's looking at the same bit of wall near the light switch where the crack has disappeared.

Other points of reference in the flat, which has become both hers and the film's world, begin to form a motif: the hall that becomes even longer and darker, and a plate of leftovers that becomes moldy and putrescent as if time is elapsing in weeks rather than hours. Finally there is the film's first outright scare: as Deneuve takes advantage of a momentary brightening of the light to view herself in a mirror, a male figure is seen standing behind her—which of course disappears the moment her expression shifts back from one of ease to fear.

Each image, a review of the film shows, has been reinforced by a specific mechanical technique. The hall is darker because of less lighting, but is also longer because Polanski has used a distorting camera lens; later on in the film, when his character's perception is thoroughly deranged, he will reconstruct the entire set with wildly disproportionate angles to the walls, ceiling, and floor. The plate of food is made to look worse and worse by a combination of lighting, camera angle and proximity, and changes to the physical property itself. The most effective device, however, is the use of sound, which for the hallucination scene becomes absent. When Deneuve sees the man standing behind her, she turns with a start, slamming the mirrored door shut and looking as if she has screamed—but the soundtrack here, and actually for the moments before, is totally blank. If the audience hears anything, it is the gasps of horror from those in the seats around. Which is most effective, for the most unnerving terror is not up there on the screen but down here among us in the seats.

Using the most basic elements of film—light, perspective, and sound—Polanski has begun conditioning his viewers to expect terror. Thenceforth every visual fright will be accompanied by a distortion in sight and a silence on the soundtrack: when Deneuve worries about the suspect light switch, for example, the perspective seems a bit off and we cannot hear her footsteps as she approaches it, which sets us up for the fright when she reaches to flick the switch and the plaster suddenly fractures apart with a startling crash that reminds us there is such a thing as sound. It is because action only intrudes into this world after light, sound, and perspective have been established as major elements that the cinematic experience becomes so fully felt.

The conditioning process becomes a thing in itself when the director feels the time has come to play with it. Because every act of terror has been accompanied with and forecast by silence on the soundtrack, Polanski knows he can play some tricks, scaring his audience by cutting the sound and then not having anything happen. What is most horrific comes not from any subject represented on the screen but from the very materials of filmmaking themselves: sound, light, and perspective, with action itself simply as a foil to these devices. Here might be a key to how Jerzy Kosinski's similarly terrifying fiction worked—not by saturating the page with cascading waves of violence, but by using the material effect of written language to condition a sense of horror.

Not that either *Repulsion* or *The Painted Bird* lacks scenes of graphic horror. It's just that such truly outlandish displays are saved, held back much longer than even the suspensefully inclined person might expect. And not just so that the wildest action can be saved for last. Those scenes alone would not be half as horrifying had not both director and author conditioned their audiences beforehand, inviting predictable assumptions and then dismantling them so that by the time something truly frightful hits the screen or the page one is virtually defenseless against it, all the customary defenses having been systematically deconstructed.

I knew this was true because at this Halloween screening of *Repulsion* I was transfixed with horror. Some in the audience, of course, had come for a scream-fest. But others of us fancied ourselves as more sophisticated consumers—and, after all, I was here to study Polanski's art. Yet well before the film's end I was twitching and howling, and even after Polanski's quietly graceful denouement—where the camera leisurely scans the shambles of the flat to settle in on a childhood portrait of his heroine where her eyes suggest the same discomfort that has generated all this horror—I was worried about the dark and spooky walk home.

That night I took the film's deconditioning experience to bed with me, and was still tossing with nightmares well past breakfast time. What woke me was the bedside phone, the incessantly rhythmic ring of which was taking me back to the soundtrack's regulated fury that accompanied the grisly, slashing murder scene (where Catherine Deneuve does in the innocuous caller whom her psychosis has transformed into a dire threat). I'd certainly made quite a state of myself, not just by seeing *Repulsion* but by getting immersed in this whole Kosinski business. As if *The Painted Bird* and *Repulsion* weren't awful enough, these two creators had suffered from life imitating art: Polanski's wife, Sharon Tate, and several of their friends had been murdered by Charles Manson's gang at a party Kosinski was scheduled to attend (he'd delayed his flight to find some lost luggage, and by not showing up as a victim pegged himself as the crime's first suspect). True, Polanski and Kosinski remained survivors, just as they'd survived equally grotesque horrors in World War II. But their survival seemed predicated by an ability to control, rather than efface, such monstrosities around them. And now I was putting myself in their orbit, scheduled to meet the more formidable of the two in just a few weeks.

The voice that roused me from my troubled sleep did not snap me into reality. If anything, it put me more firmly back in the film's world of horror, for here was a shrill, highly inflected Eastern European speaker straight from our popular culture's nightmare world of Bela Lugosi, lashing out like a whip to command my attention.

"Professor Klinkowitz!" it shrieked. "This is Jerzy Kosinski in New Haven! Will you please come and see me tonight!" It was a different Kosinski than had phoned me earlier that fall. Then he had been calm and courteous, even ingratiating. Now he seemed hurried and distracted—as if he was calling from a phone booth in a bus station just seconds before his bus was about to leave. In future years I'd come to recognize this mood as one of impatience with matters he couldn't control, almost as if talking hard and fast would gain his end. Kosinski's insistence was a force to behold, and here I was just barely awake and trying to deal with it.

At least my pure instinct for survival took over where reason may have lagged. "No!" I shrieked in return, a cry that worked as a backfire to Kosinski's raging imperatives and gave me a bit of breathing space.

"You see, a problem has come up," a calmer Kosinski began to explain. "I may have to leave the country suddenly, with very little notice. And I would like to do our interview before that happens. We must seize the opportunity! Who knows? As the saying goes, I could be dead tomorrow!"

Making it a life or death matter impressed me, and I asked if tomorrow night would be ok. That was fine, Kosinski agreed, and I set about changing my airline and hotel reservations. That was easy enough, but I'd planned on using the next several weeks to review Kosinski's work and arrange a set of thoughtful questions. Now I was taking off for a flight east with a hastily packed bag and some even more chaotic carry-on luggage holding books, offprints, and notes I'd try to get in order before meeting the man himself.

My friends Lynn and Mel Bendett met me at LaGuardia; on the way home I'd spend some time with them in New York, but for now they drove me straight up the Parkway to New Haven. I was settled into the Sheraton by seven, and phoned Kosinski to let him know I was in town. Would he be free tomorrow morning after breakfast? "Why not right now?" he asked, as I should have guessed, and so in a few minutes I was making my way over to the Yale campus through the darkening chill of this November night.

It was Sunday, with streets and sidewalks deserted. Davenport College, where Kosinski lived in a top-floor resident-master's apartment, was easy enough to find, but its aspect was foreboding, an architectural rendering of mediaeval gimcrackery that made it seem less like a university hall than the set for a mystery film. The four-story climb up the narrow, twisting stairway was a worrisome thrill of wondering what lurked behind each heavily studded oak door. When I reached the top and knocked on Kosinski's, the intimidation factor could not have been any more acute.

Yet opening the door was a gracious, beckoning host, dressed in corduroy slacks and a comfortable looking sweater; behind him the room looked warm, cheerful, and cozy. There was nothing threatening, now, in Kosinski's manner, and as he welcomed me in his only intention was putting me at ease. He introduced me to his companion, using her nickname, Kiki; I knew she was more formally the Baroness Katherina von Fraunhofer, a woman whose formidable ancestry was equaled by her success in the business world, where she had headed her own advertising agency before meeting Kosinski and dedicating herself to his work. Kiki offered to bring us some beer, and her gracious ease made me hope she'd linger with us. But after a minute of polite conversation she was off to another room, leaving Kosinski and me to settle down in his study—he behind his desk, me in a luxurious leather chair next to one of Davenport's leaded windows. Had there been a fire in the fireplace and brandy in our glasses instead of Heineken's, the atmosphere could not have been more perfect for the mulling over of literature and life.

With my tape recorder running and Kosinski's in place beside it (as a "back-up system," he explained), we began talking about the progression of events that had taken him from childhood during the war through his experiences as a student and young man in the postwar Polish collectivized state to his emigration to America in 1957. Sociology had been an interest, but also film and still photography. Did he have any continuing interests in these subjects? Not really—they were simply devices to help him escape Poland, and the fact that he had become a master of all of them was incidental.

Our conversation, which had begun about 8:30 PM, was now stretching well past ten, with no signs of lagging or abating. Jerzy was a fascinating storyteller; I was swept away by all the exotic details, and he of course (I now recognize) was enthralled by himself—egotistic, of course, but in the spellbinding way that made him a favorite guest on Johnny Carson's *Tonight Show* and other TV programs. In any event, there was energy from both sides as I feasted on the narratives that Kosinski gloried in spinning.

Then, at 10:30, the phone rang. Jerzy picked it up on his desk and after saying hello responded to his caller in French and then, as he waited for a connection, covered the receiver and addressed me. The soul of politeness, he wished to excuse himself because "the conversation I am now about to have will be in a language other than we have been speaking." Then it was back to business on the phone, where he conducted a lengthy conversation in Polish about what seemed a none too happy matter.

During this time Kiki had joined us—perhaps to offer more beer, more likely because she knew the phone call meant something serious. As indeed it did. The talk in Polish went on for about ten minutes, with Jerzy's voice a tide of stern imperatives occasionally ebbing away as he absorbed the displeasing information from abroad. Finally he said goodbye (a phrase I remembered from the kitchen Polish of my in-laws in Milwaukee), replaced the receiver, and turned to Kiki.

"That was my brother," he told her, and added—for my benefit—"in Poland." He paused for just a moment, then delivered the news.

"You see," he said to me, "my mother is very sick. In fact, the doctors say she will live only another month or two. She wishes to see me before she dies . . . and of course I would like to see her." That was why he'd phoned me yesterday to say he might have to leave the country on very short notice.

To visit Poland? "No," Jerzy said emphatically. "That would be impossible," and he motioned toward the tape machines which had just recorded his stories of covert manipulation and illegal exit. "My mother would be flown to a free city—Amsterdam—where we could spend some time together." And so was this conversation I'd overheard but not understood to plan the meeting?

Not exactly, since the flight had been arranged earlier that day. But now there was a complication. For this, he turned to his anxious companion.

"The doctors have spoken to my brother," he told Kiki. "And they say we will have to make arrangements for the body in Holland."

Kiki gasped, and even I could guess what the prognosis had been. But Jerzy repeated it nevertheless.

"The flight, they say, will kill Mama."

For several moments none of us spoke. Jerzy remained expressionless, Kiki withdrew into a worried silence, and I sat transformed. All the horror I'd thought was locked safely outside now took possession of the room, and I pondered how terror truly stalked this man, who in addition to everything else was now being placed in the inexorable position of engineering his mother's death. That he had mastered the art of horror in his fiction was remarkable, but no more so than the manner in which he was able to deal with its continual intrusions into his life.

As far as Kiki and I were concerned, the silence could have continued into the night. But Jerzy broke it, punching the red button on each recorder and answering the question I'd asked in what now seemed a lifetime before.

Our work continued well past midnight. What in the first hours of the taping had been casual banter now became rapt storytelling with me feeding on every word. The business I'd witnessed with the phone call had been unnerving, yet had given Jerzy Kosinski even more awesome stature. I was surely in the presence of not just exoticism but true greatness, for here was a man who could manage the most inconceivable terrors and not only learn from them but teach others. There were no more references to his mother or the flight, but what he did have to say—about struggling to establish even the tiniest havens of freedom in Poland, conspiring to escape the Iron Curtain, and building from scratch not just a new life in America but achieving great success in a number of diverse creative enterprises—made for one of the most compelling stories I'd ever heard, fact or fiction. Circumstances had made me the perfect audience for it, and I'm still pleased that the resulting interview turned out to be one of the most interesting in a whole generation of such work published in the 1970s.

Complementing this sense of drama was Jerzy's dedicated thoroughness. Although we'd racked up over four hours of talk, he felt we should do more, and so arranged to meet at breakfast and work on through the morning—which we did, producing another four hours of recorded conversation. This I took back home, typed up (to a total exceeding one hundred pages), and returned it—all for Jerzy's approval. I was amazed to receive another of Jerzy's elaborately stamped packages just a week later, containing the typescript with almost every line of it revised. This I typed up once more and sent to New Haven, only to see it similarly annotated before the month had ended. Thankfully the clean text proved ok this time around, and as such it appeared in the premier issue of *fiction international* (fall 1973) and again in editor Joe David Bellamy's collection, *The New Fiction: Interviews with Innovative American Writers* (Urbana: University of Illinois Press, 1974).

The interview drew lots of comments, but what I enjoyed most was telling how it took place. For most of the year afterwards, it served as my favorite party conversation, and in each rendition my sense of horror became more convincing even as the Jerzy Kosinski I portrayed became increasingly wondrous. Kosinski, meanwhile, was fulfilling his role, recounting stories on *The Tonight Show* and as Dick Cavett's guest that had similar effect on television audiences, while readers were finding that his new novel, *The Devil Tree*, could be even more effective in its literary terrorism, focused as it now was on the more familiar aspects of contemporary American culture. *The Painted Bird*, after all, could be excused as a tale from somewhere long ago and far away. Even apart from its setting in a part of Poland that seemed closer to the Middle Ages than to current reality, World War II itself as a subject was something that, for many Americans, remained physically remote. But *The Devil Tree* was situated in the upper-class world of business and finance whose manners Americans aspired to; that similar terror lurked here was unnerving indeed. And I myself had witnessed the terror in action right in Kosinski's home.

Could I convey this sense to others? After several renditions at parties and during the barroom socializing that constitutes the most useful part of an MLA convention, I believed I had my perfect audience for the great Kosinski mother's-death story one evening following dinner at the home of Professor Ihab Hassan. I'd taken Ron Sukenick up to Milwaukee for some readings on one of his Midwest tours, and following his appearance at the University of Wisconsin-Milwaukee there were eight or nine of us being hosted by the Hassans. Ihab and Sally had been colleagues of a younger but no less notorious Jerzy Kosinski at Wesleyan University back in the 1960s, and so I felt assured of their interest. Plus the atmospherics were right, because Ihab's exotic origins and rather formal European manners had prompted me to put him in the same league as Jerzy: accomplished, cosmopolitan, and definitely awe-inspiring in the experience and sophistication he could and did command. Sally herself reminded me of Kiki as a woman remarkable in her own right who had chosen to dedicate herself to the great intellectual achievements of her mate. Surely they would appreciate how Jerzy had swept me away and might wish to add details of similar rapture at his hands themselves.

My narrative did hold the listeners as intended—everyone loves a story, particularly following a great meal and accompanied with fine brandy. But as my tale concluded, its response didn't go quite right, for instead of the hushed wonder and intimidated awe I'd expected there was a knowing smile from Sally and a little chuckle from Ihab.

"How remarkable," Sally intoned, mimicking a bit the style of breathless amazement I'd used toward the end of my narration, "to think of that terrifying man, arranging the death of his mother during that phone call coming across the night from over four thousand miles away!" She smiled at Ihab, who now took over as spokesman for the audience.

"How equally remarkable . . . and perhaps more likely," he added, "to think of that phone call coming across the night from a dormitory on the Yale campus, where Jerzy's student assistant had been instructed to ring him up at 10:30 Sunday night, listen to ten minutes of Polish, and help scare the pants off Klinkowitz!"

Which was the truth? Had that warm and cozy apartment in New Haven been invaded, in my presence, by the most intimate and vexing of terrors—or had it all been arranged as a stunt? Was this Jerzy Kosinski, champion of life, survivor of the Holocaust and later calamities, caught in the most maddening and pathetic of international circumstances that nevertheless impacted directly on the most personal aspects of his existence? Or was it Jerzy Kosinski manipulating an interviewer, as he must have manipulated them all, into just the awe-struck mood he'd wanted for this talk? As with other stories he'd tell and little events he'd contrive for me to see, you can take your choice—a choice that does not diminish his effectiveness either way, because it was now becoming apparent that Kosinski had insured that his audience would never know the truth for certain. He lived secure in his secrets, for he and not his interviewer controlled his revelations. This same energy vitalized his fiction, which is what I had learned in trying to control it as a narrative strategy myself.

In time, other little cracks began to show in his legend and the stories he constructed to support it. Yet through all of this Kosinski remained a person, even *the* person, to talk about. No other current writer inspired such controversy or prompted so many stories, apocryphal or otherwise. For a time I remained immune to such challenges, such as the ones presented by Zjizslav Njader, a Conrad scholar from Poland who visited my university the year I met Jerzy. Njader was living in the United States in 1957, when Kosinski arrived, and contradicted Jerzy's statement to me that he'd abandoned photography after leaving Poland. Though he'd become "one of the most frequently awarded photographers in Eastern Europe," Jerzy assured me, he'd used this art simply as a device for establishing contacts with the West and facilitating his escape. "When I landed at Idlewild," he boasted, "the first thing I did was throw my cameras away!" Not so, Njader countered. Kosinski had sought work energetically as a photographer, and Njader recalled an entire day given over to driving Jerzy out to Long Island where he called at every company from Eastman Kodak on down. As far as precipitating his mother's death by having to fly her out of Poland for a meeting, that was utter nonsense. "Those Polish bureaucrats don't care that Kosinski left so many years ago," Njader chided me. "Jerzy must certainly know the type: they're a bunch of old sentimentalists. He'd say his mother was dying and they'd cry their eyes out as they let him in and let him out again."

But all this was just politics, I told myself. Njader was a Pole who lived in a much friendlier Eastern Europe, enjoying frequent travel to the West and even working for a time with the Voice of America. His view was too rosy for the view my myth of Kosinski demanded, which posed Jerzy at the border, being pulled one way by trench-coated government agents and the other way by freedom fighters—a scenario favored by American audiences since the Hungarian uprising of 1956.

What I should have realized was that my fascination was not with these elements as political truths (or falsehoods, for that matter) but as episodes in a grand narrative that I was as eager to compose as was Kosinski. I wanted a story, and Jerzy was the perfect person to give it to me.

As my acquaintance with him developed, this storytelling penchant became more obvious. In 1972, perhaps with Kosinski's help, I moved to the University of Northern Iowa, where Dan Cahill promised to keep my interest in Jerzy's work alive. Both Dan and I were making new friends among the legions of Kosinski supporters, and we soon found ourselves exchanging stories about the master with the élan of a preteen fan club. Which is no way for supposedly objective scholars to act. But Jerzy understood the fascination Americans have for myths and images, particularly for the way they themselves can parlay images into convincing and supportive myths, and in this regard he was surely playing us along. It never could have happened in Europe, for example, where scholarship remained so much more traditional. Nor would it play as well on the East Coast as in the Middle West, or in prestigious schools as compared to the more egalitarian and open atmospheres at newer state universities, particularly those still in search of an identity as was my own. I had this confirmed when during my change in jobs I also was considered for a position at Wesleyan University in Connecticut. Kosinski had been a resident scholar at its Center for the Humanities, and I assumed its English department would be impressed by my work on and friendship with him. Jerzy even tried to add a feather by calling me during my visit for no real purpose other than to let me drop his name. But the professors were not impressed by this or by Kosinski's work at their school; in fact, he seemed decidedly low rent, which is how they eventually wrote me off. One of the younger profs was a bit more sympathetic, but as a recent Yale Ph.D. he was able to tell me why Jerzy was a member of its Drama School rather than Department of English: he was a New York friend of Robert Brustein, but the English department wouldn't have him. Yale professors did not like being jerked around by publicity-conscious pop writers, it was implied; nor did the crowd at Wesleyan.

But at Northern Iowa Jerzy Kosinski's style of self-mystification was just what we wanted, and I'm far from convinced that our interests were so terribly misdirected. After all, what was so superior in what Wesleyan and Yale were offering? At the former school, the department head had set aside his specialty interest in eighteenth-century literature to dabble in Faulkner, something he must have found daring and exciting but which the profession received as embarrassingly amateurish work (he eventually went on to a third career sketching vermin). Yale, of course, was changing the face of criticism in America—but only to make it a decades-old copy of French literary theory, something Ron Sukenick told me was the sign of a hick university (why not, he reasoned, simply skip that phase and begin with something truly new?). In Cedar Falls, we had followed Sukenick's ideal and moved directly to what was the emerging literature of our time. Kurt Vonnegut, Jerzy Kosinski, and Donald Barthelme were obvious first choices; but there were also faculty and even students eager to do the first work on Grace Paley, Alice Walker (whom we taught ten years before the country discovered *The Color Purple*), Robert Coover, and John Irving. The Writers Workshop down in Iowa City brought a lot of these people through, but there was also the excitement of forays we'd make to New York and of sharing stories culled from these experiences. In time, they made for quite an anthology of narratives. And the advantage was that, far from being jerked around by Kosinski's manipulations or having our critical talents immobilized by awe, these stories let us see the working nature of Jerzy's genius. If we were the audience he practiced on—and he once did go so far as to admit that he liked spinning tales on talk-show television as a way of testing them out—then we were privileged to have glimpses inside his creator's workshop.

Initially, there was the pleasure of swapping such tales—like Vonnegut's readers, whose badge of membership in the club would be their favorite grimly comical line from *Cat's Cradle* or *Mother Night*, Kosinski admirers enjoyed bonding by means of the stories about him they could share. Although skeptical, Zjizslav Njader had shown the same fascination with Kosinski, who even as a subject to be debunked maintained immense stature; the energy and verve of Njader's narratives derived from the power we had attributed to Kosinski's own exaggerated stories, and challenging them only increased their sense of legend—Jerzy Kosinski was someone to be talked about incessantly and perhaps compulsively. Meeting novelist James Park Sloan, I learned Kosinski was a fellow-admirer of what I thought to be the best-yet novel of the Vietnam conflict, *War Games*; Jerzy had befriended the young writer and so impressed him that Sloan tried his hand at an Eastern European style novel in the patented Kosinski mode, *The Case History of Comrade V.* Sloan's favorite story about his mentor was funny—that Jerzy had learned English not because he'd been traumatized in his native language or because English's syntactic emphasis on the verb suited his action-based narrative but because the Slavic languages he knew lacked the proper tools for seduction. "When it comes to talking about sex," Sloan informed me, "Polish and Russian lack our subtle words and expressions: they have just the extremes, of carrying on either like animals or like angels." Apparently the newly immigrated young Pole wished to seduce all the women of New York, and had even chosen an ideal piece of furniture, a "Castro Convertible" which could be changed from a sofa to a bed with the easiest gesture, to facilitate his quests. But moonlight, wine, soft music, and roses were of no use either until Jerzy could learn enough English to murmur convincingly of love.

Sloan's challenge to Kosinski's version of being motivated toward English was instructive. Jerzy's intentions had been amorous rather than strictly linguistic, but both the purpose and effect had been the same: control by means of mastering another tongue. And so the myth-making was augmented rather than contradicted.

In time, variations would develop according to where a Kosinski story had been heard. On a visit to New York I was welcomed to Jerzy's top-floor apartment, a cozy, well-ordered set of rooms on West Fifty-seventh Street. A prominent feature was the terrace on which Jerzy was growing some shrubs and even a fairsized tree; seeing a coiled hose, I remarked how ironic it was to picture him gardening up here almost three hundred feet above one of the busiest and most congested spots in midtown Manhattan. At which point Jerzy launched into a story I swore at the time was spontaneous, so naturally did it fit within the conversation that had developed. The provocation, in fact, was not just my notice of the garden hose, but how the summer's drought must have kept him busy watering. Was that, I wondered, the reason why he'd installed such a powerful system?

"Yes, it is an extremely high pressure hose," Jerzy assured me, but then stumped me with the news that he didn't need such capacity for his plantings but "to reach over the roof and across the street."

Was it some type of fire hose? Yes, Kosinski agreed, it could perform that function, but that was not why he had it. I could feel I was being set up for a narrative, but only in the sense of being entertained, as everything seemed contextually appropriate.

"I like to use the hose on bright, dry days," Jerzy told me, "especially on days like today when there is not even one cloud in the sky." What he'd do was arc his hose over the roof and course a stream of water down across Fifty-seventh Street to the corner at Sixth Avenue below. Figures about gallons per minute and concentration of flow were rattled off—they could have been made up, but Jerzy marshalled them with such authority that I couldn't help but be convinced. "You can imagine what a pool it makes in the street!" he said, and I marveled along with him. But why create such a flood on a clear, dry day?

"So that when I go downstairs, walk to the corner, and see this great puddle, I can ask the doorman who stands there where all this water comes from," Jerzy confided with a sly smile, and I knew the best part of the story was about to unfold.

The build-up was to a moral, the most old-fashioned kind of storytelling that in the hedonistic sixties had made Kosinski's preachment a form of innovation in itself. The doorman, it turned out, was not in the least mystified by the appearance of all this water on a cloudless day. In fact, he had a story about it, almost as good as Kosinski's, mimicking his same sense of authority and conclusive judgment.

"The water comes from these tall buildings," the doorman had explained—a correct answer, but incorrectly deduced. "You see," the fellow explained in all seriousness, "having all these skyscrapers packed so close together creates an electric field." Noting Kosinski's interest, he had continued, detailing with scientific precision how vapor from the street-level activity would rise, trapped between the walls of these steel canyons, until at the top all this massed electricity would trigger a miniature thunderstorm. "You should see it come down!" the doorman marveled. "I can just imagine!" Kosinski had replied.

"You see," Jerzy now instructed me, "the man cannot rest with the phenomenon unexplained. He has to devise an answer for it—which is to say that he has to construct a myth!" This was his story's point, and a moral one indeed. What impressed me most was that it seemed to come spontaneously, prompted by my remark about the hose. Later friends would hear the same tale themselves, however, with variations according to context. Had the event ever actually happened? That was not the right question to ask, any more than asking Herman Melville if Ahab had really been dragged down by the whale—or, more appropriately, asking O. Henry or Guy de Maupassant if their exquisitely turned plot devices were based on fact.

The beauty was that Kosinski was such a fine storyteller, and when the morals of his stories complemented his strong sense of narrative, listeners could have no objection if they derived from fantasy. After all, one of Kosinski's themes and a tenet of the whole era was that the imagination took primacy over any supposed description of what passed for reality—this was the anthropological model for existence shared by Vonnegut, Kosinski, Sukenick, and most other innovative fictionists of the day. That Jerzy told different versions from time to time only meant he was tailoring them to the occasion or perfecting their form.

The dark side of this storytelling was that it sometimes took a mean and petty direction. A couple of tales, involving the low-ranking copyeditors who were given the most servile tasks during the production of his books, struck me as especially cruel. To be sure the copyeditors were not getting lazy, Jerzy would introduce deliberate and egregiously obvious errors into his typescript; later, while reading galleys, he'd let a few glaring typos stand, waiting to see if the publisher's staff found them. I knew what a mentally deadening and even soul-killing task such proofreading can be; a few mistakes can easily slip through—and a timid editor with the utmost respect for Kosinski's work might even let one of these oddities stand as intentional, a presumed idiosyncracy in this most bizarre of writers. There had been cruel tricks played on the boy in *The Painted Bird*, a novel which I thought displayed sympathy for those in helpless positions. But now I could recall how the playfulness of *Steps* turns nasty after awhile, almost as if those who are weak enough to be duped deserve it. The ultimate point flattered not the protagonist's sensibility but his power. Imaginative richness did not include taking pity on underlings, which was a weakness itself.

During the fall semester of 1975, just as this sense of cruelty in his work began to bother me, Jerzy came to Cedar Falls for a lecture at the university and a few days of visits with Dan Cahill and myself. Kiki was along, and together they formed a picture of politeness, grace, and even kindness. As department head, Dan would usually put up visiting speakers in his home, and his litmus test was the extent to which they did or did not pick up after themselves. The worst was an eminent University of Chicago professor who'd left everything looking like a pig sty. Most visitors at least kept the guest room neat, but Jerzy had outdone himself, making up the bed with the skill of a gentleman's valet, asking for the vacuum cleaner so he could sweep up, and even washing the dishes after grabbing a snack.

His lecture was a sparkling delight as he played the audience like a fine instrument, teaching them lessons about American materialism and warning them how advertising, mass market culture, and the flattening effect of television was making them as collectivized as the society he'd fled from in Poland. But his very appeal to our students was that he came across like the host of a TV talk show himself, pulling out clippings from the newspaper for sardonic comment, telling stories about the rich and famous, and dramatizing the unique cut of his own personality and habits for sometimes hilarious effect (this included exaggerating his Slavic accent when pronunciation could add to the joke). Afterwards, it seemed half the town crowded our home for the postlecture party, and Jerzy proved himself a genius at mingling about and making everyone feel special. Even Kiki performed a role, helping some of the more self-taken intellectuals in our group play out the scene from a Woody Allen movie where it's decided to sneak off to the family room and watch a basketball game on TV—it was even a Knicks game, which made the affair a perfect quotation. Yet as the evening wore on I noticed something peculiar: that Jerzy always knew where I was, and always chose a spot in the room from where he could watch the door. If I asked him where my wife or Dan Cahill or even a guest he'd met hours before had gone, he could tell me. Thus even in the pell-mell nature of this crowded social occasion, where Jerzy proved the life of the party, he was maintaining cautious control.

Before the night ended I saw that caution turn, for just a moment, into something else. Suggesting a breath of fresh air but really wishing to show off our fine yard, I invited Jerzy to step outside and take a walk around the house. Though late, there was a pleasant crispness to the fall air and plenty of moonlight, and of course the lawns were bathed with light from the bright and bustling party inside. I assumed Jerzy would be at his best out here, and that we might share a moment of silence after which he'd utter some profound and poetic truth. Instead, I found myself in the presence of a Jerzy Kosinski I'd never seen, for as we left the front steps and made our way through the side yard he became uneasy, moving in fits of starts and turns as he struggled to overcome the sudden disorientation. His eyes reflected the night's darkness, which no longer seemed pleasantly serene. Instead I found myself with a man transfixed by fear, a fear I began to share myself.

Turning to the front door's light, Jerzy hurried back inside, wasting not a single word as he fled this insecure world. What on earth was this, I wondered: Jerzy Kosinski, afraid of the dark? Or was it just the caution exercised in alien circumstances? In New York the year before, Kiki had told me, with Jerzy agreeing, how he liked to wander some of New York City's rougher streets late at night, dressed like an urban tough and flirting with all sorts of danger. Why should a neatly landscaped yard in middle-class Iowa frighten him so? Because it was not his element, and despite all assurances he was not ready to surrender himself to the safekeeping of another. Perhaps there were things about my neighborhood that I myself did not know. Self-reliance dictated that he get back inside, where his presence commanded a sense of order.

It was just after his visit to Cedar Falls that we learned about something truly scary. Jerzy had been gone for only half a day, but his phone call didn't surprise Dan Cahill, since the first words were ones of thanks for Dan's hospitality and news that the flight had gone smoothly. Jerzy and Kiki had made Iowa part of a transcontinental trip, traveling on to Los Angeles the morning after the lecture and party for an appearance on *The Tonight Show*. Getting to LA had been easy enough, but at the airport a terrifying adventure had begun.

As he helped Kiki into a taxi for the trip to town, Kosinski had noticed at once that all was not right. The cab's interior was different, there was no license on display, and the driver seemed especially nervous. The truth of Jerzy's suspicions was borne out when the driver disregarded all instructions and began driving randomly around the county, becoming irrational and rambunctious as the expedition turned into an ordeal of several hours. One proper feature the cab did have was doorlocks controlled from the front seat, making Jerzy and Kiki prisoners. They were effectively kidnapped, but to where, and for what purpose?

As Dan Cahill recounted to me what Jerzy had told him, I marveled at the adventure our two visitors had found themselves in just a few hours after leaving us. As the cab hurtled around the outskirts of Los Angeles, Kosinski had tried every trick he knew to overpower the driver and escape, but there seemed no way out. The worst part of it all was that Jerzy and Kiki didn't know their fate but had plenty of time to imagine the worst. Like many episodes from Kosinski's fiction, it was a nightmare that promised to have no end. How did it in fact end?

How did Jerzy save himself and Kiki, as he surely must have to be calling Dan late this same afternoon? "Jerzy said he eventually managed to trick the driver, and he and Kiki were able to get away and make their way to the hotel, from where he was calling," Dan said. What the trick was, neither of us could guess, and for now Jerzy wasn't telling.

Nor did he reveal his saving strategy that night on television, when he held Johnny Carson's audience in rapt attention with the same story. For years, Jerzy had been a *Tonight Show* favorite, for his stories were funny and his delivery hilarious. But this tale put his stage persona in a new light, one that was autobiographical in a terrifying rather than comical way. It was all quite perplexing, and none of us could be sure what Jerzy had in mind.

The next year, 1976, offered a clue, for to a new edition of *The Painted Bird* Kosinski added a lengthy preface, explaining how much of that novel's action, including some of its most frightening terrors, were autobiographical. This was a 180° reversal from the tack he'd taken back with the novel's publication in 1965, where he declined to make any comments whatsoever on whether or not the boy's adventures were similar to his own; his commentary in *Notes of the Author* had made a lengthy argument about why such speculation was pointless, given memory's power as a fictive editor.

Then, in 1977, he published *Blind Date*, a novel Jerzy had been writing while in close touch with all of us, and from the result it became clear what he'd been up to. Just about every story we'd heard him tell or had witnessed him act out for our own retelling was there, now in the guise of fiction (and fitting the book's narrative strategy quite well). Just a year before, during November of 1976 when Julie and I had been in New York to do some work with Kurt Vonnegut, we'd met Jerzy for a couple hours' talk at Wolfe's Delicatessen, to which he'd invited us as his "neighborhood place." There at a window table looking out at the corner of Sixth Avenue and West Fifty-seventh Street—the same corner mythologized by the doorman who'd turned Kosinski's prank with the garden hose into a meteorological legend—he went though almost a dozen routines, at his best not only to satisfy me but to impress his new listener. I should have heeded Julie's advice afterwards, that she'd found Kosinski to be not entirely trustworthy. He'd been putting us on and she knew it, wishing I'd save my critical energies for nicer people like Kurt Vonnegut. But I'm glad I was there to hear these stories, for now they and others were appearing as part of *Blind*

Date's fictive fabric, a fabric whose weave I could follow all the better for having seen it woven, in stages, by hand.

Several tales from "Wolfie's," as Jerzy called his deli, were instrumental in getting the action of *Blind Date* rolling. As the story of George Levanter, a child survivor of the war and emigré to the West who now supports himself quite well through tricky and mysterious operations as an "investor" of unknown assets in unstated commodities, the novel suggests parallels with Kosinski's life. "Jerzy," after all, is the Polish form of "George," and "Levanter" means both one from the East and one whose works are bound in fine leather, and reinforcing these invitations to identify is the fact that many of Levanter's most characteristic adventures are ones Jerzy Kosinski had been telling about himself—publically to nationwide TV audiences and privately to the critics he knew would be studying his work.

There was the oft-repeated episode of approaching Leopold Sedar Senghor, president of Senegal and world famous as a poet, at a PEN function and being mistaken for a waiter (Kosinski and his protagonist both avoid embarrassing the eminent man by giving service and even pocketing a $3 tip). This story had been told to audiences in the early 1970s, and had been printed up in the *PEN Newsletter*; then, at our meeting in 1976, he'd repeated it for Julie and myself, knowing it would be fresh in my memory when I read *Blind Date*. There was Jim Sloan's tale about Jerzy learning English so he could mount seductions; Levanter's motives would be the same. The greater part of our lunch at "Wolfie's" was given over to what Jerzy made clear was his most serious business of late, and which turned out to be a central point in *Blind Date* as well: the death of his friend Jacques Monod, the Nobel laureate in biology. Monod's death had been especially cruel, for other than a somewhat exotic blood disease he was in the best of health and spirits. The disease itself, Jerzy explained, had made him seem even more robust and glowing than ever, and in the weeks before death came—during a vacation he and Jerzy spent together at Cannes during the International Film Festival—life had seemed attractive indeed. Now it had been taken away, causing Jerzy to ponder even more deeply the wisdom he'd drawn from Monod's book, *Chance and Necessity*—that any determinations in life are coincidental with the event, and not prior to it. This, Kosinski knew, had been the unstated essence of his own work, and now (it turned out) *Blind Date* would propound this truth more overtly.

Jacques Monod himself, as a historical personage, appeared in *Blind Date*, his death in Cannes handled just as Jerzy described it the year before. But situating the narrative were dozens of other stories from Kosinski's life, and as I read this novel the author's method became clear.

Some of the correspondences are self-serving, such as the way both Kosinski as president of PEN and Levanter as head of "Investors International" free a prominent Iranian writer from jail (Kosinski's real-life doings are detailed by the writer himself, Reza Baraheni, in *The Crowned Cannibals*). Others are funny, such as the tale told on *The Tonight Show* of Jerzy and a friend speaking "Esquimaux" in a Paris cafe and unintentionally angering some Russians (whose language they are in fact using). Many of the episodes served as instructional exercises, just as they'd done when I'd first heard or experienced them, such as learning how folks like the Sixth Avenue doorman would rather mythologize to the point of absurdity than admit ignorance about something as innocent as a puddle of water, and noting how a bunch of intimidating but meaningless stickers can rush a package through the mails with the speed of light. A few match-ups were what I fancied as "auto-bibliographical," making references as they did not to Jerzy's life but to his books, such as when Charles Lindbergh describes flying over the landscape of *The Painted Bird* and an American statesman is duped with the same exchange-of-watches trick that was one of *Being There*'s funnier scenes. Moments from *Steps, Cockpit,* and *The Devil Tree* were there, too, making Jerzy's correspondences a book-length project informing every aspect of the work.

Imagine my excitement, then, when the three most terrifying stories I associated with Jerzy Kosinski made their appearance in *Blind Date*. My initial attraction to his work had been through his association with Roman Polanski—with the manner of controlling horror as in *Repulsion*, but also because of his own close call with death at the hands of Charles Manson's followers. For all the years I'd known him, Jerzy had declined to speak of that event, murmuring only that if he'd been present "things might have been different." In *Blind Date*, he puts himself there, directly in the murder scene that must have haunted his conscience for years, if only because he felt some responsibility for assembling this group of friends in the first place, having been the one to make mutual introductions a few years before. For the novel, this provided interesting experiences for both readers and author. As publicized by the media at the time, documented by Vincent Bugliosi in *Helter Skelter* and by Ed Sanders in *The Family*, and discussed by commentators later, Kosinski's involvement would be known to the more interested readers of *Blind Date*. As author, Kosinski takes this most widely shared of his experiences and fictionalizes it, for the occasion summoning his most calculatedly brutal writing style. Having invented it in *The Painted Bird* to fit adventures that by this time he had admitted were his own, he now adapts it to what would have to be a higher purpose: not to unleash the memories repressed by traumatization (for which he'd always insisted a new language, one learned as an adult, was necessary), but to detail the minute-by-minute horror endured by some of his closest friends, *when he himself was not there*. The writing here is strongest because Levanter, like Kosinski, must imagine the scene. As in *The Great Gatsby*, the narrator has not been present at the killings, and so must imagine them into existence. Responsibility for the act, then, proceeds as far as conscience will allow it; guilt and anxiety know few limits, and this energy controls the episode's style. As such, this incident becomes the novel's heart.

Yet even this scene alone would not be so effective without the process of conditioning through which Kosinski has taken us. There are many layers of experience among Kosinski's readers. Most would have heard about the Manson murders, while only a few would have been treated to the story of how he was being forced to engineer his mother's death. But the tale of that maniacal taxi driver who'd kidnapped Jerzy and Kiki in Los Angeles had been told on *The Tonight Show*, one of the most widely viewed programs in America (and, thanks to its frequent repeats, one of the most familiar). All three figured as important stages in the narrative, and as one of the book's ideal readers (having witnessed or heard these stories as autobiography) I was in the best position to see how Jerzy was using them.

Consider the taxi cab driver. In *Blind Date*, as to Dan Cahill on the phone that afternoon and to Johnny Carson's viewers the same night, Kosinski tells of getting in the cab, sensing that something was wrong, and then being held prisoner for a terrifying ride around town. The driver's irrational behavior, dangerous driving, and unspecified but very obvious threats formed the texture of

Blind Date's episode as they did for Jerzy's personal narrative. And the point was the same: that life is a blind date with destiny, every turn of which makes for an chance encounter. Yet the novel had emphasized the moral of another story, one previously kept independent of the taxi cab tale yet now so naturally associated with it: Jacques Monod's belief that determination is simultaneous with the event and not prior to it. This space between chance and necessity, *Blind Date* now suggested, was sufficient within which to create a free identity. But such freedom demanded some exceedingly brutal tasks, and the novel's first one comes at the end of the tale of kidnap. Recall that Jerzy told neither Dan or Johnny Carson how he'd freed himself from the driver, just that he'd "tricked him." Now, in the novel, Levanter goes through the same adventure, and tricks the driver into pulling inside a warehouse—where Levanter most brutally and even sadistically kills him.

Does this mean that in real life Jerzy Kosinski killed the taxi driver? It is not that simple, for the author is not so much teasing us with implications as conditioning our reading so as to take us places we never thought we'd be. As in Polanski's *Repulsion*, it is a slow and subtle affair, in Kosinski's case starting with such simple and amusing stories as the Senghor affair and the garden hose trick (the autobiographical keys for which the reader is delighted to decode and follow) and then moving on to more terrifying tales (such as the cab ride) that turn into chilling conclusions the reader would rather not reach. The same thing takes place with the mother's death story, which happens in the novel just as it transpired before my eyes and ears that night in New Haven. The son cannot return to his homeland; the mother wants to see him and insists on being flown out; the flight will kill her. Like the taxi-driver story, Jerzy had left it unconcluded in terms of his real life. Had his mother died? No one was going to be so rudely insensitive as to ask. Now, in *Blind Date*, the mother dies. But that is by no means the worst of it. Her death, and even her son's complicity in it, are far less horrifying than what the novel reveals about the life they'd once shared together: a life of happy, blissful incest.

That's the author's trick, one that successfully conditions the reader: of dropping all sorts of autobiographical hints so that one reads on happily gathering clues like a child on a treasure hunt— until the path leads to suspicions that are too horrible to entertain, let alone being too shocking and embarrassing to ask about. Kosin-

ski has not only understood readers' fascination with the correspondences between fiction and real life but harnessed that energy
to propel them through the narrative, only to have it turn on them
in the end.

It is the method of *The Painted Bird* taken one step further. Just
as style has been used to liberate not just the author's memory but
now his creative imagination, so it takes readers further along, well
beyond their depth, because the uninviting topics of physical and
mental mayhem have been safely contained within a type of prose
and activity that is perfectly acceptable and even welcoming in
terms of ease and reward. If we can read this far, we think, everything must be ok—the descriptions of the Polish countryside in *The
Painted Bird*, the funny stories millions of viewers saw and heard
Kosinski tell on TV. They are just like the first thirty minutes of
Polanski's *Repulsion*, where nothing seems more threatening than a
cheery neighborhood pub and the peacefulness of having a spa-
cious flat to one's self for the weekend. At which point both Polanski and Kosinski spring the trap, shocking us with previously
unimaginable horror that less skillful narrating would have let
degenerate into titillation or farce.

In terms of storytelling, this talent had elevated Jerzy Kosinski to a position of eminence among contemporary world writers.
He had won the top literary prizes here and abroad, and was making a serious impact as a spokesman for writers' causes as president of the PEN American Center even as he fashioned a popular
reputation through appearances on TV. Late in the evening he'd be
on Johnny Carson, and for each new novel—and they were coming
out every year and a half during the middle and late 1970s—there
he'd be in the morning on *The Today Show* or *Good Morning America*,
not only promoting his book but teaching the interviewer some lesson about life. This celebrity presence built as he involved himself
with the filming of *Being There* and climaxed when he became a
movie star himself, playing a featured part, that of the revolution-
ist Zinoviev, in Warren Beatty's film, *Reds*.

Through all of this it was obvious that Jerzy was projecting an
identity between himself and his fiction. And not just in terms of
content. It was a matter of making moral points as well, his public
life expressing the same themes and values as did his protagonists.
Most importantly, there was the identity of style. He made his way

through life exactly as his language coursed through his novels: dynamic and yet utterly controlled, warmly ingratiating but unmistakably dedicated to his own fortune. The correspondences between what he and his protagonists did became more and more emphatic, the climax coming with the hero of *Passion Play* who though in a different line of work entirely managed to do it in ways that matched both Kosinski's life and literary output.

And what about the deviations? In terms of his books' style and structure, they had helped rather than hurt; in the case of *Blind Date* the discrepancies proved crucial to making that novel read so well. But as his fiction moved closer to his autobiography in time, space, and verifiability, with chapters of next year's novel being acted out for this year's viewers of *The Tonight Show* (and privately for those of us doing critical work on him), simple contradictions of fact were popping up. Through all of this the fiction remained intact; but in terms of Jerzy's life, his stories were beginning to unravel.

His academic credentials were the first thing to be questioned. Early in his career there had been references to his doctoral studies at Columbia, with the implication he'd received a Ph.D. By the time I met him Jerzy was making no such claims. Quite the contrary, he acted as if accepting a doctorate from Columbia was beneath him. "I completed all the course work in sociology," he told me in 1971, "and had passed my comprehensive exams. And of course I had not only written a dissertation but had published it—*The Future Is Ours, Comrade*—and was well on the way to finishing a second book, *No Third Path.*"

Then why hadn't he graduated with his Ph.D.?

"At the last moment," Jerzy told me, with a gesture of impatience and disgust, "the program directors introduced a new requirement, a proficiency test in statistical research." This was patently unfair, Jerzy complained, a case of changing the rules in midgame. And so on principle he refused to fulfill this unwarranted obligation and left without his degree. By this time *The Future is Ours* had been serialized in *The Saturday Evening Post* and condensed by *Reader's Digest*. Funded with what must have been a healthy advance for his second book and preparing to wed the widowed millionairess, Mary Hayward Weir, who'd met him while doing research of her own, this piqued graduate student was now more famous and better off financially than many of his professors.

But still there was rumor, which may have helped Kosinski when his reputation had far less to go on, that he'd earned a Ph.D. I can even hear him now, emphasizing that he'd truly "earned" it, with the burden of guilt resting on Columbia's faculty for not fairly awarding it. But that was just the style of equivocation I was beginning to sense in other areas of accreditation and documentation. When I tried to remind Zjizslav Njader that Jerzy was an "associate professor" at the eminent Polish Academy of Sciences in Warsaw, Njader broke out laughing. When I showed him Kosinski's vita, listing the rank in Polish as *aspirant* before translating it to an equivalent of the second highest post in the American university system, Njader scoffed, explaining that *aspirant* meant "graduate assistant," the lowliest rank, reserved for students still working on their final degrees. But the myth Jerzy fashioned demanded that we marvel at how he'd approached the summits of Polish academic life and then abandoned it all to start from scratch in the West. Forsaking a graduate assistantship simply failed to support such an image, and so Kosinski had used our ignorance of Polish nomenclature to suggest he'd been far more prestigious than in fact.

Another myth involved his relationship with Mary Weir. She was heir to the National Steel fortune and a member of the social elite that maintains much influence in American politics. Jerzy had married her shortly after the death of her husband, whose family controlled all this wealth, and even as his novelist's career began he found himself living in the sometimes stupendously expensive world of monied luxury. In the mid-1970s Jerzy began to make his own capital from this experience, telling stories (some of which made it into print in the autobiographical preface added to the 1976 edition of *The Painted Bird*) of how his own considerable income was depleted simply by having to hand out tips to the legions of servants one met at every step of Mary's whirlwind, jet-set life. Much of *The Devil Tree*, published in 1974, draws on legend from Weir family manners and exploits.

As a fitting climax to this story, Jerzy would explain how at Mary's death he inherited nothing. "Which is how I would have wanted it, had it been my decision instead of that of the family trust." Our understanding, of course, was that Kosinski had been widowed. Which was not precisely the truth.

Dan Cahill was the one to discover this, though the evidence had been plain for anyone to see. Dan's insight came by chance while doing a bibliographic comparison of *The Painted Bird*'s several editions, each of which incorporated slight changes in the text. Now Dan noticed that there were changes in the book's dedication as well. The first edition, which we could find in libraries and buy from rare book dealers, reflected the reality contemporaneous with 1965, when the marriage was at its heights: "To my wife Mary, without whom even the past would lose its meaning." The edition most of us used was the third printing of the Pocket Books paperback issued in March 1970, two years after Mary died; appropriately, the dedication is changed to read "To the memory of my wife, Mary Hayward Weir, without whom even the past would lose its meaning." But what caught Dan's eye was the scarce first printing of the paperback as published in September 1966. As a paperback, it was not kept by libraries, and rare book dealers usually restricted their holdings to hardcover firsts. But I'd found a copy on a friend's bookshelf, offered him a new hardcover edition in exchange, and passed the volume on to Dan, who was stunned by the form of its dedication: "To my former wife Mary Hayward Weir, without whom even the past would lose its meaning."

In none of Jerzy's stories had there been any hint of divorce. Of course not. In terms of storytelling it was an unsettling distraction, and as a plot device it would undo the irony of Jerzy inheriting nothing from her estate. Our friend had never said he *wasn't* divorced, but as an important line in anyone's biography it had been dropped, leaving the implication that Jerzy was a widower rather than an ex-husband. We could see why, for his stories about Mary were not half as compelling if one knew it was not death but the divorce court that had taken her from him.

Then there were contradictions in Jerzy's public roles and the philosophies behind them. For years he'd argued that his novels could not be filmed, as cinema was a manipulative medium, part of the American collective he despised. Fiction activated the reader's imagination, while film controlled it by imposing the director's design. His own novels especially were less depictions of action than encodings of language, just the opposite of the external, visual devices upon which movies depended. All of this squared with his larger aesthetic as promulgated through his critical booklets, essays, and interviews, including the massive 1971 dialogue he'd undertaken with me.

Hence when press reports appeared that *Being There* would

become a major motion picture, I felt justified in asking Jerzy what had changed. "I *must* film this book," he told me with some impatience, "because I feel America needs to know its message." Indeed, he now launched a personal campaign to keep me informed and presumably enthused about the project; during the first six months of 1979 he must have phoned me half a dozen times, telling me not only how the preproduction work was being handled but why.

In order to keep his principles for literary art intact, he'd decided that he'd use some of the movie industry's most characteristic practices against themselves. For example, all of the minor characters would be played by exceedingly famous actors, "so well known that they themselves are institutions, just like the ones *Being There* employs." But the featured role, that of Chance, the illiterate and almost hermetically shielded gardener who blunders out into the world only to become, within three days, a worldwide celebrity and candidate for the American vice-presidency, would be played by a complete unknown, a new actor to whom the audience could have no predictable response—so that they could imagine him into existence like a truly fictive character, which is just what the world does to Chance in the novel. Here Jerzy went into great detail, announcing plans for "a nationwide talent search" for this Great Unknown Actor, followed by "filming in secret" so that fan magazines could create no expectations that would interfere with Kosinski's perfect blank of a cinematic protagonist.

Yet even as I accepted this rhetoric, it began to unravel, for soon the "people" sections of magazines and newspapers across the country were filled with news of the film's production, which had gotten underway not with an unknown actor in the principal role but Peter Sellers. Not only was he immensely famous, but in the flood of interviews conducted to promote the film insisted that he'd been promised the role eight years before!

Of course the choice of Sellers could be justified within Kosinski's theory. As a great mimic, the British actor had excelled in such a wide variety of guises that critics said his own personality could never be known, so devoted was it to the parody of others. But why had Jerzy carried on so about keeping the actor's identity secret, when now he was helping direct such a massive publicity campaign? I got the idea that there was some fancy footwork here, with my friend springing to a new position as details changed in what must have been the exceedingly fluid conditions of high-budget filmmaking.

As I planned to be in New York late that summer, I phoned Kosinski to ask if I could stop by. Perhaps a face-to-face discussion would help in clarifying these matters. But that was not possible, Jerzy explained, because he'd be out of town that week. He was coming to the Middle West, in fact, and wondered if I could see him in Oak Brook, a near-west suburb of Chicago just a few hours drive from Cedar Falls.

Was he speaking there?

"No," he said. "I'm playing in a polo tournament. Why don't you come and see the game?"

"Polo?" I asked in stunned surprise. This was something completely new to me. I'd fancied myself an authority on not just Kosinski's work but on his life as well, as interesting as that life had been with its outline of a terrorized childhood in the ravages of World War II, resistance to Soviet collectivization, and so forth. Plus he had always publicized his activities so grandly that I could not imagine how a new career in polo could have gotten underway unnoticed.

"Don't you know," he asked with apparent smugness, "I've been a champion polo player for many years!"

No, I didn't know, but there was no way I could challenge him now, for I'd been on guard for feints about the movie; this polo business was fully unexpected. Yet I had no choice but to listen as Jerzy went on with a virtual cascade of information, making me wonder where I'd been.

His new novel, scheduled to appear early in the fall, was all about polo. It was titled *Passion Play* and he said I'd have galleys of it shortly. As promised, the book arrived in mid-August, but by then I was heading to New York and didn't have time to read it. Yet the polo image continued to mystify me, and I wondered how it would resolve itself as a factor in Jerzy's ongoing life story.

In New York my principal points of business were to see my own editor at Dell, Chris Kuppig, who'd just published my and John Somer's anthology, *Writing Under Fire: Stories of the Vietnam War*, and to meet with Kurt Vonnegut about his own forthcoming novel, *Jailbird*. During the small talk that concluded my visit, Kurt asked if I was seeing anyone else this trip.

"No," I replied, stating that Don Barthelme was down in

Houston and Jerzy Kosinski was off playing in a polo tournament.

"Polo?!!" Kurt was as dumfounded as I'd been when hearing this a few weeks before.

"Don't you know," I revealed, taking great pleasure in being so up on literary news, "that Jerzy has been a champion polo player for several years?"

"That's remarkable," Kurt agreed, but now he was laughing. "Why," he continued, "I taught Jerzy how to ride in Central Park just last year!"

Nevertheless the novel turned out to be filled with the lore of polo, all of which was handled in Jerzy's manner of familiar and commanding authority. From *Passion Play* I could learn about everything in the sport, from how horses were bred and trained to the different tactics riders would use in their play. The business was particularly intricate because Jerzy had arranged it all so that it matched up perfectly with his own career as an author; his polo-playing protagonist, Fabian, writes books on the subject, and their titles and themes are systematic analogues to Kosinski's own.

As such, Fabian's parallel identity was the climax of a trend in Kosinski's fiction that had featured Tarden (of *Cockpit*) and Levanter (of *Blind Date*) acting much like their author. But something else was becoming quite obvious, too: that the worlds his heroes moved in were ones of money, fame, and flamboyance. In the past when one of his protagonists wished to score a point, it was done thanks to deftness of intellect and superiority of nerve. Now such triumphs were more simply the product of wealth and power. At times, the action even seemed shabby—not because Kosinski didn't know the glamour of this high-rolling world, but because he assumed his readers didn't and would be fooled by the tackiest flimflam, much of it along the lines of mink-upholstered Cadillacs and champagne-filled swimming pools raved about on a television show, *Lifestyles of the Rich and Famous*, which was just beginning to make impressions on the "nation of videots" that a more taste-conscious Kosinski had once censured. As a test for this opinion, I tried reading passages aloud in the smarmy Australian-accented voice of the show's narrator, a style that turned out to fit Jerzy's prose exactly.

The presumed attractions of this world left me cold, and I worried that Kosinski had been subsumed by them. Whereas the imperative in his earlier work had always been toward the hard edge of terror, now there was just one overpacked material display after another, like the curtains being opened across stages number one, two, and three on *Wheel of Fortune* or *Let's Make a Deal*. And the action itself, with everybody from the majordomo to the mailman in tuxedos, smacked of *Fantasy Island*. My God, had Jerzy succumbed to his own American nightmare and become a prisoner of TV? That was certainly what *Passion Play* seemed like with its penchant for the superficially flashy. Its women characters were glitzy cardboard cutouts with names like "Alexandra" and "Vanessa," and they towered over everything in Valkyrie-like stature enhanced by gold lamé sandals. Men were no longer men, but Argentine playboys, Caribbean dictators, or multimillionaires. The Rolls-Royces were outnumbered by private jets and helicopters whisking in with weekend houseguests. Kosinski's own attitude toward this world could be found by looking to what he always fancied as his linguistic code, a code activated by his care for each sentence's active verb. And what were these verbs? When it came to acting on the women characters, they were patently sexist, with the women always "claimed," "taken," "yielding," "surrendering," and—in the triumph of Fabian's manipulative art—being "imprinted" with desire for their master.

I regretted the loss of Kosinski's taste and judgment, but most regretful was how he was surrendering the greatest strength of his earlier work: the human will's ability to seize and fashion its own freedom. *Passion Play* was everywhere consumed by an antidemocratic fascination with the very rich. There had been none of that in *The Painted Bird* and *Steps* where society had been no nicer but at least the coin of the realm had been stark, elemental power, and not the megabucks of nitwits with jet-propelled playthings.

I was wondering how I could avoid having to comment on this disaster when a second set of bound galleys arrived, together with a note from the *Chicago Sun-Times*'s review editor, Henry Kisor, asking me to cover the book. Unasked, I would have remained silent; but facing the expectations of a reading public, before whom the reviewer stands as somewhat of a shield against an author's unfair manipulations, speaking up truthfully was easy. Besides, the last thing Kosinski needed now was a puff endorsement. He was rich and powerful and eager to advertise those facts, so how could one measly little clipping hurt him?

Of course, I worried for this turn his writing had taken, and expressed that in the review. Ever since *Being There*, I wrote, which had been Kosinski's first thoroughly American novel, he had been "struggling with this country's fraudulent currency: the superficial glamour of money and influence. Such a fine writer and insightful student of humanity should recognize how these false values jeopardize his own vitalistic ethic."

The review appeared on September 2, 1979, and I wondered what Jerzy's response would be. In a few weeks I heard—as usual, via the phone. Yet for once Jerzy was neither impatient or imperative, but seemed relaxed and considerate, if a bit indulgent.

Had he seen my review? "Of course," he remarked, adding that "it followed me around the country." The *Sun-Times*, it turned out, had put it on the wire, and as a piece ascribed to the Field News Service had appeared in cities and towns all over the country—every place, in fact, where Jerzy was traveling to promote the book and the local paper didn't have its own reviewing staff. Yet he held no hard feelings, and professed to feel as friendly towards me as ever. "As the saying goes, this is a free country," he reminded me, "and you are entitled to your opinion." But it was evident that my opinion was making no headway with Jerzy himself.

At this point, much as with my Vonnegut work but for a different reason, I felt that I'd be putting my scholarship of Jerzy Kosinski to rest. My remarriage, new literary tastes, and commencement of frequent travels to Europe had me pointed in different directions, and in Jerzy's case I no longer felt I could be the one to advocate his case. Yet the Americanists at the Sorbonne, where I'd lectured that spring, wanted to hear about Jerzy, who'd been their own guest a few months before, and so during my visit at the start of October I found myself once again on his reputation's trail. Plus this time I was going on to Kosinski country—Eastern Europe, to a Hungary and Poland still a year away from the first agitations of reform that in a decade would tear down the Iron Curtain that had been such a factor in Kosinski's life.

Heading East made me feel like I was entering that shadowy *film-noir* world of strangeness and intrigue so atmospheric of the Jerzy Kosinski I'd sought to meet back in 1971, before he'd become an almost familiar acquaintance and had also let himself be so thoroughly materialized in the commercial American manner. This was the difference between Eastern and Western Europe; Paris had become heavily Americanized, older sidewalk restaurants giving way to fast-food shops that looked like McDonalds, and in the few years I'd been making visits a McDonalds itself had sprung up just off the Luxembourg Gardens on the Boulevard St. Michel, squarely in the path Hemingway had taken on his way down from my neighborhood to the good café where he'd write "A Three Day Blow." There was little of this in Budapest, less in Warsaw, and virtually none in Lublin, the medieval university town where I spent the greater part of my stay. Even traveling was different, and in the Budapest airport I found just the prewar ambiance I'd been seeking as the old waiting room, trimmed in mahogany rather than formica, sat directly on the tarmac, with clouds of smoke from cigarettes, cigars, and pipes partially obscuring the departure board announcing flights (in obsolete-looking propeller-driven airplanes) to Prague, Dresden, and Leningrad.

On the plane, stewards and stewardesses made their way up the aisle handing out small loaves of bread from great wicker baskets; following the meal they brought around baskets of apples. At Warsaw as in Budapest machine-gun-toting soldiers had been the first ground crew to welcome our arrival, but then came the lovely custom of receiving flowers from my host. Everything in Poland seemed prewar, the only obvious signs of modernity being the war damage still visible here and there. In Posnan it was the pockmarks from machine-gun fire along the facades of some otherwise ornate buildings, and outside Lublin there was a concentration camp preserved as a memorial to its victims. Otherwise, it was as if I had stepped back into the world in which Jerzy Kosinski was born.

Yet almost at once I began hearing deprecations about the author I'd thought should be a favorite son. Some of its motivation surprised me, but then a great deal of intellectual and academic life here seemed strange, dating as it did from a different era. For example, my hosts were put off by my habit of being friendly and familiar with those serving us, and were quite upset that I was considerate and polite with the scrubwoman who cleaned the university guesthouse where I stayed. Socialism didn't translate as democratic egalitarianism, I learned; in fact, this academic crowd gloated in its own sense of privilege and superiority, and seemed to enjoy being callous, such as when my host insisted on leaving our university driver sitting in the car, unfed after a full day on the road, while we enjoyed a lavish meal in a country restaurant. Thus when a lot of these people's animosity toward Kosinski turned out to be not because of his themes or style but because he was Jewish, I wrote it off to the same ambiance that made the Poland of 1979 seem so distant from the time frame I'd left in the West.

Yet regardless of motivation, my hosts could marshal plenty of facts that made definite cracks in the image Jerzy had constructed. Learning them as I did, just after witnessing so many contradictions in his ongoing autobiography, I was disposed to receive them as more than just routine anti-Semitism or even anger about his negative portrayal of Catholic Poland during the war. And unlike my own approach to Kosinski's work, much of which relied on nothing more substantial than stories he himself had told me, my hosts' claims were based on solid scholarship replete with bibliographic citations and descriptively based comparisons of texts.

The first of these involved plagiarism and repeated something Zjizslav Njader had pointed out to me before: that *The Painted Bird*'s accounts of peasant superstitions and behavior had been drawn from a sociological text published in Poland by the eminent authority Henryk Biegeleisen in 1929, *The Healing Practices of the Polish Peasantry*. I'd made a reference to this in my own study, *Literary Disruptions*, and had Kosinski on the phone, upset with me for implying that he'd lifted his material (I thought my reference had been neutral, but Jerzy assured me that when he'd taken my book out onto Fifty-seventh Street and read the passage to the first five passersby, four of them had sensed the implication of plagiarism, about which he was extremely sensitive). Now, in Poland, I was being shown Biegeleisen's text and seeing it compared line by line with Kosinski's novel, and I had to admit that the parts quoted were virtually identical. Nor was this an isolated incident, for Jerzy's whole career had been a series of borrowings from texts unknown in America but very popular (and effective narratologically) with audiences in Poland, such as the prewar writer Tadeusz Dołega-Mostowicz's *The Career of Nikodemia Dyzmy*, a precursor of *Being There* whose success as a novel had been eclipsed only by its fame as a motion picture.

The man was a thief, my Polish friends assured me. And also a liar. I'd been taken in by his story of having to fake his references and make an illegal exit from Poland. He'd done this "with a cyanide capsule under his tongue" in case he failed, Jerzy had assured me, and this my hosts found utterly ridiculous. "He left in 1957," they said. "That was during a thaw in relations with the

West: you can look up the announcements of new procedures from the Party Congresses here and in Moscow. Visas were very easy to get; going West was encouraged. Kosinski would have had nothing to worry about—a cyanide capsule under his tongue, indeed!"

Admittedly, this took much of the drama out of Jerzy's emigration. Looking back, one could see that *The Future Is Ours, Comrade, No Third Path,* and even *The Painted Bird* were published with right-wing endorsements; like Kosinski's escape story, this marketing had pandered to Cold War sentiments, and as the chilliness of that era later eased such blurbs were dropped from successive printings of this first novel. Indeed, in the years following Solidarity's emergence and eventual triumph I'd see Jerzy moderate his hostility to the Poles and, most amazingly, see them warm up to him; by 1989 the editors of the leading literary magazine, *Literatura na Świecie,* who'd defamed Jerzy so vehemently during my visit, were assembling a special issue on him and reprinting my chapter from *Literary Disruptions* they'd previously found so flawed. Typically, these editors declined to publish the essay I'd written that repeated their initial claims and used them as part of a reassessment of Jerzy's work and the autobiographical myths associated with it. That was how dramatically the political winds had shifted, something I was witnessing for the first time but which Jerzy had gone through time and again.

My response to being challenged on Kosinski—by the Poles, by the contradictions involved in filming *Being There,* by the polo-playing business in *Passion Play,* and by the disturbing changes in Jerzy's ethic and aesthetic—was a text I felt I should write. I began it after arriving home at the end of October 1979, and by Christmas had something ready that I didn't think I could publish yet but surely wanted to be read by friends. It was a "samizdat," I realized: a piece of writing that for various reasons could not be published but which could have a life of its own by virtue of circulation as a photocopy, a chain letter to be sent around for responses, additions, and forwarding to the next interested party. I'd picked up the term from Jerzy, who'd told me it was how Russian dissidents kept their ideas in circulation when they weren't free to publish. The title reflected my motivations and also my feelings. As "Betrayed by Jerzy Kosinski," it spoke directly of what had happened, but its reference to the title of Manuel Puig's novel then current, *Betrayed by Rita Hayworth,* suggested that what happened was seductive and even pleasurable in retrospect—yet a betrayal just the same.

In writing the piece I not only organized my thoughts—and also realized what a vast number of contradictions had accumulated—but came to understand something more about Jerzy's methods. The keys involved making secrets and cloaking one's identity as a way of keeping free and secure. In sketching out the details of my first meeting with Jerzy, back at Yale in 1971, I recalled a few things that for a decade had rested in the background, but which now seemed quite telling. On settling down in his study for the interview, he'd presented me with a form to sign, giving him copyright and complete control over anything we'd tape, transcribe, and edit. At the time I thought nothing of it, but now realize no respectable interviewer would submit to such control, especially when being confronted with it only at the last minute, after all that preparation and travel. But even here was a clue, for as Jerzy checked my signature he remarked, almost as if to himself, "Klinkowitz—that's *Klinkiewicz*," just as my Polish mother-in-law habitually recast each Germanized or Americanized name back into its native form. I'd always been told my great-grandfather had changed it to sound more German while he fled one of Bismarck's East Prussian drafts. In the meantime I learned from friends with similarly changed names that every family had such a story, covering the truth that great-grandpa was really skipping out on debts or hiding from the police. As it was, "Klinkowitz" was a formula that Jerzy, like my mother-in-law, could easily decode. Making secrets was thus a game on both ends, and in the energy resultant from such codings and decodings could be found a principle for his fiction.

But what of his life itself? *Write about what you know best—* Jerzy had taken this vernacular principle from the most classic American literature and turned it inside out, for although he was writing about himself, that self was in a continual process of reinvention. It had begun with a firm-enough basis in autobiography, for no one could fault the author's life or art in *The Painted Bird*. That part of his life story was sufficient to propel the writer out of Poland and into America—no matter whether the exit had to be accomplished by subterfuge or was expedited by a thaw in politics, for the energy of such transition on its own terms was sufficient to generate another novel, *Steps*. From this plateau, Jerzy had been able to write a masterpiece, *Being There*, and even a creditable look at upper-class American manners, *The Devil Tree*. But then, as his self-invention could rest on nothing more substantial than fame and money, the slide began, with each novel becoming a bit tackier than the last, until *Pinball* found Kosinski's protagonist, always a projection of himself, devoured by the underside of the same power, money, and dominating sexuality that had taken control of his writing and his life once the earlier materials had been written out. That the urban landscape surrounding his hero was so physically blighted and spiritually morbid was simply a reflection of how decrepit Jerzy's material ideal had become.

Yet who was I to decry the lot he'd chosen. Though the world of *Pinball*, published in 1982, was in decay, Jerzy was still at the heights. In fact, there seemed no limit to his celebrity, for he was now something even more than a subject for book-review columns and a guest for the last ten minutes of Johnny Carson—Kosinski was not only an intimate of the Hollywood crowd but a movie star himself, in Warren Beatty's *Reds*. In a transition that mirrored the change in his fiction, he'd moved from the book-review pages to the style section. The climax to this came on February 21, 1982, when *The New York Times Magazine* not only gave ten pages to a lavish feature on Jerzy's life (based on material only he could have supplied), but posed the author himself on the cover, wearing polo boots and breeches and nothing else, fixing the camera with his dark-eyed stare that implied he'd taken control of the entire newspaper. In a season which had seen *People* magazine dressing Kosinski as a stand-in for his protagonist in *Pinball* and *Vogue* opening its pages to Jerzy's own chit-chat about hanging out with Warren Beatty, this display in *The New York Times Magazine* must have struck some people as too much.

On June 22, 1982, the whole caravansary that Jerzy Kosinski had so elaborately constructed fell in like a house of cards. For here were Geoffrey Stokes and Eliot Fremont-Smith of *The Village Voice* claiming that not only was *The New York Times Magazine* wrong but that Kosinski's collective behavior books had been funded and promoted by the CIA and that his novels bore so much heavy rewriting by others as to be plagiarized.

What resulted was a full-fledged media war in which Jerzy's response to these accusations was lost amid the larger forces of a literary world gone mad in a feeding frenzy over this figure who had so baited them over the years. Neither side distinguished itself, other than to show how the matter of Kosinski's unraveling biography was enough to bring out the worst in almost anyone. The *Times* editors and publisher seemed willing to forgo any research of their own and simply publish Jerzy's defense as he presented it to them; the *Voice* too often used implication rather than solid examples, while around the country book editors found I.O.U.'s being called in by an increasingly desperate author in New York. There was desperation indeed in the note I received from Jerzy. "Where are you?" his letter's single sentence asked.

I called him to say that I'd already written something, three years before, which might be of help: my samizdat, which had noted the discrepancies in his autobiography but related them to the brilliance of his fictive art; I had also mentioned in this piece that friends had told me for years that his books were ghostwritten, but how I presumed these were misunderstandings prompted by his methods of composition and linguistic research that would sometimes have him hire writers with different languages in their background to express an action Jerzy had conceived, so that he might compare and contrast their ways of handling it.

Would he like to see it? By all means. I sent it off, and meanwhile the press war continued. As with Richard Nixon and the Watergate affair, it was obvious that the response was far worse than the claimed offense, and that Jerzy's attempt to control those who wished to support him was giving this business the feeling of managed politics. My fears were justified when *The Nation* and even *The New Yorker* published satirical pieces making fun of the whole affair, for now it had become a matter in which relative claims of guilt and innocence were less interesting than the folly of it all.

Meanwhile a reporter from *The New York Times* had called— not a staffer from the *Book Review* or even the editorial pages, but John Corry, who was preparing a story for the paper's "Leisure" section. I gave him a full account of everything I knew, assuming this would help Jerzy's cause. The next day Jerzy himself called, agitated by my samizdat. "This must *not* be seen!" he emphasized, but declined to say why. When I told him I'd already sent the piece off to John Corry, at his request, Jerzy was stunned. Our phone call ended with that, and I never heard a thing from him afterwards, even years later when my occasional notes and calls to him would go unanswered. In exercising such freedom of expression, even in the unpublished format of a samizdat, which is how Kosinski himself would have had to write had he remained in the Eastern bloc, I had crossed the line, and now at least in his book I could never return.

That Jerzy got to John Corry was obvious from how my own position was represented in Corry's account published on November 7, 1982. "A Case History: 17 Years of Ideological Attack on a Cultural Target" read its title, with most of its material reprising the packets Jerzy had sent to book editors across the country that summer and fall. As for my part in the business, Corry used it as a key factor in what he presented as the root explanation for Kosinski's troubles: he was being attacked, for East-West political reasons, by the Polish military government that had been installed to crack down on the Solidarity movement. I, along with *The Village Voice*, had been an unwitting dupe of these nefarious intriguers, and as evidence Corry stated that I'd been fed this material on a visit to Poland. That the visit took place long before the military government came in and even before Solidarity was organized didn't figure in Corry's calculations, nor did the fact that my Polish hosts who'd faulted Jerzy had become Solidarity people themselves— one of them, Zbigniew Lewicki, presently being jailed by this same presumably anti-Kosinski leadership.

I found the whole business preposterous, and decided to write it off as the final chapter in a saga that had begun with extraliterary monkey business and seemed to be ending that way. I didn't think Jerzy was guilty of working for the CIA or having his novels ghostwritten. But neither did I think General Jaruzelski and a bunch of Soviet goons were troubling themselves over this writer who'd been divorced from Polish issues for almost twenty years and who seemed much more interested in polo and Warren Beatty instead. What had happened was obvious: in fabricating an identity Jerzy had gone too far. The world was content to let him invent himself as a tool for fiction, and could even admire the results. But to use this same talent for self-gratifying celebrityhood was disgusting, and for it he was being slapped down.

Did Jerzy deserve it? Recalling how fine his earlier novels were, the answer is no. But there is less of a defense for *Passion Play* and *Pinball*, and none at all considering the nature of his response. As one who has had friends in Poland suffer for their support of Solidarity, I'm disappointed that in order to ingratiate himself with a trend-seeking public Jerzy tried to ally himself with this movement, not in its early days of activism but only when he thought it could be a life-preserver to save him from being pulled down in the maelstrom of publicity he himself had helped stir up. And then, as if trivializing the fate of Solidarity under the military government were not enough, Jerzy moved on to claim an even broader kinship: with the six million of the Holocaust, for "just like them" he was being persecuted by evil forces. When I saw that line in an announcement for his new novel, *The Hermit of 69th Street*, in a Bantam catalogue, I could not believe his tastelessness could drop so low. As it happened, Bantam rejected the manuscript when it came in, and only in 1988 did it appear with a much smaller publishing house. But by then Kosinski was out of the limelight. Even a feature in *Vanity Fair*, where my samizdat was discussed again, failed to get his career back on track; when he interviewed me for the piece, the essay's author confided that he'd read an advance copy of Jerzy's novel and found it to be an almost undigestable word salad, a linguistic riot undertaken as if to prove Kosinski could do anything he wished with language—except to have it mean.

For almost ten years I did not give Jerzy Kosinski a thought. Convinced I'd do no further work on him and uneasy even with his books around, I gathered up all I'd collected and sent them off to a rare book and manuscript dealer so that they would eventually wind up in a library where they might be of use to someone who cared, for I certainly didn't. But in coming to write this present book and finishing the initial chapter on Kurt Vonnegut, I realized that friendship with Jerzy Kosinski, manipulated and even hoaxed as I'd been, was an important part of my experience as a critic. And so the chapter at hand was begun.

With only the title yet typed, I was struck by the urge to phone Jerzy. When I'd tried this before he hadn't responded—I could picture him there up above West Fifty-seventh Street, listening on his speaker-phone as I left a message with the answering service that he constantly screened, resolved not to answer. But now, almost a full decade after those events, he might feel differently, especially since I would be explaining—over that screening loudspeaker that could be heard throughout his apartment—that I was making a final pass over these materials and that perhaps he'd like to have the last word.

I didn't make the call, although I had reached for my address book and had his phone number at hand. Yet even then, Jerzy managed to have the last word, for it was Friday morning, May 3, 1991, and he was in the bathroom just off his bedroom/study, taking his own life.

That afternoon I learned of Jerzy's fate. There was his photo, one he himself had taken and credited to "Scientia-Factum," the corporation which was nothing other than Jerzy Kosinski, with the superimposition of his dates: 1933–1991. The first had been given to him by fate; only the last could he control. Kiki had issued a statement saying the heart condition troubling him for years had worsened, preventing him from working and making him fear he'd become a burden to others. He'd been depressed. All of this was on television, repeated every half-hour as part of Headline News. As in life, Jerzy was dominating the media.

Yet who was really in control? Among the very few Kosinski items I'd saved turned out to be something I can now cite as his epitaph. It was the flyleaf presentation on the copy of *Cockpit* he sent me, dated on his birthday, June 14, 1975. The book was now gone, but for some reason I'd photocopied the inscription, which now told me how I'd figured in his life. "For Jerome Klinkowitz," it read. "Watched, every man feels guilty—and is."

3

Donald Barthelme

There was always a quirkiness to dealing with Donald Barthelme, a style of behavior that fit right in with his work. As opposed to Kurt Vonnegut, who seemed the most vernacular American writer since Mark Twain, and Jerzy Kosinski, who cultivated a reputation that far eclipsed the ordinary in terms of command and control, Barthelme came across with a slightly off-beat angularity that made him behave as curiously as his fiction. Yet beneath that fiction, I came to learn, was a bedrock of popular forms as commonly American as anything Vonnegut might use. And over the years I could appreciate how underneath all those layers of acculturation—Greenwich Village over East Texas over family tastes and influences that made Don as capably cosmopolitan as Kosinski at his best—was a fellow who took pleasure and even delight in the simplest functionings of contemporary life, particularly the life whose remnants survived as traces from his adolescence and young manhood. While the reading public knew him as one of the more innovative writers in *The New Yorker* and as a commentator on the cutting edge of postmodern literature, philosophy, art, and film, I was finding a guy conversant with the routines of Abbott and Costello and whose first publications had been a cub reporter's reviews of "Singer Jane Powell at Loew's as Beautiful Texan in Paris" and "Jeanne Craine as Sorority Girl at Met." True, some of his dwarfs in *Snow White* quoted Heidegger and carried on like Merleau-Ponty; but what made that funny was their qualities as drawn not so much from the Grimms as from Disney, whose rhythms formed an important part of Don's aesthetic life.

For once, Barthelme was a writer I found on my own. In college I'd begun reading *The New Yorker*, as much to ape the manners in its ads as to appreciate the fiction. At the time, the magazine was still publishing new work by John O'Hara, and I could sense the continuum in style that carried forth to stories by Updike and

Cheever, no part of which made me think of special literary accomplishment—such narratives seemed to my untrained eye as little more than copy for the advertisements. But during the years I was buying each weekly issue, from 1963 through 1967, quite distinctive material began to appear over the name "Donald Barthelme." I'm sure I didn't read the first stories, and was reacting simply to seeing the author's rather unusual appellation appearing so frequently. When I did skim a piece it impressed me as quite different from those of the other regulars. Barthelme had begun in the back pages of the magazine, contributing what I took to be novelty items based on funny uses of language in our media-based culture—how news magazines favored colorful action verbs, how *TV Guide* could be as fragmentarily narrative as a novella by Samuel Beckett, and how reading too many issues of *Consumer Reports* could overly depress one with the facts that the whole world was sagging, scaling, or sinking in an abyss of insufficiently warrantied products. But in time Barthelme's work moved up to share the front pages with Updike and Cheever, and I could see how true stories were being devised from these same materials.

Don would find it typical that one of the most American of habits, name recognition, drew me to his work. For that was what prompted me to spend $2 for a copy of his first collection, *Come Back, Dr. Caligari*, the hardcover first of which I found in a used bookstore during a Florida vacation. That was in 1967, in the interval between moving from Milwaukee to my doctoral studies at Madison, and the coincidental publication of Don's first novel, *Snow White*, let his name catch my eye at the university bookstore a month later. Together, these works gave me a nice idea of what he was up to. Then came the recommendation of a friend. Back in Milwaukee Carl Krampf, the bass player from my old rock band and now a practicing clinical psychologist, bought Barthelme's next book, the collection titled *Unspeakable Practices, Unnatural Acts*, and began to sing Don's praises. I'd begun subscribing to *The New Republic* and *The New York Review of Books*, and found similar endorsements there.

By 1970 Barthelme was getting even more attention with his third book of short stories, *City Life*, and I'd begun teaching contemporary lit. Therefore as I sought out writers on whom to do research, he became one of the first I wrote, asking about earlier publications and whether he'd be willing to do an interview.

I wrote Barthelme in care of his agent, Lynn Nesbit, and in a few weeks I had a letter back from the man himself, saying that he "froze in the presence of tape recorders" but would be happy to answer some questions by mail.

The interview proved to be a delight, but not before some quirkiness. I'd put together a kit of sorts, with each question typed at the head of a blank page which Barthelme could fill as amply or sparsely as he chose, with the option of continuing on to another page if he wished. He'd responded with a note saying the queries were good ones and that I could expect a set of answers in about a week. When a month went by I sent him another letter, asking if by chance his materials had gone astray. This was answered by a one-line note saying he hoped to get the work done this coming week. Then another month of silence.

I was about to write him again when late one afternoon I got a phone call. The voice was clipped and mannered in a way that sounded almost British, and I was surprised to hear it was Donald Barthelme calling from New York.

"I've just put my answers to your questions in the mail," he said, and I remarked that this was good news indeed and thanked him. Yet his tone was anything but happy; in fact, he was apologizing for mailing the material, and urged that I not even open the package when it arrived.

"Are you retracting the interview?" I asked in alarm, but Barthelme assured me that he wasn't, that I could do anything I wanted with his answers. He just felt badly that "they weren't any good" and didn't want me to be bothered with such nonsense.

"I thought of pulling them out of the mailbox," he admitted, "but that would be misunderstood." You bet it would, and I could picture a beleaguered Barthelme being hauled off to jail. His greatest worry, however, was that my time would be wasted in trying to make anything worthwhile of this project. Only after I begged him to let me decide, with the promise that I'd drop all work on the interview entirely if I thought the material were not of good quality, did he seem relieved.

A few days later the big manila envelope arrived, and I was pleased to find a neatly typewritten answer to each of my queries. Everything seemed fine, and things had gotten off to a good start with the first question, one that had been suggested by Carl

Krampf: "When you improvise, do you think of the chord changes or the melody?" This, of course, was a parody of one of the stupidest questions to ask, a satire on the square interviewer using bogus technicalese to probe dimensions of jazz about which he doesn't even have a clue. Carl's posing of this question to Don, however, worked a bit of magic—for the joke in it but also for the way it associated Barthelme's fiction with the spirit of jazz. "Both," he'd answered. "This is an interesting question which I'm unable to answer adequately. If the melody is the skeleton of the particular object, then the chord changes are its wardrobe, its changes of clothes. I tend to pay rather more attention to the latter than the former. All I want is just a trace of skeleton—three bones from which the rest may be reasoned out."

From here Don went on to answer each question I'd asked, sometimes going onto a second page for details about growing up as the son of an accomplished modernist architect, living in a remarkable house that drew sightseers ("We used to get up from Sunday dinner, if enough cars had parked, and run out in front of the house in a sort of chorus line, doing high kicks"), and telling about the early writing and editing he'd done for the University of Houston *Forum* and the art journal *Location* in New York. There were comments about his method of breaking up abandoned novels into stories (the relationships among which remained evident), his fascination with fragments and collage, and a joke made from my own question as to whether he had any favorite comedians and reasons for liking them (his answer: "The government"). Nor did Barthelme's answers stop with my questions. Ending the twenty-some pages of material was a question he'd devised himself, "In your story 'See the Moon' one of the characters has the line, 'Fragments are the only forms I trust.' This has been quoted as a statement of your aesthetic. Is it?" His answer was set up as if typographically in a newspaper:

No. It's a statement by the character about what he is feeling at that particular moment. I hope that whatever I think about aesthetics would be a shade more complicated than that. Because that particular line has been richly misunderstood so often (most recently by my colleague J. C. Oates in the *Times*) I have thought of making a public recantation. I can see the story in, say, *Women's Wear Daily*:

WRITER CONFESSES
THAT HE NO LONGER
TRUSTS FRAGMENTS

Trust 'Misplaced,' Author Declares

DISCUSSED DECISION
WITH DAUGHTER, SIX

Will Seek 'Wholes' In Future,
He Says

CLOSING TIME IN GARDENS
OF WEST WILL BE EXTENDED,
SCRIVENER STATES

New York, June 24 (A&P)—Donald Barthelme, 41-year-old writer and well-known fragmentist, said today that he no longer trusted fragments. He added that although he had once been "very fond" of fragments, he had found them to be "finally untrustworthy."

The author, looking tense and drawn after what was described as "considerable thought," made his dramatic late-night announcement at a Sixth Avenue laundromat press conference, from which the press was excluded.

Sources close to the soap machine said, however, that the agonizing reappraisal, which took place before their eyes, required only four minutes.

"Fragments fall apart a lot," Barthelme said. Use of antelope blood as a bonding agent had not proved . . .

Why had Don been so disappointed with his work on this piece? Much of it read as entertainingly as his fiction, and I know he fancied the writing he did here—over a decade later the passage about the press conference, replete with its jokes, appeared in one of his short stories. I wrote back to say how much I liked his answers, and why. Seeing the style of questions he liked, I added a few more, which he answered promptly. Then, after he approved the full text, it went into editor Joe David Bellamy's *The New Fiction: Interviews with Innovative American Writers*, which the University of Illinois Press published in 1974. At the same time I put together the chapter on Don's work for my own *Literary Disruptions: The Making of a Post-Contemporary American Fiction*, which Illinois brought out the following year.

Throughout this period I'd be in touch with Barthelme by letter, asking him to clarify bibliographic details and let me know if any of his stories might be appearing in places the standard indexes would miss. He was always helpful. No request went unanswered, and to save me the inflated costs rare-book dealers were charging for the exhibition catalogue he'd prefaced on five millennia of women in art, *she* (Cordier and Ekstrom Gallery, 3 December 1970 to 6 January 1971), he sent me a photocopy of his typescript. But his letters were exceedingly concise, usually just one line typewritten on a plain sheet of bond—which was always enough to satisfy the matter at hand.

In spring of 1975, however, my work found a new form of expression, to which Don's response was enthusiastic and even exuberant. The occasion was the publication of my first "superfiction" essay, a piece done in the manner of Ihab Hassan's "paracriticisms." Hassan had found the conventional essay form limiting and boring, and began incorporating aural devices (such as transcribing a tape recording to counterpoint his main line of commentary) and aligning his text in various formats (lists, quotations, and so forth) in order to break up the page and reflect the dynamism evident in his thought. To Hassan's method I added graphic effects, such as different styles and faces of type and collages; with the help of designer Roy Behrens each page was set up as an element in the essay's composition, and with the argument being made by such juxtapositions a great deal of tedious critical analysis could be dropped. Appearing in the spring 1975 issue of *Critique*, the balance of which was devoted to conventional essays on Don's work, the piece was visually stunning. Roy and I had sent camera-ready pages to the magazine, and in them viewers could see critical fragments pertaining to Barthelme's work bounced off examples of his work itself. Framing the piece were Joyce Carol Oates's complaints about the aesthetics of fragments and Don's tongue-in-cheek press conference answer from our interview. Nine collages by Roy, done in the manner of Max Ernst which Barthelme had himself been toying with in stories since *City Life*, made the fourteen-page essay an attention-getting delight. And the reader most delighted of all was Barthelme himself.

I'd sent him a copy of the magazine, as I'd done with pieces of my earlier works on him before, and this time instead of a line of thanks received a full page, single-spaced letter literally bursting at the margins with appreciation and encouragement. Even the salutation was multiform, expressing Don's wish that our acquaintance become less formal: in overlapping typescripts he'd aligned three greetings, "Dear Prof. Klinkowitz—," "Dear Mr. Klinkowitz—," and "Dear Jerry—," and went on to say how he liked the superfiction piece so much that it made him uncomfortable, for "you damned critics are pushing us damned writers a little too closely, formwise." Yet he confessed to having been uncomfortable already, so it was no great matter. What he did feel strongly about was that we should get together for "a drink or many drinks" and specified why. "Your effort affirms what I am always in doubt about, that I am a writer," Don explained. "May seem to other people that one is doin' pretty well, but always seems to the midget in question that he has just fucked up again maybe not so badly as last time but still behind the door when the brains were passed out. I think only very good or really terrible writers have confidence, for the rest of us it is Anxiety City, forever." In its own way this reminded me of what Kurt Vonnegut had said in his own first letter back in 1972, that I had been "useful" to him in "caring about" what he did.

Elsewhere in Don's letter were offers to help straighten out his primary and secondary bibliography, references to other critical pieces he'd liked (singling out essays by Charles Samuels and William H. Gass), and some tips on how Roy Behrens could get rid of the "telltale white outline" when pasting collaged elements onto an engraving, "a thing I learned by hard experience." To establish that he wanted things to proceed on a first-name basis, his letter was signed "Don."

Would I come to see him? Absolutely. In late September I'd be on the East Coast, and made tentative plans to see him. Don himself would be away during my first swing through New York, but after a weekend in Boston I could easily shuttle back down. The Boston adventure, however, erred on the far side of having "a drink or many drinks," and with a sickening hangover I phoned Don to say I'd taken ill and was heading directly back to Cedar Falls. Two weeks later I was back in New York, rescheduling the meeting with Don and resolving not to let things get out of control.

On a lovely October evening I left the Royalton, Vonnegut's old hotel on Forty-fourth Street, and took the subway downtown. I thought I knew Greenwich Village pretty well, having spent time with Clarence Major at his apartment just a half block off Washington Square, met Steve Katz and Michael Stephens where they lived in the loft district of SoHo, and even coursed through the commercial desolation of Hudson and Bethune Streets when visiting Gilbert Sorrentino. But Don's neighborhood, in the block of West Eleventh Street running between Sixth and Seventh Avenues, was something I hadn't expected. This didn't seem like the urban mass of Manhattan at all, for as the rumble of the Seventh Avenue subway faded behind me I found myself walking up a tree-shaded sidestreet of two and three story townhouses, each with its neatly fenced front yard. Strollers waved to friends in windows or sitting on the steps, and up ahead Sixth Avenue offered nothing more imposing than a corner grocery store, a liquor shop, and a pizzeria. I could have been back in Cedar Falls. But in a moment Don would have me moving back in time and place even further.

His address turned out to be a small apartment building. In the lobby I found a mailbox labeled "Barthelme/Knox," and taped to it a scrap of bond paper with the neatly typed message, "Bell broken. Stand at window and yell." So back I went into the yard, and beneath the large overlooking window began shouting "Don! Oh Don? Hey, Don!" I could have been a ten-year-old back in suburban Milwaukee, calling for Kurt Osborn or Jay Smaltz to come out and play ball. Hadn't Don's letter said venturing to publish new work made him feel like a midget, and that my scholarship gave him a sense of stature? Well, in a harmlessly comic way his doorbell note had reduced mine, and as I saw him come to the window and motion me in I was once again humble enough.

Inside I met Don and was introduced to Marion Knox, a researcher at *Time* magazine who in 1978 would become his wife. We settled down for a couple scotches, Don sitting in a straight-

backed cane rocker that made him look very upright and nine-
teenth century in a rather stern Scandinavian way. Yet all was
friendly, and at seven Don suggested the three of us walk down the
block for dinner at a new restaurant on Sixth Avenue called Hopper's.

As we headed down West Eleventh to the corner I had the
feeling that I was being walked not just through Don's neighborhood but through one of his texts as well. Six months later I'd
encounter it as a piece of writing in a format he'd only recently
begun, an unsigned contribution to the "Comment" section of
those front pages in *The New Yorker* under the weekly headline,
"Talk of the Town." In 1978 the best of these would be collected in
a small press edition, *Here in the Village*, published by the Lord John
Press in Northridge, California. The piece in question concludes
that volume, and follows the narrator as he strolls these same environs, noting the children's art from the grade school next door dec-
orating the windows of Ray's Pizzeria, the books stacked along the
windowsill in Ramsey Clark's apartment (all hardcovers Don
pointed out to me then and again in this text), the recommended
books meriting window display at Igor's Art Foods on Sixth ("We
are a bookish community," Don remarked, again both to me and
his *New Yorker* readers when the column appeared), and other residences and shops that made this stretch of the West Village so
accommodating. Don had lived here, in this same apartment, since
coming up from Houston to edit Harold Rosenberg and Thomas B.
Hess's magazine, *Location*, in 1962. From here had been written
Snow White and the hundred stories already published, most of
them in *The New Yorker*. This work, which to most critics had
seemed so angular and abstract, was coming from a familiar environment, Don seemed to be implying now as we walked past the
apartment where Snow White and her boyfriend-dwarfs might
have lived quite happily.

I was getting the picture, yet Don continued. I should have
realized that dining at Hopper's would be instructional, too, given
the routine I'd been put through with the doorbell. The first Donald Barthelme story ever, published in 1961 as "The Darling Duck-
ling at School" and retitled "Me and Miss Mandible" when collected in 1964, had placed a character in just such circumstances, as
a thirty-five-year-old insurance adjustor suddenly finds himself in
a sixth-grade classroom, his adult stature, manners, and instincts

crammed into this hothouse of adolescence and pubescence. Like Kafka's classic, Barthelme's story had presented this single premise and then let everything else follow naturally—which despite the narrator's even tone cannot be natural at all, but is instead a hilarious attempt at coming to rational terms with the unreasonable. I'd had that feeling, decked out in my professor's corduroy and lugging my bibliographer's kit of first editions (to be signed) and unattributed book reviews (to be identified) to Don's door, only having to step back and make contact like a school kid. Now at this trendy new Sixth Avenue restaurant I was to see another Barthelme narrative take place. Only this time, for the author, it didn't go so smoothly.

"Good evening," we were greeted after having been given menus and seated. "My name is William, and I'm your waiter . . . The young man was about to ask if we'd care for drinks when Don looked up and addressed him in mock severity.

"No you are *not!*" Don announced, underscoring the last word with a nod of authority.

"Sir?" the waiter asked, genuinely puzzled.

"I said you are *not* a waiter!" Don repeated. He moved his head from side to side, taking in Marion and myself for the bit of wisdom to come. "This is Greenwich Village, young man. You are really an actor, or a painter. Maybe even a writer struggling for a break. But you are most certainly *not* a *waiter!*"

The restaurant was filling with customers and young William surely had enough to do already. Marion and I had become uncomfortable with Don's teasing, and I could tell she was about to intercede and ask for more scotch as a way of smoothing the waters. Which is just what I didn't want to have happen, given my overimbibing at Dan Wakefield's in Boston less than two weeks before. Thankfully William stood up for himself.

"I'm sorry sir," he said with firmness, "I *am* a waiter and a damn good one! May I please have your order?"

He wasn't getting one from Don, who reacted with a moody silence and downcast glance that didn't rise 'til William had left. Marion ordered chicken Kiev for Don and lamb for herself. I opted for the lamb and said we wouldn't be needing any drinks. Finally, with this chapter of the restaurant story having turned on its narrator, we settled down to sipping at our ice water and reestablishing a more social mood.

Which came easily enough. The food was delicious, the service excellent, and I could sense Don's smug satisfaction when William brought us complimentary brandy afterwards, though the motive was surely less one of apology than an attempt to salvage his tip from this prime table. With the bill, however, came a chance for Don to get involved again. Even as William laid it on the table, Don was reaching across to cover it with his American Express card, angled so the waiter could read its boldly stamped name: DONALD BARTHELME. The caps reminded me of how Don's name appeared at the end of each *New Yorker* story, and it struck me that now he was signing this one. Another routine, and this one at some small cost, because when making the date I'd asked if I could pay for the dinner.

Back at the apartment we fixed more drinks, Don switching from scotch on the rocks to scotch with water; I stayed with the former so as not to kid myself about how much alcohol I was taking. Marion joined us for a while, talking about how the reviewers she knew at *Time* had handled Vonnegut and recalling how my own *Vonnegut Statement* had won coverage there (in an issue Don had saved since its feature story was on Janis Joplin, whose career began in the same southeastern Texas orbit as his own). When Marion left to do some work in her own study down the hall, I felt somewhat abandoned; the age we shared, a dozen years younger than Don, made us allies, especially against the posturings he'd undertake—without her at the restaurant Don's scene with the waiter might well have turned ugly.

Yet without Marion as an audience his penchant for display seemed less keen, and for most of the following hours he allowed the focus of our conversation to be on me. His position, however, remained superior, and as we discussed other writers he seemed determined to counter my own tastes, associating his preferences and even his work itself with a more conservative crowd—Walker Percy, Joyce Carol Oates—as opposed to the camp of innovative revolutionaries in which I sought to place him. At one point he tricked me by raising expectations: reaching to the bookcase behind, he said he would give me an extra copy of the novel that had interested him the most. Would it be by Beckett, or perhaps someone younger—LeClézio, Sollers, Butor, Handke, or Wittig? Nope, I could hear Don saying to himself as he read my eager thoughts; it was *A House and Its Head*, by Ivy Compton-Burnett. As if to mystify and frustrate me further, he then went on to say the most interesting writer at work today was Anthony Powell, even coaching me on the right pronunciation ("Pole") so that I could carry this unwelcome information back to the waiting world.

Now came my time at bat, for Don had pulled down another book—the copy of *Literary Disruptions* I'd sent him at its publication earlier that spring—and ran down its list of my own favorite writers, most of whom were getting their first chapter-length coverage in a university press publication.

"Kurt Vonnegut," he began, looking at my first chapter. "No question about that—absolutely first rate! We're friends, you know," Don added, and I recalled silently how Kurt had once told me the basis of their friendship: each was the son of an architect.

"Now this next fellow, 'Barthelme,'" Don continued, turning to chapter 2. "I have no idea whatsoever about him, but for the third one I think you're making a mistake."

"Jerzy Kosinski?" I asked. "Don't you like his work?" This worried me, for I'd made Kosinski's privileging of the imagination an important link in the book's alignment of technique with theme, and feared Don would be shooting down my thesis before it could get off the ground.

"*The Painted Bird* is good," he counseled, "but halfway through *Steps* the writing begins to lose substance. And since then he's done absolutely nothing."

I felt compelled to argue, and asked if Don didn't think that *Being There* was an exquisite practical joke.

"A joke—yes," he replied, but with such a disapproving glance that I felt ashamed for proposing practical jokes as art.

"LeRoi Jones," Don continued. "Hasn't written fiction for years. Probably never will. James Park Sloan—a one-book man." As my hopes visibly faded, Don perked up a bit, enjoying his triumph enough to offer some praise. "Now, Ronald Sukenick. He hasn't done his best work yet, but he's obviously thinking. Sukenick—ok."

"What about Raymond Federman?", I asked eagerly, hoping Don would see the link with Sukenick.

"Nope."

"Gilbert Sorrentino?"

"Nope." With that, Don closed the book and returned it to the shelf. Facing me from that sternly upright rocking chair, he assumed an even stiffer posture and began what was surely a prepared lecture.

"Now if you want to be the top-dog critic," he began, "and you surely do, you're going to have to be right a lot more often than you're wrong!"

I did a quick count in review, taking credit for Vonnegut, Sukenick, and Don himself, and felt I'd been slighted. "Isn't three for eight a good average?" I asked. "That's hitting .375, good enough to lead most leagues!"

"But you're not the hitter," Don countered. "We're the hitters. You're the fielder, and you're not going to get anywhere if you keep dropping every other ball!"

For this I had no ready answer, and Don sat there in satisfied silence. Then we heard Marion's voice from down the hall. "Why, Donald," she was saying, and I could see her coming up behind his chair. From Don's point of view the timing was perfect, and I could see from his smile that he was anticipating some praise, some marvel about himself that his fiancée had just discovered.

"Why, Donald!", Marion repeated, now standing just behind his chair. "Your father's is bigger than yours!"

With a lunge forward Don fought not to choke on his drink, from which he'd been taking a pleasurable sip to accompany Marion's expected praise. As his complexion struggled through differing shades of red, blue, and white, I could see Marion enjoying her trick on him—and also to what she was referring, for in her hands was the latest edition of *Who's Who*, where she had doubtlessly just compared the entries for Donald Barthelme, Senior and Junior.

From then on Don became a less intimidating figure. His very posturing was of the sort that set him up for a fall—for a pratfall, in fact, that he seemed to enjoy taking. The book he was just about to publish—his second novel, *The Dead Father*—based both its thematics and techniques on that style of inevitable deflation, and it seemed appropriate that I had pried loose an advance copy from a friend at the Strand Book Store and had it here for Don to sign. The games he played with me were probably along the lines of how he related to his younger brothers, Rick and Steve, both of whom wrote fiction. A year before I'd met the conceptual artist Joseph Kosuth, and during our dinnertime conversation had heard Joseph's verdict on these younger siblings' work, a line that doubtlessly originated with Don: "Nothing grows in the shade of a great tree." For Kosuth, it was just a one-liner, but in both Don's life and work I was beginning to see how such statements never stood alone but were always challenged by both text and context. Take a look at almost any page of *The Dead Father* and you'll see it—lines that deconstruct themselves as objects refuse to hold the message carried by the verb, leaving the subject sitting there holding the bag. It's how the Dead Father himself speaks, and how his words are undercut by the contrary language of the young women around him. It is his formality that is both funny in itself and hilarious when festooned with the colored streamers of Julie and Emma's more lively dialogue. It was, in fact, just what I'd heard as Don's self-satisfied little lecture about my chances of being "top-dog critic" wobbled off its seat of authority in the aftermath of Marion's little joke with *Who's Who*.

The subject poses, upright and noble, impressed with its own feeling of command. A statue, noble and erect; a veritable monument. But life isn't so static. As language, it is all motion and change, the forward pointing arrow of the transformational grammarian keeping everything in flux. The women of *The Dead Father* understand and appreciate that flux, and best of all can enjoy the humor of their superannuated male protagonist trying to resist it. As a generating force for narrative, it is classically simple, a line as straight (and yet as liable to obstruction and distraction) as the path taken by the crew hauling the old man to his grave. It was the image Don had fun in cultivating, whether it be making the comment about nothing growing in the shade of a great tree (sound of buzz saws off stage) or playing his little game with the waiter (and ending up by giving the waiter the best line).

One year later a glimpse of Don, caught across a crowded room, confirmed this image. It was during the time I'd brought my fiancée Julie to New York, meeting Vonnegut, Kosinski, and the others I'd done work on. It was November and the weather was chilly, but the Strand Book Store, just below Union Square on the Village's northern edge, was warm and cheerful, for here Burt Britton was hosting the book party for his *Self-Portrait: Book People Picture Themselves*. The room was awash with literary celebrities, so packed that one could hardly move. I was glad Julie had the chance to meet Kurt and Jerzy at restaurants uptown, and that others had been found at less frantic parties, for unless the author in question were jammed into one's own corner you could only wave and smile. In this madhouse I could see Donald Barthelme, looking more nineteenth-century Scandinavian than ever, like an Ibsen rector staring sternly across his oddly cut beard and standing so erect one might think his back were braced or his ribs in terrible pain. Don's height made him stand out half a head above the crowd, but it was his manner of dress that made him look so singular: bundled into a heavy topcoat and wearing a outdoorsman's cap, its earflaps firmly fastened beneath his chin.

He stood out, of course, like a sore thumb. But amidst the party's bustle it seemed a perfect image, a rock-solid probity that loomed above the chatty social currents like a mountainside over a fjord. As I continued reading Don's work, these alternations of movement and stasis would characterize his style for me, a style in which a steadfast object would stand amid the narrative like a word's resistance to the blankness of a page. Quite often such objects would function this way by means of off-beat cleverness, such as the scene in "Critique de la Vie Quotidienne" (collected in the 1972 volume done with Farrar, Straus and Giroux, *Sadness*) where the hapless father accompanies his little daughter to nursery school, only to find the children merrily making death masks— what better object to halt the father's unassuming joy and create that little narrative hitch that made the story so characteristically Barthelme? Because one never knew where a death mask might pop up, the storytelling would have to proceed like walking on eggshells or thin ice, a manner which becomes even funnier when the obstructions are so quotidian in themselves:

> I remember once we were sleeping in a narrow bed, Wanda and I, in a hotel, on a holiday, and the child crept into bed with us.
> "If you insist on overburdening the bed," we said, "you must sleep at the bottom, with the feet." "But I don't want to sleep with the feet," the child said. "Sleep with the feet," we said, "they won't hurt you." "The feet kick," the child said, "in the middle of the night." "The feet or the floor," we said. "Take your choice." "Why can't I sleep with the heads," the child asked, "like everybody else?" "Because you are a child," we said, and the child subsided, whimpering, the final arguments in the case having been presented and the verdict in. But in truth the child was not without recourse; it urinated in

the bed, in the vicinity of the feet. "God damn it," I said, inventing this formulation at the instant of need, "What the devil is happening, at the bottom of the bed?" "I couldn't help it," the child said. "It just came out." "I forgot to bring the plastic sheet," Wanda said. "Holy hell," I said. "Is there to be no end to this *family life*?" (p. 7)

As in the routine with the waiter and the business with Marion and *Who's Who*, this scene from "Critique de la Vie Quotidienne" is pure Barthelme. Like Don in his general approach to life, it ventures out in cautious, tight rhythms, holding a narrow sense of balance so that nothing can tip things out of line. Order would come from the incantation of repetitive elements—we said, the child said, all limited to the world of the feet at the foot of the bed. The debate is as systematic as a dispute supervised by the courts, and as the case is won (at least on rational grounds) the narrator allows himself a longer sentence that subsides, with the kid's whimperings, in a series of legal references—final arguments, the verdict in. As with his Dead Father figure, Barthelme has played at controlling language by limiting his sentence to balanced exchanges and anchoring each so firmly with such extremely limited syntactic alternatives—the feet or the floor. But language is not only order but play, and relearning this lesson is the motive behind all Don's fiction. Notice how the child opts back into the game on the game's own terms, seizing a legal phrase of its own, "not without recourse," and moving the action forth by a quantum leap— wetting the bed. With this bed-wetting the narrative is once again moving, and now on a higher level, that of the nuisances of family life. What can the narrator say? We can almost hear the Dead Father in one of his useless yet thoroughly self-fancied pronouncements— God damn it! Holy hell!

Language is order, but also play, and exploring this tension in narrative situations creates a style of fiction that becomes so characteristically Barthelme's. I learned this from his stories, but also from his conduct that evening in New York. The other lesson had been taught to me during the business with the broken doorbell, and in reviewing the story that exploited a similar situation of returning an adult to certain circumstances of childhood—"Me and Miss Mandible"—I could appreciate both how true and how narratologically effective it was. Signs are signs, the narrator of this piece learns, but some of them are lies. As such, the story becomes an exercise not just in readings and misreadings, but in writings and miswritings. "Miss Mandible wants to make love to me," it begins, "but she hesitates because I am officially a child." That's what all the signs of institutional authority say, for her gradebook and the card index in the principal's office list the narrator as being eleven years old and not the age thirty-five that he really is. Yet a contrary set of signs—from another system, the physiological— attests the opposite: "I've been in the Army, I am six feet one, I have hair in the appropriate places, my voice is a baritone, I know very well what to do with Miss Mandible if she ever makes up her mind" (*Come Back Dr. Caligari* [Boston: Little, Brown and Co., 1964], p. 97). Notice how the signs are parallel but contradictory, just as the horror of the first sentence, implying an adult having sex with a child, is undercut by the narrator's smug assurance of carnal knowledge and even expertise. As a routine, it was similar to what Don put me through in the scene outside his window: not just that I as a thirty-one-year-old was being forced to act like a little kid, but that the sentence he'd constructed for me allowed me to play my part so effectively even as I shuddered at its function.

Don understood the nuances of American life and its popular forms of behavior; that's why me standing out on the lawn to call for him was so funny, and why the narrator's situation in the story was so telling, poised as he is between two sign systems, the terms of which can be read by the other group but not necessarily understood. How clever to have the sixth graders of Miss Mandible's class puzzling over the headlines of the year's ongoing fan magazine story, the romance of Eddie Fisher and Debbie Reynolds with its mortal threats from Elizabeth Taylor. That these materials come from the moment's pop culture is just one stage in the author's perception; fictive art becomes apparent when the classmates, some of them aged eleven and some twelve, either guess smugly at the references or sit there without a clue—and even more charming are the parallels some of the brighter young readers can draw to their own situation developing at hand among the narrator, Sue Ann Brownly, and Miss Mandible, especially in the ways Miss Mandible can be read as Elizabeth Taylor and any Disney film's Wicked Witch all at once.

Like all good narrative artists, Don was reading his culture semiotically. Signs are signs—not symbols for something deep or metaphors for things far reaching, but encodings meant to convey simple messages as clearly and as obviously as language itself. Yet for signs as well as bits of language, some of them are lies, and learning how to interpret them is an important part of growing up into the transformational business of life. Barthelme's genius was to place the action of his stories on this level, not among the attitudes represented but within the sign-making activity itself. In this way his thoroughly accessible fiction was achieving the goal Samuel Beckett had set for the greatest innovation: that the literary work not be *about* something but *be* that thing itself. The thing in question, Don had learned, was semiotic activity, and his brilliance was to see how such business took place on the most familiar levels of life, fashioned with materials as familiar as any lowbrow reader's fan magazine.

Barthelme's predecessors in *The New Yorker*—O'Hara, Updike, and Cheever—understood this process, but in a manner dating back to Henry James and Edith Wharton followed the texture of semiosis as woven into the threads of behavior known as social manners. Manners themselves are a form of camouflage, however, and by the time they are taken into a story it is even easier to let them disappear within the flow of life; as a result, readers can receive such a work as being about something rather than existing as a thing itself. With Don's stories, however, the signs were much more apparent by virtue of their action being his very point. In a Cheever story as well as one by Barthelme, the signs are there, but in the latter they are used in a way not so much to tell readers something about the character (he's rich, he's an alcoholic, he's worried about his job) as about how the signs themselves function (the classmates are reenacting the Eddie-Debbie-Liz triangle even as they puzzle over headlines about it).

This was the process I'd observed in Don's way of living in the Village. We weren't just going out to dinner, but were *going out to dinner*, every action of which could be fashioned in a self-referential way, just as calling for him at six had been made so literal. At Burt Britton's party, he'd made somewhat of a spectacle of himself, walking in bundled up to the nose in that overcoat and with the earflaps of that preposterous hunting cap tied down. Julie had thought the get-up was charming in its own way, and said he looked like a troll. Don surely was a caricature of himself that night, and appropriately so, for Burt's book was a collection of amateur self-portraits that writers had scribbled for him when dropping by to sell review copies at the Strand. The same attitude is apparent in the send-up of Carlos Castaneda's pop anthropology collected in *Guilty Pleasures* (New York: Farrar, Straus and Giroux, 1974), "The Teachings of Don B.: A Yankee Way of Knowledge," in which the Yaqui sorcerer becomes the *New Yorker* writer and the remote village of Ixtlan refocuses as the West Village environs of Don's neighborhood. The humor of this piece is two-edged, as all semiotically based parody must be: not just with the nuances, so easily joked about, in Castaneda's work, but in the way Don's own quotidian habits in the Village take on similar proportions when recounted in that same style of breathlessly anthropological discovery ("He showed me into a small but poorly furnished apartment containing hundreds of books stacked randomly about. In the center of the room a fire was blazing brightly. Throwing a few more books on the fire, Don B. invited me to be seated . . ." [p. 54]).

As I continued my acquaintance with Don and continued to learn more about his past, the reasons for his semiotic orientation became obvious. Far more so than O'Hara, Updike, and Cheever, he was visually oriented and tended to make his telling juxtapositions in terms of space rather than time. Consider a typical short story by John Updike. Its style is primarily a treat for the sensitive ear; the sound of those wonderfully complex yet ever-flowing sentences is certainly more pleasing than the task they set for the reader's eye. The characters' activity will be social, and their doings form a stream whose meanings follow naturally toward implications of myth. Updike's world, then, is at once identical to ours and much larger, and can be taken as easily or as profoundly as one wishes.

For Donald Barthelme, trained as a journalist, experienced as a managing editor (adept at solving problems of layout and design), and conversant in the terms of postmodern art (having worked both as a contemporary-arts museum director and editor of an innovative art journal), the world is seen in different dimensions. His sentences are often clipped and short, building on rhythms that are typographically obvious (recall all those we saids, the child said, the feet, and the bed from "Critique de la Vie Quotidienne"). Neither will his characters' actions flow through the complex social currents Updike favors; instead, their postures stand as monuments rooted as the subject part of a transformational grammarian's sentence, waiting to be swept away not by some business at the bar or the country club but by the inexorable syntactic force of the active verb that follows. Barthelme's paragraphs are put together in the way a layout editor composes the page, with a steady flow toward the central anchoring element. When presenting a narrative, thought must always go toward supplying the right amount of visual elements; Don had this in mind when setting up features in *Forum* and *Location*, and he surely had to take it into consideration when preparing an installation at Houston's Contemporary Arts Museum, where the viewer's walk through the galleries (a narrative) had to be paced through the spaces occupied by the artworks themselves.

This was why Don's favorite form of expression was collage. By virtue of spatial juxtaposition, two or more elements from different sources could be combined to form something new (a product of visual contiguity) while at the same time remaining themselves (thanks to their visual trace of origin). Later he would add collages to his own stories, first as illustrations to the text and then as interactive devices which by virtue of clipping and positioning told their own stories (such as the tiny figure of Napoleon staring up at the page-high portrait of Tolstoy in "At the Tolstoy Museum" from *City Life*). Yet the key remained *seeing* the pictorial aspects of our culture and *reading* them as signs, and stories such as "Robert Kennedy Saved from Drowning" and "Views of My Father Weeping" are visually rich and spatially juxtapositional thanks to this ability to remember that signs are first of all signs.

The most obvious biographical clue to understanding Don's work as a fiction writer was that it didn't begin until he was aged thirty. Like Kurt Vonnegut's training in the sciences (chemistry, biology, anthropology) and Jerzy Kosinski's work in sociology, Barthelme's experience made him anything but a typical English major graduate about to embark on a career in the tradition of Henry James and F. Scott Fitzgerald. He trained as a student journalist, doing features, columns, and reviews for the University of Houston's student paper, *The Cougar*, becoming its managing editor by his sophomore year. Soon he was editor-in-chief, and was also working for the university's news service. In July 1951, Barthelme stepped directly from *The Cougar*'s summer-session coverage to a job with *The Houston Post*, where in addition to news reporting the young journalist published signed reviews of movies and stage shows on a thrice weekly basis.

A journalist is trained to see the world differently than is a literature student. Don was aware of this difference of orientation, and occasionally made fun of it in his *Cougar* columns, regretting that creative-writing instruction seemed to be supplanting creative writing itself and filing a story that detailed how an English major's complaint about grammar and usage had upset the paper's production schedule and almost prevented any news from appearing. Studying literature prompts one to see the world in terms of themes and images; the journalist sees functions, and must be able to describe an action without making suppositions as to its form or purpose until the verdict is in. Here could be roots for Barthelme's appreciation of collage, particularly the humorous applications of the collage principle; for maintaining an identity of function even as unlikes are placed together is something his eye was trained to do. Many years later, in his new career as a fiction writer, Don would exploit this talent in his novel *Snow White*, but even as a student journalist he could play with such materials in a similar way. In an entertaining little piece titled "Grimm Revisited" from *The Cougar*'s July 13, 1951 issue (p. 2), Barthelme takes two such unlikes—witchery and unionism—and combines them in a hilarious account of a witch named Jane who fails in her attempt to steal a child and is drummed out of the witches' union. A literature student, perhaps in one of those creative-writing workshops the young Barthelme had deplored, might fashion such materials into a thematic tour de force; the journalist, however, respects each element of the composition for its original function, thus allowing the story's collage effect of witches acting like witches and the union behaving just like a union, the humor coming from putting the two self-integral activities together to form something that is unmistakably the writer's own.

"Greer Garson a Shady Lady in Doubtful Game at Loew's." "John Ireland Carries Word to Custer at Metropolitan." "Mr. Disney's 'Wonderland' with Charm at Majestic." These headlines, reviewing a weekend's fare at the three major Houston movie houses, show just how American popular culture and its icons were washing over the young reporter. Again, he was both in the story and above it, watching the films with hundreds of other townsfolk (and millions across the country) yet also taking note of the effectiveness of their art. A semiotician could plot the several lines of activity that Barthelme was here collapsing onto a single plane of action: whereas an actor named John Ireland was portraying a soldier carrying a message to another actor in a location filmed to look like the Little Big Horn River, in a film which was being shown at a theater called the Metropolitan, the headline mixes a personal identity (John Ireland) with a portrayed one (Custer) and has the message carried not to the battlefield but to the movie house. Though physically impossible, such activity is precisely what takes place in the viewers' imaginations, as all three realms of action—dramaturgical, historical, and mechanical—are experienced as one. Don's genius even then was that he could distinguish all three parts as themselves even as they came together under the illusion of cinema art.

All of these materials came to light during the next stage of my work on Donald Barthelme, which this time around involved compiling a full descriptive bibliography of everything by and about him. Asa Pieratt, who'd collaborated on the Vonnegut bibliography, helped me describe the first editions and acquire publishing histories of all the foreign translations, while Robert Murray Davis joined our crew to look through all those old newspapers down in Houston. Remarkably, Bob uncovered no less than 430 such items, the gamut of which found Barthelme doing everything from covering Ronald Reagan and Doris Day movies to interviewing actor Fess Parker (of "Davy Crockett" fame) who was changing planes at the airport. Here indeed was a full career, practiced for a decade before writing fiction became a possibility. What an encyclopedia of pop culture Don had compiled, both in its original form and in its workings on the public. And what interaction the young writer could boast, working with a lead time of just hours and reaching one of the broadest audiences possible.

Don's interaction with the American middle class, on the level of its most commonly shared imaginative level, reminded me of how Kurt Vonnegut's writing had taken similar root: graduating from student journalism to the world of publicity in which he had to make readers appreciate how at General Electric the product was not only all the comfort of modern life but something as fundamentally American as "progress" itself. Kurt had also trained as an anthropologist, devising a scheme by which the cultural origins of narratives could be determined by plotting their structures, and when in 1950 he began his fiction writer's career (at age twenty-eight, just a year and a half younger than Donald Barthelme at that similar stage) it was to a field replete with identifiable formulae for structural manipulation, the short-story market of the great family weeklies, *Collier's* and *The Saturday Evening Post.*

Here, for most of the early 1950s, the careers of the two authors who would be America's leading fictive innovators of the 1960s coincided. As Don covered films by Burt Lancaster and Ray Milland and wrote praise for the Empire Room's musical program of hits from *Oklahoma!*, Kurt published story after story generated by the same interests. The entertainments page of *The Houston Post* and the fiction pages of *The Saturday Evening Post* shared the same readership, and their materials were drawn from aesthetic concerns of this same range of American life. Years later, critics coming upon their first Barthelme in *Come Back, Dr. Caligari* and getting an initial look at Vonnegut in *Cat's Cradle* would despair at rationalizing such apparently avant-garde work, not realizing that at the heart of each writer's method was an understanding of how sign systems work in a popular culture plus no small amount of love for the comedy of such workings.

As close as he was to the popular culture, Don's track record through the 1950s reflected what to more liberal eyes of the late 1960s and early 1970s would be embarrassing. Which should not be embarrassing or a surprise. After all, Vonnegut had prefaced *Wampeters, Foma, and Granfalloons* by swearing he'd never reveal the whereabouts of the three or four fugitive stories I'd yet to find, and then let the cat out of the bag by revealing one of them was an unabashedly sentimental piece about the romantic literature his family's black cook would read to him on lonely afternoons. (There's the possibility that some of this missing work may have included minority references accepted during the 1950s but awkward and inappropriate later, such as the ending to "Hal Irwin's Magic Lamp" from *Cosmopolitan* of June 1957, whose plot turns on the agency of a stereotypically portrayed black maid; the most offensive lines were dropped when collecting the piece in 1961 for *Canary in a Cat House*, and the entire story was the only one not repeated in *Welcome to the Monkey House* in 1968.) In Don's case, the troublesome piece was an editorial for *The Cougar* endorsing the anticommunist work of the House of Representatives Committee on Un-American Activities and agreeing that offending directors and producers in Hollywood should be exposed and controlled. When

Bob Davis uncovered it I wrote Don to let him know. Don wrote back expressing surprise that he'd ever written such a thing. I assured him that our description in the bibliography would steer clear of political implications, and in abstracting the piece I kept to painfully neutral language; but for the fun of it I sent the original photostat to Don in New York, who replied that our bibliographic research had indeed finally nailed him.

The bibliography itself was published late in 1977, and in addition to detailing the extent of Don's work among popular culture as a journalist it established the great range of his writing. There were theoretical essays on experimental literature and art, commentaries on the use of language and image in advertising, book reviews, movie reviews, and any number of satires and parodies. These last he had initially collected apart from his mainline short stories as the volume *Guilty Pleasures*; when I asked him why they had to be sequestered apart from his regular canon, Don replied that they really shouldn't be collected at all, that their more narrowly focused comedy might encourage a too-reductive reading of similar elements in his more serious work. Yet here in the mid-1970s he was at least bringing them together. Four years later he'd take an even greater step toward enlarging his canon (and thus allowing broader interpretations of his work) by putting his name to a batch of the unsigned *New Yorker* "Comment" columns and publishing them in a small press edition, *Here in the Village*.

As the late 1970s turned into the early 1980s, I noticed a change in Don's work. On the surface, his fiction might have seemed to be turning slightly more realistic. Locations were increasingly identifiable as Don's neighborhood in the West Village, and his protagonists' doings conformed to his own. These trends were identifiable because the short stories were becoming more like his Village-based "Comment" pieces, while others of the "Comment" variety were taking on characteristics of his more venturesome stories. Meanwhile there were still other writings being published as art catalogue notes, editorial opinions (including one in *The New York Times* regarding Grace Paley's arrest for protesting at The White House), and symposium commentaries. Yet in all such work there was the unmistakable presence of Don's style: not so much a written English as a carefully spoken, somewhat self-conscious Americanese which even as it struggled for a weighty seriousness could break into a hilarious bit of lower New York street-talk or East Texas cowboy lingo. You could identify it in a moment, the same way just a snatch of Miles Davis's trumpet or John Coltrane's tenor sax stood out whether heard as part of a small group or a larger band.

Three volumes published in New York with Putnam's signaled the integration of all these various writings. In two big collections that established what Don obviously felt was his short-story canon, *Sixty Stories* (1981) and *Forty Stories* (1987), several of the previously sequestered parodies from *Guilty Pleasures* were allowed to mix with stories from his other collections; more importantly, a few previously unsigned "Comment" pieces were now included the same way. Recalling Don's earlier worries about oversimplified interpretations, I could appreciate how he was feeling comfortable with the broader range of work and how one part of it could only enrich (and not reduce) the other. But a third volume—what would be the last gathering and arranging of previously uncollected material in his lifetime—showed how such integration of materials was in fact extending his style to almost breathtaking new dimensions.

Overnight to Many Distant Cities (1983) was composed like none other of Don's previous collections. There were a dozen stories, true; about a quarter less than usual, but as such reflecting a slight drop in production that had become evident as other concerns, largely academic, had taken time away from writing. What was different was the way these twelve were presented, each of them prefaced (in the manner of Ernest Hemingway's *In Our Time*) with a brief untitled piece of writing, all of it set in italics, and identified on the table of contents by its initial three or four words. These shorter pieces, just two or three pages in length apiece, came from all over. Some were unsigned "Comment" columns; others had been first published as stories, some in *The New Yorker* and others elsewhere, but all in the manner of the more limited entertainments of *Guilty Pleasures*; one was carved out of a longer story from *Penthouse*; and one, "*I put a name in an envelope . . . ,*" had been written for and first appeared in the catalogue for a Joseph Cornell exhibit. Their function was obvious: to establish a reception for the book that would anticipate not morally pointed or even referential stories but rather a style of reading that could take delight in the wash of intelligent and lively language over the world's curious and striking objects. As such, they made what would otherwise be conventional stories about life in the Village (in any village—in the human village) seem magical, infused with the same sense of life Don felt

when walking these streets and taking in their little presents of existence. It was the tone of *Here in the Village* extended not just to fill a
much longer book but to comprise the world view that had been
generating short stories for the past twenty years. All the strengths
of Don's earlier work were here—the fascination of fragments, the
integrity and range of collage—with none of the jerkiness that at
times had threatened to pull things apart. I thought back to Don's
coda to that 1971 interview we'd done by mail, about the laundromat press conference called to announce the search for a new bonding agent. Here, in *Overnight to Many Distant Cities*, he had found it.

During the 1980s my own travels bypassed New York in favor
of many distant cities, while my reading switched from current
American fiction to the unclassifiable prose of Roland Barthes and
Peter Handke and then to the memoirs written by Britain's RAF
pilots of World War II. Yet even here my studies kept me close to
Don's work, for Handke's marvelous diary of the phenomenology
of daily existence in Paris, *Das Gewicht der Welt*, succeeded in the
same way as *Here in the Village*, while Barthes's ability to read the
signs of popular life as a textured narrative found affinity with what
Don had been doing these same years; completing the circle was
that as I pored over the annals of knightly combat in England's skies
during the Battle of Britain, Don was writing a historical romance
that reshaped the Arthurian legends for this same time period, a
work published posthumously as *The King* (New York: Harper and
Row, 1990).

Don and I never talked about these matters. I wish we had, but
I didn't realize the confluence of interests until it was too late.
There'd be letters and an occasional phone call, one especially memorable for having taken place during a crashing thunder-and-light-
ning storm here in Cedar Falls, the sounds of which had Don quite
alarmed in New York. But the 1980s saw us switching roles a bit, as
I began writing fiction and much more generalized commentary
while Don became, for half of each year, an English professor, honored with an endowed chair at his alma mater, the University of
Houston. As Kurt Vonnegut learned at Iowa and other writers have
found out there and elsewhere, those token three or six hours a
week of teaching can come to dominate one's entire life. The better
are one's students the more pleasurable such dominance can be, and
from his earlier days as a part-timer at the City University of New
York Don had won the reputation of being a gifted and committed

teacher. The university community can be a very enjoyable one, and because it is a community one is rarely alone. And here may have come some dangers to Don's health that made it impossible for him to survive his fifties. At C.U.N.Y and again at Houston he taught evenings; this kept the more energized part of his day free for writing, but also placed him in the potentially dangerous circumstance of having evening seminars spill over into sessions afterwards with students and colleagues in the bars.

Don certainly had this proclivity, and one of the deepest impressions about him recalled from talk with others came from Michael Stephens. Don had been helpful to Michael, yet even as he made recommendations, opened doors, and offered tips on publishing Don had impressed the much younger man as being overly stiff and formal. "Then somebody told me what I was doing wrong," Michael confessed. "I was seeing Don too early in the afternoon. 'Wait until after five or six,' I was cautioned, 'or better yet, catch him after his night class.'" Why so? Because this writer, like so many American men of his generation, needed a few drinks to loosen up.

I thought of those lines from "Critique de la Vie Quotidienne" where the narrator, facing an evening that "seems fraught with the absence of promise," finds there is "nothing to do but go home and drink your nine drinks and forget about it." I thought of Don's protagonist "Slumped there in your favorite chair, with your nine drinks lined up on the side table in soldierly array," hoping his world will hang together for at least a few more hours (*Sadness*, p. 4). It doesn't, and soon the "nine drink" rule is broken along with the evening's peace, just as in other stories the "five o'clock rule" and several other such gestures toward discipline are brushed away in favor of the cleansing wash of alcohol. It's a leitmotif in the fiction and figures in one piece from *Here in the Village* where the author ponders a questionnaire he's received that seeks correlations between the writer's life and hard drinking. I thought of Don's offhand remark, made in the days before Singer's and Bellow's Nobel Prizes, that of America's eight laureates in literature "six were alcoholics, one had a serious drinking problem, and the other was Pearl Buck." I also thought of how Michael, who'd dried out on his own several times before getting a permanent cure at the Smithers Institute in New York (just after John Cheever and before Dwight Gooden), became almost rhapsodic in recalling what he'd learned about the after-five and over-the-limit Don Barthelme: "Ah, he was a famous drinker!"

That's the danger of living a collegiate life when one is no longer of college age: one drinks and smokes and carries on like a twenty-one year old in a way that a forty- or fifty-year-old body cannot handle. The nighttime ambience is always there, accompanied by flexibly light academic schedules that allow even the worst hangover to be slept off past noon. Late afternoons can be awkward—I thought of Michael feeling Don's tenseness at those hours, and my own embarrassment at the scene with the waiter—but then comes the recurrent promise that everything will be just fine. Which is of course just the opposite of a fresh renewal every morning followed by a well-earned rest at night.

Yet Don's annual semesters in Houston must have been happy ones, and I really don't imagine him out drinking every night. His story "Sinbad," in fact, makes fun of a first-time day class after years of teaching at night (when the parking lots are infernos of yellow light, the cleaning staff makes long-distance phone calls from professors' offices, and petty felons carry off the department's electric typewriters to sell for drugs):

> The students, no doubt, whispered about me:
> "I heard this is the first time he taught in the daytime."
> "They wouldn't let that sucker teach in sunlight 'cept that all the real teachers are dead."
> "Did you get a shot of that coat? Tack-eeee."
> I stood in the corridor gazing at them from behind my shades. What a good-looking group! I thought. In the presto of the morning, as Stevens puts it. (*Forty Stories*, p. 32)

And that sense of *presto* did apparently carry forth, for the story ends with the narrator neither counting the hours to five nor lining up his measured drinks for the evening but rather triumphing with the day. "Nonetheless, I said, I have something to teach. Be like Sinbad! Venture forth! Embosom the waves, let your shoes be sucked from your feet and your very trousers enticed by the frothing deep. The ambiguous sea awaits, I told them, marry it!" (*Forty Stories*, p. 34).

About this time, in 1986, I exchanged my last letter with Don. I'd written him in New York and received his reply from Houston.

We were both putting things in order. Not expecting to do further work on him, I'd packed up my bibliographic archive for storage and was placing the three- or four-dozen letters from him with an archivist in California who'd eventually put them in a library or museum. Did he have any objections? Of course not; he only wondered if this letter would go, too. Don's little joke seemed wistful, as did his inquiry as to whether I knew anyone who might want to update his bibliography, as there were some funds associated with his chair to cover expenses. I think he was hoping I'd do it myself, but with my head in the clouds of the Battle of Britain and my affections out on the baseball field (where I was both writing fiction about a minor league team and helping run a real one) I just said I'd ask around. I had no idea that this would be the last time we'd share contact; my intentions were simply that an old interest was being shelved for the time being. Now, looking back, it seems a terribly flat way for such an enjoyable working relationship to end.

Yet it didn't end. With my RAF and baseball books published and not yet quite ready to begin writing about my third great preadolescent love, jazz, I had just finished a book on Kurt Vonnegut's *Slaughterhouse-Five* I'd been arm-wrestled into writing when Ihab Hassan called from Milwaukee, asking if I'd speak to his postmodernism seminar on Barthelme's *The Dead Father*. I tried begging off, saying that I hadn't even read Don's last batch of stories and wasn't that fond of the novel in question. But as with the Vonnegut project, I was trapped by the ground-floor work I'd done on Barthelme so many years before. With that aristocratic tone and instructively imperative style that made each encounter with Hassan something beyond the ordinary, I was told that "it was *expected* I would give this new generation of doctoral students my thoughts on Barthelme's masterpiece." Was *The Dead Father* indeed a masterpiece, the center of Don's career? That notion intrigued me, for it would entail the same approach as to Vonnegut's *Slaughterhouse-Five* I'd resisted writing but which turned out to be such an easy and pleasurable book.

Taking down *The Dead Father* from the shelf, I opened it to find Don's inscription from that evening back in 1975. At that point the book hadn't even been formally published. Now it was a masterpiece. Yet all I could think of was the context of that meeting so long ago. I'd seemed so young back then, and Don's business with the doorbell had made me feel even younger. Now I was a year older than he'd been at the time, with more books published and, in terms of pay and attractively flexible duties, set up in just as good a professorship. What had remained constant? The book itself and my memories of the night Don signed it. And so to keep those memories intact I sat down at the typewriter and began writing, beginning with my impressions of how friendly and appealing West Eleventh Street had looked that early evening in 1975 when I'd discovered this was where Donald Barthelme lived.

By July 20, 1989, when I met with Hassan's seminar, the memoir had grown into the first chapter of what promised to be a book. From the manner of Don's play that night I'd devised a methodology for understanding the novel's play with signs and language, and from there had looked back to his earlier work, the innovations of which impended toward this design, and then onwards through his subsequent fiction, most of which settled into a more comfortable style of realism kept tempered by the semiotics established in *The Dead Father*. A day later I returned home and began the book's next chapter and rediscovered the joy of reading those stories from *Come Back, Dr. Caligari* and *Unspeakable Practices, Unnatural Acts*. Then the phone rang with an unlikely call from the usually late-sleeping Richard Kostelanetz in New York. Donald Barthelme was dead.

I was shocked, but so was everyone else, even those who'd kept in touch with Don. There'd been some cancer, but he'd been treated and given a clean bill of health. Then, during a trip to Italy, symptoms had recurred, and a doctor in Rome rushed Barthelme back to the States, where he'd died. He was fifty-eight years old.

My imagination abounded with metaphors, some of them crudely ironic in my shock and dismay. Since leaving graduate school I'd worked exclusively on living authors, albeit with the thoroughness one associates with subjects long dead. Vonnegut had teased me about practicing therapeutic vivisection, but now, for the first time, I'd lost a patient on the table. Don had seemed so alive in my typewriter; now he'd changed tenses on me, and I actually had to go through those first two dozen pages with a bottle of opaquing fluid, whiting out all those *es*'s and inking in *ed*'s.

My most striking feeling, however, was one that turned back upon myself. In beginning the book and speaking to Ihab Hassan's seminar I'd felt so senior, so adult; but now, like a young child losing a parent, I felt terribly abandoned. Every other time I'd written something on Don he was only a letter or phone call away. Now, as I looked forward to discussing books I'd yet to bibliographically research, it struck me that I couldn't dial his number in New York and ask where that third or fourth interpolation from *Overnight to Many Distant Cities* had first appeared or if he'd had any unsigned "Comment" pieces in *The New Yorker* of late. Now, for the first time, I was alone, having lost a father figure of sorts. And to think that I'd been priding myself on having reached the age of Don's own great ascendency, earning as much money and publishing as many or more books.

Had someone told me then, "Why Jerry, your father's is bigger than yours," I couldn't have been more abashed. Don's oeuvre was bigger, and no matter what I did it always would be. That was one of the lessons from *The Dead Father*: that sons can aspire towards fatherhood themselves, but that in the true sense no son can ever be a real father as such, for a son he must always remain.

4

Ronald Sukenick and Raymond Federman

"Sukefedermanick," we wound up calling them, taking the lead from Steve Katz, a third writer close enough to Ron and Ray to be linked with them in name as well. These were the true avant garde of innovation, never getting the broader audience Vonnegut, Kosinski, and Barthelme enjoyed but using that writerly freedom to push fiction well past the limits their more popular brethren might test and tease but never fully surpass.

For a while I called Sukenick's and Federman's work "experimental," but Ron objected to that, rightly, as a denigrating and ultimately dismissive label. It meant *unperfected*, not fully viable, he said—as a passenger would I want to fly on an experimental airplane, or eat a restaurant's experimental hamburger? It was a way traditionalist critics wrote off innovation, Ron believed, and I came to see how he was right. Yet "innovation" seemed not much better. I'd used the title *Innovative Fiction* for my first anthology with Dell, and had to laugh when Michael Stephens asked if the next one would be called *New and Improved Fiction*. Better living through chemistry. Progress is our most important product. Wouldn't you really rather have *this* year's model? I was confusing fiction with cereal and appliances!

The strategy Ron preferred was to insist that "traditional" or "conventional" fiction was in fact the flawed product. Because realism, just one of fiction's many possible forms, was being received as the only valid type, its conventions were no longer acknowledged as such but had become petrified as absolutes. Imaginative writing must remain bright and flexible, and a self-apparent honesty about its artifice of form was essential to keep things working. Flourishing as it did in the American 1960s, such an ideal for fiction fit right in with the cultural transformation that was questioning axioms of political, social, and moral life that had stood for decades as certainties.

It was in just such a transformative world that I first encountered Ron's fiction. With fall 1970 had come my second year of being an assistant professor and the first in which I felt capably in control. First semester the year before had been a hassle of rummaging through notes and preparing classes, and in the spring I'd been surprised with a new course on the contemporary American novel. It was then that I'd rediscovered Kurt Vonnegut and found in his work an analog for all the radical changes I was seeing around me. Teaching *Mother Night* the morning after Kent State was an awesome lesson in how life can sometimes imitate art, and now in late October I was about to experience a similar correlation. Private lives had become more public as they moved in synch with the exuberantly adventuresome culture, and soon my own life took that form. The younger end of our university community—its assistant profs, instructors, and extremely hip students, most of them bright kids from the Chicago suburbs—had chosen a lifestyle compatible with the new countercultural values, and to the renaissance of brilliant rock music and elaborately expressive artistic forms we were adding our own sense of more widely ranging sexuality. Rather than as couples, folks would form little societies of seven or eight, and as such would be living an increasingly communal style of life. Friendships eclipsed earlier physical bounds; older conventions were seen to be just that, arbitrary provisions devised for circumstances that no longer prevailed. Identities were not something we were born with, but rather something that could and should be created at will. So we did, and into this life came a work of fiction that might have been its Bible: Ronald Sukenick's first novel, *Up*.

October 28, 1970—I wrote the date on the book's endpaper, tossed it on the bedside reading table, and then kept my wife awake late into the night, jiggling the bed with suppressed laughter—as I careened through the wild comedy and formal wizardry of Ron's novel. I'd ordered it thanks to the same device that prompted me to buy Donald Barthelme's first and second books: name recognition. Two years previous, when getting study materials lined up for my doctoral exams, I'd bought the paperback of Ron's critical study, *Wallace Stevens: Musing the Obscure* (New York: New York University Press, 1967). Now the name "Sukenick" had jumped out at me from the Dell college catalogue. The notion of a published college professor writing fiction was intriguing, and the cover pictured in Dell's ad appealed to my curiosity: a square of four silkscreens of the author's face, one of which would have been conventional enough as a back-flap photo but which here, structurally replicated yet varied in color and shading like a series of Warhol prints, seemed brashly revolutionary.

In the ongoing history of American literature, as scholars plot trends and debate the merits of canon formation and certain books and authors make it into hierarchies of study, one should note the importance of those college catalogues hitting all the young profs' office mailboxes almost daily. Publishers were booming back then, acquiring new authors and spending ample budgets distributing examination copies free to anyone who wanted them. Schools themselves were crowded with that huge crop of new Ph.D.'s produced during the hyperactive sixties when jobs were plentiful and universities were funded without limit according to how many of the more expensively remunerated graduate credit hours they could generate. There was, of course, a similar phoniness on both ends of this world: there really weren't enough university teaching jobs for all these graduates, and much of the publishers' profits were coming from stocksplits rather than sales. But in 1970 there were plenty of eager young assistant professors sufficiently uninhibited to take advantage of these economic go-go conditions. Our senior colleagues would never dream of requesting an exam copy unless they were seriously considering adopting such a book; we grabbed everything the sales reps seemed eager to send (one measure of their own success was how widely each title sampled). And what kind of books would we ask for: more tired old editions of the nineteenth-century and modernist classics we'd just finished studying to the point of tedium in grad school? Or such wild looking stuff as the catalogues presented so attractively: those Richard Brautigan novels with the unlettered hippy-dippy covers, Richard Fariña's fetchingly-titled *Been Down So Long It Looks Like Up to Me*, or Ronald Sukenick's book that brought the same sentiments down to just one word, *Up*.

The novel's story was certainly revolutionary: of a protagonist named Ronald Sukenick who is struggling to write a novel titled *Up* while dealing with the hassles and delights of living in the world from which this novel springs. We see him in his neighborhood and at home, with friends and with antagonists—and occasionally having discussions with his own characters and debates with himself about strategies of writing that become part of the novel's action, which is of course its own being. Near the end he celebrates with a party, inviting friends from real life and creations from his novel to mix over drinks and hors d'oeuvres. Ron's real wife, Lynn Luria-Sukenick, meets his novel's fantasy girlfriend. "I thought she'd be prettier," Lynn says.

All that was clever, and behind it was something sharply intelligent: a challenge to the notion that for fiction to succeed its readers must surrender to the suspension of disbelief and thereby receive the novel as they would a work of history or the news. From this crucial difference Sukenick would develop a full aesthetic for the era, one that not only fit the fiction of our times but seemed to spill over into the new styles and ethics were were developing in our lives. And this latter affinity was what I was sensing and so much enjoying that night as I read *Up*.

As portrayed in the novel—as he generated its existence, more properly—Ronald Sukenick seemed one of us. In the novel as in real life, he was a fresh young Ph.D. struggling through a ghastly first appointment as an assistant professor teaching in a dull department chaired by Professor Whitebread Blackhead, author of a dissertation on the fart in Chaucer. He'd spend his lonely office hours counting the few fives and singles in his wallet from his last and final paycheck, then train back from Long Island to his room in the slums (actually the culturally vibrant East Village, about which he'd write in *Down and In: Life in the Underground* twenty years later). There he'd work on two books simultaneously: a revision of his doctoral dissertation (which would become his Wallace Stevens book I'd read back in 1968) and the novel I was reading now, *Up*. It was a total integration of art and life, a seizing of the energy of existence and using it to create both the life of fiction and the fiction of life. Art is not about experience, Ron would say later—it is more experience. And his model for integrating such life and art would be identified as Henry Miller. No one back then thought of comparing *Up* with *Tropic of Capricorn*, for Miller was still alive, a resident titillation in *Playboy* and a staple in the Grove Press catalogue and therefore not yet fully in vogue. But in later years the analogy became a compelling one, one we should have noticed earlier as Sukenick's example made its impression on our own lives—especially since the impulse to make contact with him as I was about to do with Barthelme and Kosinski seemed such a natural thing.

His name was in the Modern Language Association directory, listed as a visiting professor at Cornell. By this time I'd learned he'd done his B.A. there, and I had copped a review copy of his 1969 collection with the same publisher that had done *Up* in 1968, the Dial Press of New York. Several pieces in *The Death of the Novel and Other Stories* were set in the Cornell environment, which reinforced the connections with our own campus life. I explained my interest in his work—how I'd noted that many new novelists were academics with scholarly books I hoped could be correlated with developments in their fiction. Would he be willing to discuss these ideas with me and help fill in some bibliographical gaps?

Sukenick's answer came back from southern California, where he'd taken a similar visiting job at the University of California-Irvine. He was living in Laguna Beach, a pretty toney address for a gypsy academic and radically innovative writer, I noted. Later I'd learn he had a talent for taking advantage of off-season residencies to sublet virtual mansions for very little money, getting a fantastic home on the ocean for the same low price he'd paid for renting a stately property in Ithaca while the owners wintered in Florida. In terms of his current interests, my inquiries were equally off the mark. He was grateful for my comments on *Up* and *The Death of the Novel*, but preferred to tell me about the book he was "really in love with at the moment," a new novel called *Out*. As for the correlations I hoped to draw between his fiction and his literary analyses, he was dismayed that I'd seek too easy answers. *Up* was not written to exemplify any ideas in *Wallace Stevens: Musing the Obscure*, he stressed. And, above all, would I please forget the appellation "academic novelist." That sounded stultifyingly dull, and made him think of people like Elder Olson and Lionel Trilling. Please don't put him with that crowd, he begged, and I thought of those painful scenes in *Up* when young Dr. Sukenick is taken through the wringer by his boss, Professor Whitebread Blackhead, who doubtlessly remembered *The Middle of the Journey* as his high point of recreational reading.

Over the next year we exchanged more letters, and Sukenick got me in touch with someone else interested in his work, Joe David Bellamy. Joe had interviewed Ron before he left Cornell, and the piece would be appearing in the spring 1971 issue of Joe's magazine, *The Falcon*. I in turn had been in touch with editor Rob McKean of *Chicago Review*, singing Ron's praises, and could now report that there was another section of Bellamy's interview and large parts of *Out* yet to be published. My own essay on Sukenick's work, which I'd first anticipated as a stuffy Modern Language Association convention paper on the academic novel, took form as a more lively essay titled "Getting Real: Making It (Up) with Ronald Sukenick," and in offering it to Rob McKean swung a deal whereby the same issue of *Chicago Review* would feature Joe's interview and a chapter of the forthcoming *Out*. This was how things were done, I was learning—not so much a network of professional connections as a chain letter of future friends getting in touch to share a common interest and enthusiasm. Rob replied with a deal of his own: he could get University of Chicago funds for a Sukenick reading—not much, but if I'd do the same at my school and perhaps book one other for Ron his trip might be made worthwhile. A few phone calls later the event had grown into a significant production, for Ron would not only speak at my university but would be the featured guest at the Illinois Interpretation Festival, where we'd mount a readers' theater production of *Up*; in addition, my old department head at Marquette, where I'd done my first two degrees, said he'd hire Sukenick for a lecture (having admired his Stevens book). And so Ron would not just be visiting, but would be reading, lecturing, and produced. One of his own friends was working at the University of Wisconsin-Milwaukee, so we'd make a social stop there. In all, I'd be spending a week with Ron at home and on the road, and felt proud of becoming part of his life of fiction.

It all happened in April of 1972. By this time I'd run through a similar routine with a visit from James Simon Kunen, had visited Jerzy Kosinski, and had worked by letter and phone with Donald Barthelme, so meeting Ron at O'Hare wasn't in the least intimidating. If anyone was rattled it was Ron, who arrived complaining that the flight hadn't been "right." Turbulence? Delays? No, just a very old airplane, old magazines in the seat pouches, and even "old, beat up stewardesses." Did he fear he'd been transported into the twilight zone? No, just that it all kept him uneasy. He'd been uneasy on the way to the airport, he confessed, and said that three or four times on the drive from Laguna Beach to Los Angeles he'd asked his wife to stop the car so he could check to see if his briefcase (with the manuscript of *Out*) was in the trunk. Now he was worried whether he'd picked it up at the baggage arrival. I said he'd been carrying it off the plane, but Ron insisted that I pull over so he could look in the trunk. When it wasn't there he panicked until I got his attention and pointed it out in the back seat.

Ron finally settled down when I suggested that he pick out some music. I'd tossed in quite an assortment of cassettes before leaving, including some jazz, but he surprised me by choosing a Mongo Santamaria tape. "I really like this stuff," he enthused. I guessed that it reminded him of his lower East Side neighborhood in New York, the *Up* neighborhood, and he agreed, but said the music's real significance wasn't exclusively Latin. "It's the first real synthesis of everything American," Ron explained. "Hispanic, Black, rock and roll, blues, and jazz." Properly synthesized, he settled back for the rest of our hour's drive. In a while Ron began tapping out the rhythms, and I joined him with the baritone sax's part to "Watermelon Man" as I'd played it night after night with Junior & the Classics, earning money for grad school. We were loose and happy, and probably each thinking about how his story "Momentum," from *The Death of the Novel and Other Stories*, ends in a cascade of ongoing rhythm I was finding essential to Ron's work and happiness: "i got some good music i started singing along with the radio i felt wonderful in fact the last time i felt just this way was when i finally left cornell both times singing like a maniac both times total enjoyment of driving a big american car on a smooth american highway with jazzy american music" (p. 39).

This momentum carried us through the rhythm of the next six or seven days. First there was Ron's speech, a little commentary on his fiction followed by the reading of a section from *Out*. There were over five hundred students, faculty, and townspeople in the audience—these were the days when even an unknown writer could draw such numbers on a campus, part of that same turn of the sixties energy that affected so much of our life. I was asked not only to introduce Ron but also to take a few minutes to situate his fiction within the literary tradition. I'm sure my department, which was coughing up $400 for the event, expected me to relate Ron to Faulkner and Bellow (the latter of which had spoken here the year before), but I found it more appropriate to bring a little book from my children's library, a Sesame Street volume titled *The Monster at the End of This Book*, and point out how its strategy of having the protagonist, "loveable, furry old Grover," spend the narrative worrying over its title, trying to hold back, tie down, and eventually brick over each page to forestall the supposedly terrible ending, when in fact the monster is just Grover himself, is the same that Sukenick used in *Up*. This was evidence, I suggested, that Ron's work was less part of a foggy and distant avant garde than a response to a new aesthetic developing right under our nose— unseen because we were giving more attention to Faulkner and Bellow than to what our own kids were reading.

As I welcomed Ron to the podium, he took a moment to give me some advice. "Jerry," he said, "you should really be an agent instead of a professor!"

"Why an agent?" I asked, worrying that as Dr. Sukenick he'd somehow disapproved of my introduction.

"Because you've got this enthusiasm for our fiction," he explained, "and can convey it so well." I paused as Ron indicated the audience; they did seem nicely warmed up, and his hour's reading went nicely, especially for an auditorium the first rows of which were filled by some of my senior colleagues who may well have written their theses on the fart in Chaucer, but whose grand-kids had the Sesame Street book.

Next night was the readers' theater production of *Up*. I'd written the adaptation, which thanks to the commercial expertise of a visiting drama prof from Hollywood turned out ok. Sydney Smith was an old Culver City hacker who could still be seen on reruns of "Wagon Train" (as the chuck-wagon cook) and "Perry Mason" (as a bailiff). Some of Ron's stuff mystified him, but he had a brilliant command of blocking and timing; through eight weeks of rehearsal we'd tinkered with various styles of presentation, and each night I'd head home for another rewrite. But between the student-actors' natural feel for what Sukenick's novel was doing and Sydney Smith's physical mastery of stagecraft we got it all together. "This is a little like Firesign Theater, right?" the lead actor, portraying both Ron the author and Ron the protagonist, asked. "That scene with Strop Banally and his secretary should be played like carnival vaudeville," Sydney Smith urged, and gave the youngsters a run-through of how county-fair comedy had looked in the thirties. What resulted was a synthesis—Ron's key to everything—that for the two months of rehearsal and week of production made us a communal entity.

Two of the actors were part of our own communal group, and at the party for Ron following the Interpretation Festival it seemed like *Up* was happening all over again. The play had delighted him. "It felt as if I were sitting there in the back row watching all these characters come out of my head," he marveled. Then, at the party, it struck him that the same thing was happening, as the house was packed with scores of students and young faculty members who'd either already been living their lives like the action in *Up* or had taken a cue from having read the book. Not that there were outrageous acts or unspeakable practices; there's nothing obscene or even overt in the novel, nor did our gathering turn into anything scriptable as a triple-X video. It was just the sense of intimacy, imagination, and highly charged excitement that was making Ron's visit an experience, giving people the same feeling as when attending a great rock festival or other shared event.

Afterwards, in the privacy of one-to-one relationships, things may have gotten a bit polymorphously perverse. Ron was booked into a room at the student union, and a few of us planned to meet him there at ten for breakfast. But after an hour of waiting only one of our crowd showed up. "I don't think we'll be seeing much of Ron for a while," she confessed. "He must have had too much to drink—he keeps saying 'This is what F. Scott Fitzgerald must have felt like.'"

Finally, just before noon, Ron came down and let us order a belated breakfast. Following that I took him into the student bookstore, which had made a display of his novel, story collection, and Stevens book. To my surprise he grabbed up every unsold copy of *The Death of the Novel*. "The book's gone out of print," he explained. "I tried to get some last copies but the publisher said they had all been shipped." His appearance at Northern Illinois University had cleaned out the warehouse, and now he needed to save these copies before they disappeared into oblivion.

That afternoon we drove into Chicago. There the *Review* crowd made him feel right at home, and I could sense in a moment not only the difference between the U of C and my bushleague school but how Ron's style was so much a part of the former. Joining us was Chuck Russell, a recent Cornell Ph.D. who, as an undergrad in the sixties, had assumed Ron's lease on the *Up* apartment. Suddenly I felt the lower-middle-class poor kid in the company of these Ivy League-educated sons of prominent dentists and bank presidents. Yet Ron's reading, for this much hipper crowd, was a pleasure, and afterwards we motored up to Milwaukee where

Chuck had attached himself as an apprentice to Professor Ihab Hassan at the University of Milwaukee-Wisconsin. This was an even more exclusive and mannered world, and only my association with Sukenick justified my presence. At Chicago, Rob McKean had stacked the room with copies of the special Sukenick issue, and folks had commented politely on my essay. In Milwaukee, Hassan seemed quite curious about my interests, particularly as I'd "discovered" a novelist a few steps ahead of his own concerns. The real fun, however, was at Marquette, where my old profs from the early 1960s, none of whom had much of an idea that even the 1940s had yet happened, were alternately amused and mystified by Ron's discussion. To be anti-Aristotelian was one thing; but the faculty at Marquette had received their Aristotle via Thomas Aquinas, and their tone was so medieval that I could imagine Ron being tied to a stake and burned as a heretic. Yet the department now boasted a world-class Joyce scholar, Robert Boyle, S.J., and his intercessions saved the day.

A year later my new job as a senior professor at the University of Northern Iowa made it possible for me to bring in Ron again. This time the big event was a "Survival Conference" my colleague Loree Rackstraw had organized, bringing together a wide range of authorities on all aspects of our physical and imaginative environment to discuss how the earth and its inhabitants might survive. We almost didn't; though scheduled for the hopefully balmy second week of April 1973, the unpredictable Iowa weather presented us with a record snowstorm, locking us in with twenty-seven inches of slush and ice. Supreme Court Justice William O. Douglas, scheduled to speak on environmental issues, was snowbound one hundred miles away at the Des Moines airport. For a while Loree considered arranging for an off-the-road vehicle to bring him up to Cedar Falls, until our fears of what might happen to the seventy-four-year-old judge strapped onto an ATV and taken on a six hour trip through frozen open country convinced her this might be a bit much. But we did have Joseph Meeker, William Irwin Thompson, and several other ecological and new-age philosophical superstars, plus Ronnie to represent the arts. He in turn was supposed to bring along his shaman, Leonard Crow Dog, who in Carlos Castaneda–Don Juan fashion had been speaking for the magical properties of imaginative reinvention. But during an American Indian Movement demonstration at the Rosebud Reservation a few days before Leonard had been arrested and imprisoned under several thousand dollars bond—for having a broken headlight on his wife's car. We wired him the money as an advance on his appearance fee, but the weather kept him from getting to our town.

It was at this conference that I saw Ron in one of his favorite roles, as irritant to any established position. From the start, others didn't want to accept him as having any validity; they were the scientists, the thinkers, the true authorities, while he made up stories. Although Meeker and Thompson had made great capital of walking away from conventional university professorships, they and the others still dressed like academics and spoke like Professor Whitebread Blackhead. Ron was in jeans, a loud shirt, and a more quiet sweater, and soon found out that during the panel discussions Thompson would be argumentative and even antagonistic when Ron had the sweater off, and then get more agreeable when Ron covered up his screaming shirt by putting the sweater back on. Meeker and Thompson took special offense at Ron's dismissal of traditional fiction for its demand that disbelief be suspended, while he in turn regretted their inability to see its political implications. "You have to be very careful about how you imagine things," he cautioned, "or else somebody else will do your imagining for you." Ron's examples were the unquestioned acceptance of socially realistic fiction, the techniques of advertising, and the control by totalitarian governments. He'd take his sweater off, and William Irwin Thompson would object; the sweater would go back on, and Thompson would agree.

During this same visit Ron did a reading for the English department, presenting the section of *Out* (which was being published soon by the Swallow Press in Chicago thanks to another set of contacts) in which the protagonist meets the Indian shaman Empty Fox in South Dakota. At the time this business struck me as being much like Carlos Castaneda's *Journey to Ixtlan* and *The Teachings of Don Juan*, books my students had showed me back at Northern Illinois. We talked about this afterwards with my colleague Robley Wilson, who agreed to print this passage from *Out* and my response to it in the summer issue of *The North American Review*. There the two appeared, in June 1973, as "On the Wing" and "A Persuasive Account: Working It Out with Ronald Sukenick." Between us we were suggesting how good fiction functions anthropologically, just like a shaman's tale, offering not a scientifically monolithic view of reality—for there is no one reality—but rather a persuasive account of one version of it. There are many versions, of course; that's the richness of human experience that the literary artist tries to emulate. Yet even as he or she presents the account, the reader must remain aware that it is a fabrication, or else the joy of the experience will be lost. At the time it struck me as so much better (and so much more promising of survival) than the other conference speakers' agendas, all of which seemed extremely limited yet immensely self-taken. They all wanted the authority of science, and each thought he had it, whereas Ron was the only one even coming close.

A year before, in Chicago and Milwaukee when Ron had got caught up in his special crowd, I'd felt dismayed by his rich-kid, Ivy League ways. But now in Cedar Falls Ron could fault me for the other side of this, as he got fouled up in the oligarchy of our own small town. Social life for Loree's conference was the domain of the area's political elite: our young mayor and his gorgeous, showpiece wife; the local hanging judge, a white-haired, red-faced muncher of Valium pills who slept with a .45 holstered on his bedstead as insurance against the convicted felons who'd sworn to kill him when eventually released; plus various attornies and doctors and their spouses whose thoughts for the environment extended only as to how many parties the conference could produce. I kept away from all this but Ron, as one of the star attractions, couldn't. Yet he gave me the full story, a persuasive account in which he found himself with the others at the judge's estate, getting the full treatment of indoor swimming, wet and dry saunas, and romps in between out in the back yard, rolling naked in the two feet of snow.

What was so bad about that, I wanted to know.

"Well, there was this really strange feeling to it," Ron explained, "as if there was a subtext, another story that nobody was admitting but was really going on all the time."

"Some of Loree's big-roller friends do give me that sense," I agreed. But where was the danger?

"It kept happening in the sauna," Ron told me. "The swimming and the snow runs were ok, because everyone was moving around. But back in the sauna the mayor's wife kept playing footsie with me."

"No kidding!"

"And then the judge's daughter."

"Those are some pretty nubile young women," I observed.

"That was the problem. I figured if I did anything at all, all these goons would jump on me, like it was a set-up or something, an excuse for a pogrom." I could see Ron was worried about what I'd brought him into, this strange land so different from his native New York and adopted California, this part of the country called the Midwest.

Though we always kept in touch, as l worked with him more closely than any other writer and would see him frequently in New York and other places, Ron came back to Cedar Falls only once after that. I'm sure he wasn't suspecting any traps, but our small-town, medium-college atmosphere wasn't one he could enjoy. I know that, because for his last swing through he offered more than a persuasive account. Like any act of his fiction, it was that and much else too, no small part of which was parodic comedy.

It began in Iowa City, where he was giving a reading and being partied afterwards at the Writers Workshop. Since the departures of Vonnegut and Robert Coover almost a decade before, the Workshop had been anything but a home to innovation; John Cheever and Raymond Carver were the honored visitors, and the new realism—minimalism, some called it—was the style of the day. Ron was uneasy, and so was much of his audience. But some pranksters were eager to recover the excitement of the mid-1960s even if that meant reducing it to a childish stunt. Ron walked right into it; after reading an introductory section of his new novel, *98.6*, which the Fiction Collective would publish next year (in 1975), he reached for the pitcher and drinking glass so thoughtfully provided. "I need some water," he rasped, poured a full glass, and drank deeply. "That's not water!" he said, now gasping and turning crimson. "But I think I'll drink it anyway." And from there the reading went downhill as the audience became less interested in the succeeding parts of *98.6* and Ron slowly but steadily drank the pitcher's contents, nearly a quart of straight vodka.

Ron never actually got drunk. Better that he had, for it would have made the stiffness of the party afterwards less trying. All any of the workshop staff wished to talk about was M.F.A. politics; to Ron, with his Ph.D. and faculty (rather than writer-in-residence) appointments, it was all Greek, and thoroughly boring to me. On the two hour drive up to Cedar Falls I'd hoped we could enjoy my new toy, a classic Mercedes-Benz sports car, a 1961 190SL, jet black with red leather upholstery and a car stereo primed to knock Ron's socks off. But there was no singing along down the highway. He asked for no music, and no talk either, and by the time we hit Cedar Falls we felt like strangers.

As our houseguest for the next couple days Ron was never unpleasant, but I could tell he was annoyed at the idea of being trapped in Iowa so long. He surely didn't care for the workshop's new style of realism, but he seemed to have brought with him its taste for alcohol. In classic Cheever-Carver fashion he kept asking for drinks, and when my bottle of Jack Daniels was gone several hours before his reading he turned up his nose at what I had left, a fifth of Early Times. "You want to make me sick on that rotten Cabin Still or whatever?" he chided, and waited for me to offer to run out for another bottle of Jack Daniels. This was not the Ron Sukenick of *Up*, I thought, but someone more like Frank Sinatra. Yet with the cabinet restocked with JD he got happy enough, and seemed especially pleased that my wife devised a way for him to take some along to school, in one of our kids' old baby bottles dug out from the closet.

The reading went well enough, but wasn't perfect. A few months before I'd heard Ron read the "Palestine" section of *98.6* up at the University of Wisconsin-Milwaukee, where the internationally recruited faculty and heavily East Coast cadre of graduate students made it feel more like Ron's home. The audience loved it as he played comic games with such notions as "the state of Israel," where everyone's personal ecology was balanced perfectly by the "PH factor," which meant "pure horniness." Here in Cedar Falls, where an entire Woody Allen film could be shown without getting a single laugh, much of the ethnic Brooklyn humor was lost, and Ron had to rummage around elsewhere in the novel to find something that would sell. Which certainly didn't make him happy.

There was a party at my home afterwards, and in time it developed into the more comfortable style of communal gathering we'd always favored and at which Ron had felt so comfortable before. But in the first minutes after the reading, when Ron and I arrived to find the living room crowded with early-arriving guests—the town's bigwigs and poseurs, who hadn't even heard Ron speak—I feared the worst. And the worst did happen. Ron made an initial circuit of the fifty or so guests by continuing right on with his reading from *98.6*, this time adding further dramatics by shaking each man's hand ("Hello, I'm Ronald Sukenick") and asking each woman "Do you want to fuck?" First in line were the mayor and the mayor's wife, of sauna fame; maybe this was what had started Ronnie off. No one showed any sign of being shocked, and some guests even laughed along. But then Ron turned back for a second time around the room, saying hello to each man again but suggesting to each woman, "Let me try something different: would you care for some sexual intercourse?" Nobody thought this funny, and a few people quite honorably left. Which helped get things settled in a better orbit; the hours drew on and the party loosened up, and eventually we had our old Ron back among us. But it remained an experience neither of us ever wanted to repeat.

Our doings of the next decade and a half remained friendly but were determinedly professional—rightly so, for there was a great deal of work to do. For a while Ron's writing took back seat as he became somewhat of a committee person, helping organize The Fiction Collective (which allowed authors to produce their own books, ones the commercial houses wouldn't touch), chairing the Coordinating Council of Literary Magazines (which distributed government grants money), publishing *The American Book Review* (a survey of what the bigger journals deliberately overlooked), and even getting on the executive council of the Modern Language Association. I objected to his manner in some of this, that it was overdoing the egalitarian bit by forsaking the drama of a revolution for the benefit of letting things be run by the lunchroom committee. But there was plenty we agreed on. He had me write for *ABR*, and I talked him into collecting his literary and theoretical essays into a book for my series with the Southern Illinois University Press in Carbondale, appearing at the series' head in 1985 as *In Form: Digressions on the Act of Fiction*. Not the "art" of fiction; that was Henry James. *Act*, as in the action of Henry Miller's life becoming the essence of his art. Art is not about experience, it is *more* experience. Television gives us the news, fiction gives us our response to the news. What does the imagination do? It reaches out and establishes a relevant relationship with the world, thereby making the world more real. An era's fictive aesthetic can be found in this book.

For a while, even though letters, phone calls, and publishing deals continued, I felt somewhat distant from Ron. I'd remarried in the interim and found myself reevaluating friendships through my new and quite different wife's eyes. Julie and I enjoyed a month's honeymoon in Paris and around France during June of 1978; Ron was living in a grand apartment down on the Place St. Michel, one of those remarkable sublets of which he remained a master (before turning his talents to buying equally fine properties on the cheap), but we didn't see him, so guarded were we about fouling our new-found happiness and stricter values. But then, as I kept returning to Paris for a month or so every spring and fall and Ron gravitated more and more toward the city, meeting there became inevitable.

It happened in early May of 1981, in the unlikely company of my mother. I'd taken her abroad for her seventieth birthday, and before visiting her ancestral homes in Buckinghamshire and County Limerick we had arranged for a week in Paris. Ron would be there, and he wanted me to meet the person who was with him: his own new wife, Julia Frey. And so we arranged for Ron to meet my mother and myself at the Hotel du Pantheon, have lunch, and then take my mom back to the hotel for an afternoon's rest while I went over to Ron's sublet in the Beaubourg to meet Julia.

If Julie changed me, Julia surely transformed Ron. Or maybe it was just being on his turf, his new turf, Paris. Now I could see the advantages of Ron's upbringing and education, as he acted the per-fect gentleman and made my mother feel like the toast of Paris. We lunched at Hemingway's old haunt, the Brasserie Lipp, and as we strolled about afterwards Ron pointed out literary landmarks of my mother's own generation. Then, after settling her at the hotel, we walked across part of town to Ron's neighborhood, pausing in a working-class bar on the fringe of the Marais for some fresh coun-try wine. These were the same kind of places Ron liked in Brooklyn and parts of Manhattan, places not unlike the corner taverns I'd played in with polka bands back in Milwaukee. It was as nice an afternoon as we'd had back in 1972, pounding along with those Mongo Santamaria tunes on the highway from O'Hare to DeKalb. Now, at their apartment, I met Julia, and could see how it was so much easier for Ron to behave. Who could be selfish or infantile in the presence of such a remarkably stable, assured, yet extremely kind person?

Ron's marriage to Julia Frey, a French professor with a book on Flaubert and plans to buy an apartment in Paris, made for an interesting circle, for as we sat drinking still-fresh Beaujolais that day I could tell Ron that just a block or two away in the Marais was the childhood home of Raymond Federman. Raymond was my close friend and, thanks to me, Ron's friend and collaborator in promoting innovative fiction. If there's any reason for my name to be remembered in literary history one hundred years from now, it will be for the same reason the scholar-critic Evert Duyckinck is recalled. On August 5, 1850, having made sure each writer would know something of the other's work, Duyckinck introduced Herman Melville and Nathaniel Hawthorne. Each was then working on his major work, *Moby-Dick* and *The House of the Seven Gables* respectively, and found in the other not only a basis for lifelong friendship but a strong literary affinity that summoned new achievement from each. In 1971, just as Sukenick's work was impressing me as the leading edge of this new movement in fiction, I was informed of Raymond Federman's fiction, and as I learned about this new factor it seemed a perfect equation with Ron's writing. Before meeting either in person, I told each about the other's work; then, having met each of them face to face, devised a way for them to meet and did all I could to see they hit it off. That happened during a mutual visit to New York late in 1972, and from there on Sukenick and Federman's friendship flourished.

I remember the occasion well, an MLA convention party to which I'd invited both Ron and Ray. By this time they'd read each other's work—what little there was of it so far—and seemed to get along well on a professional level. But their personal friendship and the ongoing fun it would involve began with a bit of adolescent horseplay suffered by a young woman with an editorial interest in this new style of fiction. Her college major had been in French, which Ron found out and used to start charming her with his own schoolboy command of the Gallic tongue. It was the same proper and correct French I'd hear Ron using a decade later in Paris when ordering lunch for my mother; he'd spent a Fulbright year in Paris following his doctorate studying the impressionist poets, and seemed as smooth in French as in English. But then Raymond cut in, and with his vernacular speech ran circles around Ron and had the young woman's head swimming. Each remained gentlemanly, and the young woman seemed delighted by this linguistic display and courtly combat for her attention. My own French, limited at that time to a cursory reading level, kept me out of it except to realize that there was an amazing life of fiction being created here, all quite properly so because it was in a language fully artificial to all of us except Ray, who hadn't needed to speak it as a native since leaving France in 1947.

Indeed, even in 1972 Raymond had been speaking English for a greater portion of his life than French, for he'd emigrated at the age of 18. In America he hadn't found any rarified expatriate's world, but had plunged right into the main currents of popular American life, living in a lower-class section of the Bronx while washing dishes and bottles, working in a lampshade factory (which he considered grimly ironic, having just evaded the Nazis' concentration camps), and then moving to the black ghetto of Detroit where his friends became a bunch of future jazz musicians, including Frank Foster, Tommy Flanagan, and Kenny Burrell. In their company he picked up tenor sax and became good enough to jam along; one night Charlie Parker, on a visit from New York, sat in with them for a full set, borrowing Ray's tenor while the young Frenchman played Bird's alto. Then back to New York, where he was inducted into the Army. He'd wanted to be a frogman (as his friends had been calling him "Frog"), but was routed into para-trooper school instead. All this time his English must have been improving, becoming a capable Americanese sharpened by talk with his fellow workers in Brooklyn, his ghetto pals in Detroit, and now in the barracks with his G.I. buddies.

Yet to this day Raymond's accent remains so heavily French that one must imagine him drilling on old Maurice Chevalier songs and movies to keep it so sharp. I can see why: it is part of not just his personality but his fictive image, based as almost all his novels are on the linguistic vacancy of his family lost in the camps (an XXXX, for his absent father, mother, and sisters) and the alphabetic infinitude he generates as a writer to fill the gap. It's the making of a second life, a coda to one that should have ended on July 16, 1942, in that great sweep the German occupiers made of the Marais, rounding up the city's Jews for shipment to Auschwitz. Raymond's mother had hid him in the closet, where he cowered for several hours before coming out into a silent, vacant world. As an instan-taneous orphan, he sneaked out of the city and fled to the south, working on farms for two years until the occupation ended and he could return home. But there was no home there. For two years he struggled to make his way, until an uncle in America found him and arranged for passage to New York.

Raymond tells that story in his first novel, *Double or Nothing* (Chicago: Swallow Press, 1971), and hearing it in his heavy French voice augments the experience. It is an accent that I'm sure he cannot abandon, having given up so much else in his life and replaced it with things he's made from scratch. Yet it is also wonderfully comic. Just a few years ago Raymond and his wife Erica stopped by Cedar Falls. Erica herself had been an immigrant, born in Vienna, but her speech could not be distinguished from a native American's. Raymond's French accent, however, was as strong as ever— maybe a bit stronger this morning over breakfast as he poured it on to impress my own young Francophile wife. Soon Erica began imitating him and making jokes about how he sounded like he was just off the boat. They'd been driving cross-country from Buffalo, where Raymond taught and Erica worked in the university's administration, and the roadmap of American cities and towns had made it a linguistic carnival.

"You can't believe what I've had to put up with," Erica complained with a laugh. "Just listen to this," she warned us, and turned to her husband. "Raymond—say 'Indianapolis.'"

"Indiana Police," he obliged, accenting the last syllable with a sibilance straight from the cafés in Montparnasse. Ev'ry leetle breese zeems to whispa Louieese. We loved it.

I'd met Raymond Federman thanks to a poet who was equally enchanted with Ray's words and how he could generate a narrative from the music within them. Michael Anania had done a graduate degree under Federman at the State University of New York in Buffalo, then left for an editorial job in Chicago with Swallow Press. In 1971 he gave a poetry reading at my university, and as my home had become the party house for such occasions and my communal gang the obliging hosts I found myself talking about books and writers with the young man.

Discerning my taste in fiction, Anania began pumping something that was presently in production with Swallow: Federman's *Double or Nothing*. "You won't believe this book," he insisted. "If you like innovation, this one's so innovative that we couldn't even figure out how to print it!" Each page was uniquely designed, typed in formats like a secretary's game. Swallow had given up and decided just to photographically reproduce Ray's typescript. A few months later Anania sent me an advance of the book, and there it was: 203 pages of typing-size paper bound together yet insisting that each page be read as an integrally yet idiosyncratically designed element. There were lists, squares and other shapes of type, blank spaces, and even different colored pages, one of which was printed in reverse so that one had to hold it up to a mirror to read it. Another page was typed in a circle; imagine having to read it in public, spinning the book around thirty or so times before getting to the end in the page's center! That page told about some wild activity that seemed like a maelstrom, and so that's how the page looked. For each stage in the narrative, Federman had contrived a set-up for his page appropriate to the subject and action. Here indeed was fiction as itself, for one could never forget that there was a book in one's hand. The formats were also a discipline, as quite often I'd see Raymond fashioning lines so that all the margins conformed, meaning if the first line was sixty characters and the next line was fifty-eight or sixty-three, he would go back and rewrite it choosing some shorter or longer synonyms. Like a sonnet's form, this forced him to think up new styles of expression. In his next novel, *Take It or Leave It* (New York: Fiction Collective, 1976), one section would consist of comically exuberant love-letters written for his buddies at a standard fee by the young French paratrooper. The language was a tour de force of excruciatingly awkward choices in diction and construction—"My BIG Dear Turnip, My SAD Muscular Paratrooper, My Lonely Prune, Dear J****," one of the girlfriends would write back, trying to emulate the bizarrely overwrought style—but having seen the original typescript I knew Raymond had been forced into these constructions by virtue of making each line count out the same, even though when published the secret disappeared in the mechanics of typesetting. But once again the action was on the page, reminding the reader at every stage that this was a work of imaginative artifice and virtuoso display.

At Michael Anania's urging I wrote Federman in Buffalo, telling of my interest in innovative fiction in general and in Ron Sukenick's work particularly. Raymond wrote back, thanking me for alerting him to *Up* and *The Death of the Novel* but confiding that no matter how good these books were, *Double or Nothing* would be better. Other letters followed from both sides, and I began to take delight in Ray's uninhibited style of self-promotion. Once I had his voice to match it, it all became quite natural, a style of Gallic showmanship right out of the old movies of my childhood. "Kleenk-oweeetz," he'd be saying to himself as he addressed the letter, "if you are really a professor and this 'Northern Illinois University' is really a school, why don't you come to the MLA convention in Chicago and meet me; Mike Anania is having a big party at Swallow Press for my book, and you can meet everyone!" I did, and the occasion was memorable, the party being held down on South Wabash in the combination warehouse and loft that served as Swallow's offices. There, amid steel-case shelves stacked high with *Double or Nothing*, I met Raymond (was warmly embraced by him, in fact) and socialized with his entourage from Buffalo and other points East. Leslie Fiedler, his department head, was there. Robert Creeley was also along, I was told, but in the crush never found him. Anania prompted me to review the book, and gave me several extra copies to push on other potential reviewers; these I sent to Sukenick and others whom I wanted to know about Raymond's work.

Two years later Anania and Swallow would be publishing Ronald Sukenick's novel, *Out*. It had been rejected everywhere else and the Fiction Collective was yet to be organized; who knows if otherwise the book would not have been published—it certainly would have been delayed, in turn throwing off everything else. How tenuous are all these little connections that, nearly a quarter century later, can be seen to have made a genuine advance in American literary history. But then there were all sorts of delicate little bridges being built all over that would eventually become conduits for the flow of literature and the ideas about it. John O'Brien was poking around New York and finding Gilbert Sorrentino and Clarence Major; I gave him a copy of Ray's book and he gave me sets of theirs. Larry McCaffery feasted on Robert Coover's work, while Tom LeClair was Fulbrighting in Athens and learning about a virtually unknown writer named Don DeLillo. One way or another, the good writing got through.

In any event, Ron and Ray became fast friends, and a consideration of their joint projects would fill a chapter. Both were active on the Coordinating Council of Literary Magazines and in the Fiction Collective; this meant business meetings but also panel discussions for audiences at hosting universities. At the University of Louisville one such program began with the two plus three others of their sort seated behind a table across the stage. After their introduction, Federman and Sukenick rose together and began talking at the same time; then they sat down and two others rose to do the same. A long minute of silence followed, then all five rose to speak. This little bit of nonsense served to demystify the panel's role and put to question the whole notion of such joint discussions. I'd have to guess that between 1972 and the present Ron and Ray must have made up to a hundred such appearances. It spread to Europe, where Malcolm Bradbury, Marc Chénetier, and Heide Ziegler had organized the Common Market's younger Americanists into a "trilateral" group that virtually took over university programs and publishers' series; Sukefedermanick were frequent visitors and collaborators in their projects. Ron seemed happiest tweaking the noses of the sometimes stuffy Germans; Raymond, however, found his greatest acceptance there. A young graduate student named Peter Torberg, having done his M.A. on Vonnegut, wrote me to ask for some newer American writers. I suggested Federman, and soon, by virtue of Peter's critical essays and translations, Raymond was launched on a career that far exceeded anything he'd enjoyed in the States: published by the leading house, Suhrkamp, his German-language editions were printed in runs of fifty thousand, with adaptations for television and even ballet. In America Raymond and the other innovationists would be lucky to move two thousand copies; even Donald Barthelme, far more famous, was being published in first editions of five thousand copies, most of the earlier ones never selling out (later initial printings of ten thousand copies eventuated massive remainder sales). By the early 1980s the Sukefedermanick craze had spread to Israel, where each writer made several extended academic visits.

Yet the essence of Federman's appeal was that unique blend of romantic Paris and the utterly vernacular American that is surely the essence of our country's culture, made as it is of formerly European elements turned to radically new purposes in conditions the Old World never imagined. Ray's life was just such an invention, and using it not just as a subject but as a generating principle for his fiction was a natural. My fondest memories of Raymond, though I've met and worked with him scores of times, are from his first visit to Cedar Falls back in 1973. He'd make two appearances: the second to read from his fiction, the first to speak on the subject of his doctoral research and several critical books—Samuel Beckett. Over the years he and "Sam" had become very good friends, drawn to each other by what they shared in common, including writing in each other's adopted language while maintaining an almost nativistic personality based on one's origins. Our student newspaper publicized the events as front-page features, running the striking, deeply shadowed photograph of Raymond that appears on the back jacket of *Double or Nothing*. That might have been enough to draw good crowds, but the room, one of our largest science lecture halls, was packed with over six hundred eager listeners. The paper had misread the information I'd given them, and instead of listing Ray as the author of several books on the latest Nobel Prize winner described Federman as the latest Nobel laureate himself. Ray handled the flub wonderfully, prefacing his remarks by saying that he did not deserve such a prize and was therefore returning it with apologies to the Nobel Committee. The newspaper, however, remains one he treasures to this day, and I've seen that front page photo and Nobel story framed in his study.

The turnout for Raymond's fiction reading the next night was just as heavy. We knew he planned to read from the opening of *Double or Nothing*, the section where the protagonist determines to hole up for a year in a one-room apartment and write the great American novel. He sets a goal of so many pages per day, and counts on the calendar to do the rest. But first he must compute how many essentials he'll need to survive: how many rolls of toilet paper to buy (based on sheets per day, just like the pages from his typewriter), how many tubes of toothpaste (based on squeezes per brushing), and how many boxes of the cheap, essential, unperishable foodstuff he'll need to eat: noodles. These computations are immense and complex, of course, and before we know it we're on page 203 of the book—a complete novel but a flawed one, because it is on that page that the protagonist-narrator discovers that he has miscounted his funds and that "it won't have to be noodles after all!"

To flatter Raymond and get him in one of his more theatrical moods, we'd sent some students over to the science lecture hall an hour before. There, amid the demonstration table's sinks and hoses, they'd stacked up rolls of toilet paper, tubes of toothpaste, and boxes of noodles where he would be reading. He loved it. The reading was a great success, the audience alternately rolling in laughter and commiserating with the narrator's pathos as he struggles to write his book. Then Raymond read from his new novel still in progress, *Take It or Leave It*—the French loveletters, which were a scream, and the "Buick Special" passage where his protagonist tells the love story of owning his first American car and then losing it (even as it saves his life) when careening off a snow-covered mountain road into the branches of a huge pine tree just below.

The Buick Special story was an ideal one for Raymond to read, for it allowed the exuberance and flamboyance of his voice to pace itself against the narrative's extravagant action. Nor was it just a vocal performance, for the tale's ongoing energy was just the style that brought out the best of his storyteller's art. He was spellbinding, winning his listeners' sympathies by virtue of his eminently persuasive account. That it was such a ridiculous story made it all the more effective, for the audience didn't have to suspend their disbelief—they knew that even though some of it may have happened in fact, the best parts were those Raymond was making up. What he was dramatizing up there on the podium (and up there suspended in the pine tree's limbs while his Buick's engine ticked over for the last time) was not some documentary truth but the brash display of his own creative imagination. This is what Ron Sukenick was doing in his own work as well, as became obvious to any listener or reader.

Afterwards Raymond continued having fun, his audience milling about while he alternately signed copies of *Double or Nothing* and boxes of noodles. The usual party afterwards at my home was fun, too, especially when the rarest of all coincidences took place. Among the dozens of faculty and scores of students who'd followed us home was a young red-haired kid I didn't know; he didn't know us, either, but just had been wandering down the hall of the science building when he heard all the laughter coming from a roomful of listeners hearing Ray tell of noodles and toothpaste tubes. The kid eased in, and was lucky enough to hear the full Buick Special story. Charmed by Raymond, the story, and the coincidence of having walked in on it, he'd asked what was going on and learned about the party. Now here he was, asking me if he could speak to Federman. I called Raymond over and the kid spoke his piece.

"Mister," he began, "I really don't know who you are, but I think you'd like to see what I have here out on the street." Ray looked perplexed, but I motioned that everything was ok. I stood in the doorway as Federman was led out onto the sidewalk and to the street, where parked at the curb was the kid's car, an immaculate vehicle with the classic split windshield, toothily grinning grill, and three chrome donuts along each front fender that marked it as a 1947 Buick Special, the automobile of Raymond's young manhood and of his fantasies ever afterwards.

I won't tell stories of how taken Raymond was with seeing that car, or of all the other special little things that happened now and then ever since. Just that he has been a salutary influence on my life as well as my work. Steeled as I was against all the pressures of academic modernism and Eurocentric influences, Federman was the way these interests made their ways into my experience. This ran the gamut from learning how to eat (when Raymond for once and for all put an end to my habit of ordering a hamburger and beer even in the finest restaurants) to learning some manners. Inveterate gentleman that he is, Raymond ascribed this latter influence to my new wife, and he even made quite a scene of doing so. On a trip East a few years after our marriage Julie and I stopped to meet Raymond and Erica in Buffalo. Schedules had never allowed me to fulfill my promise of treating them to a three-star meal in Paris, but now there was a little country inn across the border in Canada which promised cooking almost as good, so we spent a long evening there enjoying ourselves as Raymond made a typical production of enjoying our company and the food. Afterwards, in the lobby, he drew me aside, and in a whisper staged just enough so that Julie could hear it told me "Klinkowitz—she's so lovely!" Then he had some words for Julie, supposedly just for her but loud enough for me to hear. "You know, I knew Jerry before, and he used to be a real *animal*! But you've changed him, and now he really isn't bad after all!" This was not just the postmodern but the postfeminist 1980s, yet Raymond managed to get away with such comments and even flourish in them. It was part of his life of fiction, we realized—a life of fiction that was being lived for our benefit and appreciation.

What is Raymond Federman's importance? He has all the life and comedy and unfettered imaginativity of the other innovators, but also something more: not so much a subject, something forbidden in these days of antirepresentation, but an absence. At a time when one of the initial events in his life, the Holocaust, has been almost crushed by the weight of historical study and trivialized by the maunderings of too-predictably realistic fiction, Federman has taken those four X's that life left him in 1945 and turned them into an alphabetic infinitude whose generative power has kept him rolling for another fifty and more years.

Consider the irony: hidden in the closet in 1942, struggling to make his way in the wasteland of what had been the Parisian Jewish community in 1945 and 1946. Then coming to America as a teenager in 1947 and within just a couple years sharing a stage with Charlie Parker, blowing Bird's horn while Parker wailed on Raymond's tenor.

Think of the Count Basie Orchestra blasting out "April in Paris." The lead tenor sax carrying the melody's great sweep is played by Frank Foster, Raymond's buddy from Northern High in Detroit. Then listen to Parker himself, his alto singing out that same tune. By virtue of his French background and thoroughly American foreground, it is Raymond Federman's song. Not just a kaddish for all those losses, but, in addition to that, a celebratory improvisation of the life of fiction and fiction of life that have followed for him ever since.

5

Gilbert Sorrentino and Clarence Major

Like Sukefedermanick, Gilbert Sorrentino and Clarence Major were paired—not really one to the other, but in the ways I met them, worked with them, and eventually lost interest. Each was an experimentalist to be sure, but their personalities and critical opinions eventually came to be more important than their fiction. Both Gil and Clarence were spokesmen for a specific style of writing, as were Sukenick and Federman; what made them different was the distance they put between themselves and other writers one would think were allies. Don Barthelme might object kiddingly to some of the company in which I placed him, but Gil would rage against it. The letters he wrote me—long, detailed, and monstrously opinionated essays often running several single-spaced pages each—are now at the University of Delaware with his own papers from earlier years; Stanford has the rest, and in each collection researchers can treat themselves to reams of vitriol and bile directed at his contemporaries. Gil knew this was an excess and took a comic attitude in unleashing it, yet the bitterness was there. Clarence's initial distance was measured from other black American writers—not just the realists but the innovators, too, including Ishmael Reed and Amiri Baraka. Each had his own ideas, ideas that made both of them cranks. But then both of them were right.

Jack O'Brien, my one and only doctoral student (in the program at Northern Illinois), brought back the news of both Sorrentino and Major. Jack's dissertation was a collection of interviews done with the black American innovators who, forty years after the Harlem Renaissance of Jean Toomer and Claude McKay, were creating a new style of fiction known as "Renaissance Two." Beginning with a few veterans from the generation just before—Arna Bontemps, Ann Petry, and Ralph Ellison—Jack proceeded to meet and talk with some experimentalists of the early 1960s, including Ernest J. Gaines and William Demby. These writers in turn directed him toward younger figures just emerging with their first or second books: Alice Walker, Ishmael Reed, John Edgar Wideman, Charles Wright, and the most critically articulate and radically committed of all, Clarence Major. Moving in their circles in New York, mostly down in the Village, Jack picked up information on what white innovators were doing as well. Most of these— Sukenick, Barthelme, Katz—Jack didn't care for. But there was an older guy, born a few years ahead of the others in 1929 and active as a poet in the 1950s' Black Mountain group, who'd begun publishing fiction in 1966 that Jack found intriguing. His name was Gilbert Sorrentino, and his influence on my student could not have been greater had he appeared as an Old Testament prophet. In his scornful diatribes Gil could in fact be like that, for the jeremiad, as a lamentation of fallen standards and ideals, seemed Gil's natural form of expression. O'Brien's dissertation was published as *Interviews with Black Writers* (New York: Liveright, 1973), one of the stately Gilbert Harrison's last acquisitions before selling both his publishing house and his magazine, *The New Republic*. Yet Jack would do little else with this body of literature, for his mania had become Sorrentino—not just Gil's works, but his attitudes as well. Soon Jack had me infected as well, and I began the task of culturing Gil into the colony of innovators I considered the future of American fiction. It was a hopeless task.

I met him in December of 1972 when his poetry had gone neglected, the little magazines on which he'd worked were long dead (*Kulchur, Yugen, Neon*) as were some of his co-editors (notably Frank O'Hara), and what existed of his fiction was being remaindered at the Strand. It was during the Modern Language Association convention in New York; Gil would not have gone within ten blocks of the affair, but in my enthusiasm I'd bought two dozen copies of his recent novel, *Imaginative Qualities of Actual Things* (New York: Pantheon, 1971) for $1 apiece and handed them out to the most influential scholar-critics I could find, including Robert Scholes, Leslie Fiedler, and Benjamin DeMott (each of whom subsequently wrote on Gil). Then, with Jack and our friend Kathie Hinton, we trained down to the West Village one evening to meet Gil.

Heading along Hudson Street to Bethune, I recognized the neighborhood as a place I'd been taken a year before: to the White Horse Tavern where Dylan Thomas had gone on his last binge before being carried off to die at the nearby St. Vincent's Hospital.

Behind all of this, on West Street, was a somber-looking building Jack identified as the old Bell Telephone lab where television had been invented almost fifty years before. Now it was an apartment building offering subsidized housing for writers and artists and their families. I recognized Ed Sanders's name on the directory near Gil's, and in a moment we were up the stairs to meet the man himself.

The jacket photo on *Imaginative Qualities* catches the image that confronted us at the door. There Gil, hair combed back severely and as jet black as the turtleneck shirt he wears, scowls at the camera looking for all the world like a disciplinarian at an old-fashioned Catholic boys' high school. Until he recognized Jack among us, that was the expression he wore; then, seeing the young man who'd become not so much a friend as a virtual acolyte, he broke into a wide smile and welcomed us in.

We spent most of the evening there, Gil supplying such excellent wines and cordials that I had to object that we must be drinking him out of house and home. "Don't worry," he advised, "that's the one thing we have plenty of." We knew, because he was so proud of the fact, that he had very little money; he and his second wife and eight-year-old son survived on the $4,000 he could earn annually from reviewing and free-lance editing. There was an occasional writing course he'd teach at the New School which sometimes raised his income to $6,000, but that was it. The books were earning nothing, though Jack and I were soon able to do a little something about that. Yet Gil could offer us the finest vintages and selections, because he and Victoria had plenty of friends who were working, some of them doing quite well. "Bottles of good wine are what everyone gives us," she said. "Too bad you can't sell it," I joked, and Gil scowled.

He seemed pleased enough that I cared for his work, and when I mentioned that I was planning to spend $30 for a copy of his long-out-of-print first book, a poetry collection titled *The Darkness Surrounds Us* (Highlands, N.C.: Jonathan Williams, 1960), he scoffed, walked over to a large trunk sitting against the wall, and opened it to reveal what must have been six or seven hundred copies of the thin, stapled paperback. "Here you go," he said, taking three and inscribing one for each of us. When I tried to tell him how there could be a market for these and urged him to get in touch with the bookseller, he scowled again and pointed to the cover where the price was printed. "It only cost $1.50," he grumped, and I dropped the subject. But a month later, when I convinced book dealer Peter Howard of Serendipity Books in Berkeley to buy up the several thousand copies of *Imaginative Qualities* being remaindered, Gil consented to Peter reselling them at cover price ($6.95) as long as there was any demand. He also accepted Peter's unrequired generosity in paying him standard royalties on all copies sold. But only if the price was held to that printed amount, $6.95. Gil wanted no part of a "rare books" scam. "They call this a rare book?" he laughed, waving my copy of *The Darkness Surrounds Us* where 70% of the print run still sat.

Though I've never really figured out Gil's poetry, an epigraph on that first book's cover clued me into his attitude toward almost everything. It's a quote from one of those Old Testament prophets, and reads "The wise man's eyes are in his head but the fool walketh in darkness; and myself perceived also that one event happeneth to them all." That was the two-edged sharpness to Gil's sometimes vindictive sword: not just that the damn fools around him couldn't see, but that the same things were happening in front of them as him. It's the caustic humor that motivates *Imaginative Qualities*, a vicious satire of the New York art and literary world of the late 1950s and 1960s that Ron Sukenick assured me matched up with obviously recognizable people, most of whom had been Gil's friends in those days. What Gil was like back then can be gathered from Hettie Cohen Jones's den-motherly account, *How I Became Hettie Jones* (New York: Dutton, 1990); as far as the vitriol goes, he was apparently keeping it all in until it burst out in this novel written almost a decade later. But it too was something of a jeremiad, lamenting a fine world now lost and railing against the trash that had replaced it.

I really wasn't the kind of person to be dealing with Gil. He took a great deal of what he considered nonsense from me, yet also could object with no small vehemence when I went too far. My enthusiasm for popularizing innovative fiction struck him as goofy and misinspired. That first night, as I gave him a copy of my anthology *Innovative Fiction* and regretted that I hadn't learned of his work early enough to include it, he surprised me by saying he would not have wanted to be part of it. Why not, I stammered. "Just look at this," he gestured toward the book, which he'd placed on the table and seemed determined never to touch again. "Kurt

Vonnegut! For Christ's sake!" What was wrong with Vonnegut? I suspected Gil would consider him artistically lightweight and be put off by his popular success, but argued that it would be much better to have people reading Kurt's work and thereby being drawn to more innovative stuff rather than staying stuck with social realism. This was the wrong approach, for Gil went into a diatribe about popularization, using jazz as an analog. "It's like saying Cannonball Adderley is spreading jazz," Gil complained. Wasn't he, I asked. "Not at all," Gil insisted. "He's just playing watered-down music that has nothing to do with the real stuff." But so many people were listening, and better to Adderley's popularizations than to disco. This made Gil even madder. "You want to know what I consider the best? The best music and the best way to play it?" He drew back and painted the necessary picture. "Take a small jazz club in some out of the way neighborhood in New York, maybe down the street here. It's two o'clock in the morning, and the place is empty. Everybody's gone home except the bartender, and he's not listening. And you have this quartet with a trumpeter, and he plays the greatest solo of his life. And what makes it great is that nobody has to be there to know it. *That's* the best way for art!"

Considering Gil's standards and his way of living up to them, I couldn't fault him. It was true he gained advantages from some of the things I did, even as he mocked those activities, just as the relocations of space within narrative time that characterized his first two novels, *The Sky Changes* (New York: Hill and Wang, 1966) and *Steelwork* (New York: Pantheon, 1970), benefited from having obstructing conventions and traditions cleared away by the more radically innovative fiction of writers he didn't wish to be associated with. As an eager young critic, I was set upon charting literary history even before the ink had dried on the page; Gil, having been through at least two literary revolutions already, viewed this with a tired eye, and simply wanted to be left alone to do his work. His unstated point was that he would have proceeded this way whether or not Ron Sukenick had written *Up* and Kurt Vonnegut had published *Cat's Cradle*, so what was the issue? I tried to build interest in similarities and affinities; he instructed that perceiving the essential differences was what mattered. Jack O'Brien, of course, ate this up, and in time became an image of Gil himself in everything from the way he exercised his standards (sternly) to how he expressed his opinions (abruptly). Yet through all of this I persisted as myself, impressing Gil as an overenthusiastic young hick (he once told Jack that he liked me nevertheless, for not even attempting to hide it) and winning myself a parodied role in the novel Gil wrote to consign all such innovation to silliness, *Mulligan Stew* (New York: Grove Press, 1979), where a critical advocate named Professor Roche behaves the way Gil must have thought I had back then.

My "undisguised careerism" was something else Gil told Jack that he liked about me, emphasizing the adjective rather than the noun. That careerism is what touched his own life more than any of my literary ideas, for in the bustle of activity I was orchestrating there were sufficient currents to pull him along when the direction suited his way. My role as a professor at middle-range public universities bearing names of impossible states amused him. Northern Illinois, then Northern Iowa—I'm sure to Gil this sounded like Southeastern North Dakota State University at Hoople, and in *Mulligan Stew* he gives Professor Roche a similar address. In the novel Professor Roche begins by seeking out the novelist-protagonist with promises to advance his career, and then winds up creating all sorts of trouble. That's surely the way Gil viewed my first efforts, but by the end things turned out much better for him than his writer-victim in *Mulligan Stew*.

Consider the first event. In fall of 1973 Ron Sukenick's friend Chuck Russell, working at the University of Wisconsin-Milwaukee, found he could tap funds from the school's Center for Twentieth Century Studies to mount a major conference on innovation in the literary and plastic arts. There would be minimalists and conceptual artists: Carl Andre, Joseph Kosuth. Art critics, including Jack Burnham. Writers we both liked: Sukenick, Raymond Federman, and William H. Gass. Ihab Hassan would be the premier literary scholar, but Chuck said he could get me a pretty fancy honorarium too. That wouldn't be necessary, I replied; just give me a couple hundred dollars for expenses and use the rest to hire Gilbert Sorrentino. I knew Gil could use the money, but even more wanted him to be part of this event from which I knew important things would develop. The affair, lasting three days, was well attended, getting national exposure and attracting several young Americanists from universities in Europe, all of whom were eager to find new writers to translate, teach, and publish on. I made Chuck and

Jack O'Brien (who also knew about my offer) promise not to tell Gil how we were financing him.

Sukenick, Federman, Gass, and Sorrentino got along famously, enjoying each other's readings, interacting well on the panels, and having a hilarious time at the conference's nonstop parties. The next week Gil would write Jack O'Brien defaming all three of his colleagues, disparaging their works and complaining about the stifling academic atmosphere that had forced him to wear a pasted-on smile that nearly made his face shatter. But the truth was that Gil enjoyed himself as the center of attention, winning audiences with hilarious portions of intentionally bad writing from his novel in progress ("Synthetic Ink," which became *Mulligan Stew*) and entertaining virtual crowds at the parties with routines he must have practiced at the Cedar Tavern back home. Wowing the yokels is probably how Gil viewed this, but he deeply enjoyed doing it, reinforcing as it did his prejudice that such outsiders could never understand the real stuff, limited as it was to those living and working in New York. And of course he took the money, a sum enough to increase his annual income by no small amount.

Gil exaggerated everything to Jack. The conference was academic but far from stifling, and he had a good enough time horsing around with these other writers, no matter what he thought of their work. Best of all, as a nonacademic he brought a frank style of shop talk to the discussions that made everything seem more real, including discussions of "reality" itself. During one panel session where Sukenick and Federman and Gass may have been wandering too far into their own doctoral specialties of Wallace Stevens, Samuel Beckett, and the philosophy of metaphor respectively, Gil jumped in to complain that every culture has its own limits to what's considered real. "Look at the Egyptians," he broke in, "they knew exactly where the world ended: right over that hill there," gesturing past the stage and mugging along to the audience's laughs. Afterwards he regaled the partygoers with tales of what really went on in editorial meetings (such as when he'd worked at Grove) and how the whole reviewing system was predicated on petty and ridiculous prejudices. Throughout all of this he sparkled, eating well and drinking freely at the university's expense and taking home a pocket full of cash.

Less of a crank now in favor of good humored teasing, Gil had fun kidding me about Milwaukee, which happened to be my home town. On the final night, when we had left the last party tired but hungry, he chided me that it would be hopeless even looking for someplace to eat at this hour, so square was all the Midwest. "This is Milwaukee?" he'd ask. "It looks to me like Newark." Hadn't he seen how the Midwest was developing, how nice Minneapolis-St. Paul had become? "Two Newarks adjoined," Gil replied. Now, as we cruised the streets at 2 AM I heard all the predictable lines about the sidewalks being rolled up at ten and so forth. He was right in that nothing near the university or downtown was open; even my old standby for getting food and coffee after a band job, the Belmont Coffee Shop, was dark. Finally, as we swung across the viaduct spanning Milwaukee's industrial valley, Gil let loose with an "Oh Christ, we really are in Jersey!" and I decided to let him have it back. Not with any lines of my own but with a bonafide hamburger and coffee I knew could be found.

Here, on the city's south side, I pulled up to the curb in a working-class neighborhood where a genuine all-night place, George Webb's, was bathing the street in light from its tall windows. Its formica counter and plastic seats were lit like an operating theater, and we winced as we entered the place and grabbed five stools in the center. A few rummies and hookers looked up from their eleven-cent cups of soup and dime coffees, and were dismayed to see Gass and myself in suits and ties, Sukenick in one of his loud California shirts, and Sorrentino wearing a plush purple jacket set off against his inevitable black turtleneck. Ray Federman was dressed more conservatively, but what a gathering of not just fictionists but critical theorists we had here on South Sixteenth Street. I was carrying Gil's first two novels, each of them now a rare edition, and Gass's *Fiction and the Figures of Life*. As we talked, the books were passed among us, each writer looking over the other's work and making remarks on what he'd read. Gass happened on the pages in *Steelwork* listing "Sexology: One Hundred Facts," a compendium of an eleven-year-old boy's misinformation about the act and all he and his friends could imagine it might involve, and drew some looks of shock from the other customers as he read them aloud. When I asked Gil to sign the book, he inscribed it "#101: Do not eat hamburgers at George Webb's," though he happily wolfed down several baskets of the fifteen-cent sandwiches. Sukenick had been admiring the jacket cover of *The Sky Changes*, photographer Robert Frank's evocation of a lonely highway stretching to infinity across the desolate Southwest where much of the novel's action is set. Now Gil took the book, advised me how rare it really was, and after my name and before his drew a roadsign with the legend SLOW CURVE. There was plenty of serious talk and a great deal of fun, too. We didn't leave the place until after 5 AM.

Gil's work got a full chapter in *Literary Disruptions*, a book that brought some interesting attention to both of us. In 1978, three years after its publication and long enough for it to become a frequent reference in contemporary studies, I was nominated for a chaired professorship at the University of Scranton. The salary would have nearly doubled the good money I already earned, and the position included a research budget on which I could have traveled the world several times over. Visiting the school, I dickered over how much teaching they'd want; I preferred a single class meeting just one day a week (my mad idea was to commute from Iowa), while Scranton argued for a six-hour load and two days in residence each week. Before this could be resolved my own university stepped in with a counter offer good enough to keep me in Cedar Falls, but instead of breaking it all off I urged the University of Scranton to hire Gil Sorrentino instead. They did; Gil must have felt like a millionaire, and even arranged to keep living in New York, bussing up for one day's class, staying overnight in the German hotel downtown, teaching another course and then heading back home. Then two years later Stanford University picked him off for its distinguished Wallace Stegner chair in creative writing. It meant giving up New York for California, but Gil seemed willing. That spring Will Stone visited from Stanford to evaluate my own department and confided that he and his colleagues had learned of Sorrentino's work from *Literary Disruptions* and then convinced Stanford's skeptical administration that Gil was for real by showing them my chapter on him in a second book, *The Life of Fiction*, which I'd published with the University of Illinois Press in 1977. Stegner himself, in retirement, had been furious at having such a radical innovator hired; but the fact that there was so much scholarship on Gil by now—more than on Stegner, in fact—sealed the case.

To see what moving West did to Gilbert Sorrentino, check out his photo on the back of his collected essays, *Something Said* (San Francisco: North Point Press, 1984). He's grayed, but healthily, and is splendidly tanned. No more harsh turtleneck, but rather a soft, open-collared white sportshirt. And he's smiling, almost irrepressibly. In almost every way, the pressure was off: out of New York's confinement and into the open beauty of Stanford and its campus, where many professors did their work in open-air backyard studies amid the flowers and fruit trees; into a salary twenty times what he'd lived on back on West Street; and light years away from that world in whose aftermath he'd still be bumping into old friends who'd become new enemies. True, he was on campus and a professor himself; but its sophistication was a far cry from the University of Southeastern North Dakota at Hoople, and the conservative ways of Stanford's professorate surely fit Gil's more serious style.

His writing changed as well. For one thing, I was no longer getting 1500-word letters arguing vehemently (plus brilliantly and effectively) with whatever topic I'd dared to introduce. Now everything was pleasant and serene. At the same time Jack O'Brien, who was Gil's real friend, would get letters that remained minor essays but were far less combative than in the past and much more devoted to the leisurely exploration of subjects for which Gil now had the time (including thoughts on a whole generation of neglected Irish and French writers whom Jack was soon to publish in his new ventures, *The Review of Contemporary Fiction* and the Dalkey Archive Press). The greatest change, however, was in his novels themselves. Whereas so much of his initial work had been motivated by things to argue, by genuine beefs—the insipid decay of a marriage in *The Sky Changes*, the loss of childhood's neighborhood in *Steelwork*, the pettiness and stupidity and incompetence of the literary and art world in *Imaginative Qualities of Actual Things*—Sorrentino's new work was immensely more relaxed and lyrically expressive. The transition started in New York and can be seen in his novella, *Splendide-Hôtel* (New York: New Directions, 1973), an almost copybook-like exercise in which each letter of the alphabet prompts the author's thoughts and opinions on a specific subject. There are plenty of complaints, but also lots of pure beauty, and I'd guess that writing it taught Gil that he didn't need a narrative justification (the blight of a failed marriage, of a lost neighborhood). But the grand purge of everything vexing this man takes place in *Mulligan Stew*, including both his anger with commercial publishing and his exasperation with the innovative fiction I was proposing instead. This novel mocks it all, and published as it was at the decade's close effectively brings the whole 1970s' movement of disruption and transformation in fiction to a hilarious but also self-damning end.

Now, writing from his new home in California, Gil had a new publisher as well. And what a supportive one. Whereas for each of his earlier books he could tell me a story of failure and perdition ("Arthur Wang dealt me a shabby hand on that one," and so forth) and *Mulligan Stew* itself had begun with a collection of rejection letters utterly comic and exaggerated to the point of being ridiculous (except that during the book's four-year quest for a publisher Gil had reported receiving notes of just this kind), now a new quality venture—the North Point Press of San Francisco and Berkeley—would virtually adopt his canon, publishing his next four books and printing a revised version of his first novel. This, of course, seemed too good to be true; but when North Point began to go under, Jack O'Brien came to the rescue and offered the same supportive services with the press Gil's ponderings had inspired.

Thanks to all this, Sorrentino in the 1980s doubled his production. The work itself, however, was of a different tone and style. Lacking the motivation that anger and crankiness provide, novels such as *Crystal Vision* and *Blue Pastoral* (done with North Point in 1981 and 1983) take the lyricisms of *Steelwork* and its actual subjects as well and amplify them to the point of self-taken exaggeration. In similar manner *Odd Number* (North Point, 1985) and Gil's first two books with Jack O'Brien's Dalkey Archive Press in Elmwood Park, Illinois, *Rose Theatre* (1987) and *Misterioso* (1989), are constructed as variations upon the characters and action in *Imaginative Qualities of Actual Things*. The promptings here are innovative, a writerly lesson in how supposed facts assert themselves through the various encodings of experience fiction can provide; if readers try to receive these encodings as absolute truths, however, they will be frustrated—in all fiction, but especially so in these works that Sorrentino constructs in a way to frustrate such readings. Here is where Gil's affinities with innovators such as Sukenick and Federman begin to fade, for whereas Sukefedermanick's works had been prompted by an anger and frustration with the inhibitions of realism's conventions, now Sorrentino's response was based not on crankiness with the forms themselves but rather curiously with a work of his own making. It made for a crucial second remove, and surely a backward step from truly deconstructive and defamiliarizing inquiry to a rather Wildean and Pateresque penchant of art for art's sake (or at least of Gil's work for Gil's work's sake).

If there's a bit of *Finnegans Wake* to all this, it should not be surprising, for Sorrentino was always a Joycean. During the years he wrote the more lyrical parts of "Synthetic Ink" (which then became swept up in the vicious parody of *Mulligan Stew*), he treated himself to rereading one page of *Ulysses* each day. One finds plenty of Rimbaud in *Splendide-Hôtel*, while the spirit of Raymond Roussel haunts a similar novella, *Under the Shadow* (Dalkey Archive, 1991). Some say that postmodernism is simply the failure of modernism in our latter half-century; perhaps Gil, like the more obvious efforts of Guy Davenport, was trying to recover the modernist ideal for this fallen world. That would certainly fit the tone of his opinions expressed to me and to folks I knew and with whom I was swapping stories about the man.

What matters most about Gilbert Sorrentino's work, however, is not its structure but its voice. In the essay "Genetic Coding" that concludes his collection *Something Said* (North Point, 1984), Gil reminds us of the source of that voice: the heritage of his Irish mother and Sicilian father. "Both the Italians and the Irish have an understanding of the essential idiocy of living, the former possessing the Mediterranean tragic sense of life in a pure state, and the latter cloaking their despair under violent, savage, and heartless comedy, comedy that Beckett calls the 'mirthless laugh . . . the laugh of laughs, the *risus purus*, the laugh laughing at the laugh.'" This certainly matches up with the voice I'd hear and read when dealing with Gil and his work. But it is only significant when coupled with another factor, Sorrentino's adoption of the outlook that "The Italians and the Irish hold reality cheap, and the brilliance of the art produced by these peoples is, by and large, the brilliance of formal invention used to break to pieces that which is recognizable to the quotidian eye" (p. 264). Combine these attitudes and you have the man driven to fury by the shenanigans of his colleagues in the literary world and inspired to write both the hysterically bitter satire of *Imaginative Qualities* and the soaring (yet ever referential) lyricism of *Steelwork*.

Gil's work is brilliant, but what I found most impressive was his influence on others. He argued enough that I'm sure he tried to influence me, probably to no avail, but his impact on Jack O'Brien has literally changed the world, at least as far as those who care about books and writers go. Jack, of course, remains uncritical of Gil, and I think this uncritical attitude prevents him from seeing some roots of the man's genius. Such insights, however have been made by another who was once a Sorrentino protégé, the writer Michael Stephens. As an eighteen-year-old returned from a half-year's work on a trans-Atlantic ship with a novel about growing up in the chaos and mad poetry of an Irish-American family, Michael became one of Gil's authors at Grove—but only as a momentary acquisition, for before the book could enter production the press changed hands and the less promising contracts were voided. Yet Gil stayed with Michael, seeing in his sardonic humor and lyric voice a style much like his own. On my visit to Gil's apartment in 1972 he showed me a copy of Michael's novel, finally published as *Season at Coole* that year with Dutton. This was a writer I should be studying, not Sukenick, Federman, or Vonnegut. "This one's the McCoy," Gil winked, and I took him absolutely seriously.

An age later, in 1986, I'd become an editor myself, building the Crosscurrents series for Southern Illinois University Press, and among the first books I commissioned was Michael's study, *The Dramaturgy of Style*. One of its finest chapters was on Sorrentino, with whom Michael had enjoyed and endured a relationship as typical as for any of Gil's friends. Unlike Jack, Michael could begin with something critical yet insightful: that Gil had a tragic flaw, but from that flaw flowed the essence of his work. What was it? "A wrathful judging of others" (p. 86), Michael explained. "There must have been a particular day in his life, sitting in the Cedar Bar, when Gil Sorrentino grew tired of his friends' talking about writing, and having made his own personal commitment, however eccentric, to Art and Literature, he let the bar talk stay in the bar, and he went home to write." At home he notices something left on his desk: the newspaper's comic strips "dwelling on Moon Mullins and Kayo, Mamie Mullins and her drunken-loutish husband. I suppose the old friends in the bar never forgave Sorrentino for this brilliant inspiration, using two rhythms of experience to shape his mature fiction—the funnies and the Cedar Bar" (p. 87).

It is this unique voice that skewers his characters, dancing around his subjects in the layering and embroidery that distinguishes the most characteristic Irish and Italian narratives, particularly jokes. The voice is one of ferocity and venom, but such that these qualities transform reality rather than repress it. Like the prophet's line on the cover of his first book of poetry, it is the rage one feels not at just seeing what is happening but seeing it happen right in front of those who cannot or will not see. Yet the result is not just rage, but a prophet's verse. Transposed to California for the century's end, it becomes more softly lyric: but that fits too, for I picture Gil out there, a continent removed from what he once thought was the center, stringing arabesque improvisations of great art and beauty like his ideal jazzman so early in the morning in that totally empty club.

Clarence Major was a lot like Gil. Seven years younger and a Midwesterner like myself, he seemed less a sternly critical uncle and more a fondly worshiped older brother to me, yet certain essentials of his background matched up closely with Sorrentino's. There was the influence of storytelling in his family; not of course Gil's melding of Irish and Italian but a similar combination of his mother's urban Chicago style with that of his relatives down South (whom he'd visit for extended stays during summer childhood years). Then there was the way he came to literature: not through the schools, though he was a brilliant student, but through work. In the early 1950s Gil had been one of several ex-Army vets who in their workshirts and jeans sat around corner stores in Brooklyn to thrash out a new aesthetic; Hubert Selby was there, feasting on Gil's every word. Disliking what they saw in literary magazines, Gil and his crowd started their own. In time it took them over to Manhattan, where an entirely new litworld grew—one Gil eventually soured on, prompting *Imaginative Qualities of Actual Things* and an entire voice for transforming an undesired present. Clarence's entry into the artworld was even less professional or academic. Leaving Chicago one weekend for a party in Omaha, he fell in with a group of new friends there and decided to stay, getting employment in a steelyard. Given the unpleasantness of such work, almost anyone can sign on for work in a foundry; but Clarence's talent soon led to an apprenticeship in welding, and from there to the yard's most prestigious job, operating the crane that carried steel from one part of the plant to another.

It was highly skilled but physically easy work, and often hours would pass up there between calls. To fill the time Clarence began taking books to work, and could often finish one each day. In time the notion struck him that he could write books as good or better than he was reading. He also noticed that much of this writing was coming from little magazines, operations small enough that anyone with even a middle income (such as a crane operator earned) could finance the production. Thus Clarence found himself editing and publishing the journal *Coercion* in the same manner that Gil Sorrentino had brought out *Neon* from his Brooklyn apartment in the previous decade. And like Gil's efforts, which took him across the bridge to Manhattan and its literary culture and business, *Coercion* brought Clarence into contact with the new world of innovative black writing making its appearance in the middle 1960s. Coercion Press was formed to publish Clarence's first two books of poetry, and by the decade's end he was in New York, his anthology *The New Black Poetry* (1969) and his seminal *Dictionary of Afro-American Slang* (1970) having been picked up by International Publishers, a remnant of the American Communist Party's interest in the literary work of black America. Clarence was in no way "CP"; he had in fact been working for the government, picking up employment in an agency's survey of the civil disturbances in Milwaukee and other cities in 1967 and 1968. Yet there was a deliberately subversive intent to both volumes. In the first, Clarence announced that "I see our poems, social and political, as scientific new music" by which the "inner crisis of black reality" (p. 11) could be used to "renew the world, especially to authenticate this [visionary] society" (p. 12). The *Dictionary* showed how Clarence found this process already taking place in black slang, a "so-called private vocabulary" that "serves the users as a powerful medium of self-defense against a world demanding participation while at the same time laying a boobytrap-network of rejection and exploitation" (p. 9).

The key to Clarence's genius was his ability to translate both this vision and the means for realizing it into fiction. Through his fiction was how I met him, and various fiction projects kept us in league for the next decade and a half. In all of Jack O'Brien's interviews, Clarence had the most striking ideas and sharpest talent in articulating them. Ishmael Reed's piece had funny lines to be sure, such as dismissing the work of militant essayists as opposed to his own "hoo-doo" fiction by saying "You guys go after the cop on the beat while we go after the Pope, and let's see who causes a *real* revolution!" But that was just glibness compared to Clarence Major's care in explaining how a novel is first of all words, and that any reality it conveys is primarily a construct of the author's imagination brought to life by creative interplay with the reader. This was, of course, just what Gilbert Sorrentino, William H. Gass, and Ronald Sukenick were arguing in their essays, but in Clarence's case the judgment was reached and the verdict rendered thanks to the case of actually living black experience. That was why his first novel, *All-Night Visitors* (New York: Olympia Press, 1969), was so compelling. Though it was located in two supposedly distinct realities—a black American's experience in his own ghetto neighborhood and as an infantryman in Vietnam—the novel's determination as a work of language rather than of simple representation served to make the two locales indistinguishable. Which makes for social commentary to be sure, but one that is based on the workings of the imagination, as expressed in the system of language, rather than in political machinations that barely scratch the surface. Language generates our reality, philosophy had been teaching since Wittgenstein; and now deconstructionists were showing how such workings could be traced and uncovered. But among current writers only a few, like Sukenick, Sorrentino, and Major, were actually using the innate properties of fiction to do it.

Clarence's move from poetry to fiction again paralleled Gil Sorrentino's career (and in a way recalled Ron Sukenick's critical interest in a poet, Wallace Stevens, that preceded his own fiction). As with Sukenick and Ray Federman, I felt these folks should get together, and so from Cedar Falls, Iowa I wrote letters, made phone calls, and coordinated readings and invitations in New York in order that Clarence, my new-found pen pal, could get in touch with such obvious colleagues. It happened in 1973; Sukenick was reading at Brooklyn College, and Clarence—coincidentally filling the same visiting slot in creative writing at Sarah Lawrence College Ron had enjoyed before leaving for Cornell and then California— followed my advice and attended. I'd been showing the work of each to the other, and so when Clarence introduced himself both felt like old friends. Within a year they were cooperating in helping found the Fiction Collective (which later published the bulk of their work); a few years later, after Clarence had been promoted through professorships at Howard University and the University of Washington in Seattle and Ron moved into an influential appointment at the University of Colorado, Ron arranged for his new friend to join him on the faculty there; and when Sukenick founded *The American*

Book Review. Clarence Major became an editor. It was critically important for Clarence to begin publishing with these people, whose connections were far better than he'd been suffering with the Reds and borderline pornographers (Clarence admitted that Maurice Girodias had accepted *All-Night Visitors* mostly for its frank sexual content).

Then there was the other plus of critical advocacy and promotion: putting some cash in an admired writer's pocket. It was a practice that soon drew complaints, notably from editor Gordon Lish, who in his foreword to *All Our Secrets Are the Same: New Fiction from "Esquire"* (New York: Norton, 1976), objected to "an outlet called Klinkowitz" for such a franchise "doing fire-sale business on every campus" (p. ix). I could see Lish's point, for we really were fixing the market, as I at Northern Iowa, Jack O'Brien at Illinois Benedictine, Steve Katz at Colorado (another of Sukenick's hires), and Larry McCaffery at San Diego (recommended after I declined a job there) invited someone for a good-paying reading and then kept his or her books in print thanks to perennial classroom adoptions. Yet Lish could see how well this worked, particularly in educating a new readership for fiction; within a few years he was working the campuses himself, offering writing seminars which both cultured acquisitions and strengthened sales of his existing list.

Clarence visited my school on April 17, 1974; I know the date because it is the earliest inscribed on the books of his I own. We'd been corresponding for three years previously. His first response was a happy one, saying how long it had been since he'd received such a full and chatty letter. Thanks to Jack O'Brien's work I felt I already knew him, and from then on letters flew back and forth between Cedar Falls and East Waverly Place in New York on an almost weekly basis. The occasion was UNI's annual conference on literature and social concerns, this time titled "The Black Artist in White America." From the drift of our correspondence I wondered how appropriate this topic would be, for while Clarence agreed with certain innovators, such as Ishmael Reed, that saying the best black writing was Eldridge Cleaver's *Soul on Ice* was tantamount to claiming the finest works by whites were Richard Nixon's *Six Crises* and Dwight D. Eisenhower's *Stories I Tell My Friends*, he seemed to have no great personal affection for Reed and others presumably on his side. Nor did Clarence have much patience for black novel-

ists committed to social realism. Only now was he being introduced to any number of sympathetic white writers, and so I
guessed that Clarence Major must be a pretty lonely guy.

The truth, I'd learn, was that Clarence was less lonely than
happily solitary. What he hated most were the petty organizational
hassles always springing up when writers tried to work together. It
misdirected and eventually drained away energy into silly but con-
suming animosities, and he wanted none of that. Meeting him for
the first time at the airport, I was struck by how quiet and gentle he
was. My students were similarly impressed, expecting (from the
conference's advertised tone) a firebreathing radical and getting
instead a soft-spoken, kindly individual who wanted to speak
against labels rather than paste on new ones.

That was the problem authors such as himself faced, he told
the afternoon's assembly. "In America we have this tradition of
Jean Toomer in the 1920s, Langston Hughes in the 1930s, Richard
Wright in the 1940s, Ralph Ellison in the 1950s, and James Baldwin
in the 1960s," he announced. What was wrong with that? I could
see my students looking perplexed, for these were the very authors
they knew, and proudly so. "Don't you think there might be someone else?" Clarence asked. That was the problem, that our culture
has this tradition of "one black writer at a time—and only one."
Nor was it just tokenism, he added. "People tend to receive a novel
by a black person not as art but as social testimony," Clarence
advised. "They react as if to an anthropological curiosity. They say,
'Oh, how he or she must have suffered!'" All this came across so
plaintively that we laughed in sympathy.

Back at my home, where he'd stay for the night, Clarence was
happy and relaxed. It was the first day of Iowa's spring, and in my
study we threw open the windows and enjoyed the fresh breeze.
He signed my growing collection of Clarence Major books, played
with my children, and enjoyed talking with several students who
stopped by for a personal meeting. Then we had dinner, spent the
evening sitting around drinking and listening to music, and the
next morning headed back to the airport.

From then on I was seeing Clarence several times a year, with
our lives taking on interesting correlations. In July he was driving
cross country and spent a night in Cedar Falls; by now we really
were close friends, but he also enjoyed seeing again several of the
students he'd met in April. Then in August I flew to New York to

drop in on several writers. Clarence welcomed me to his place on Waverly just a block east of Washington Square, and I was impressed with how perfect it looked: neat white walls displaying several of his paintings (impressionistic but also vaguely figurative, with a heavy application and working of oils); his writing desk organized for work; and a couch beneath a broad picture window looking south, framed like a Mediterranean villa with dozens of hanging plants. He had copies ready of his poetry books, and had fun signing them in various colors. Then his wife Sharyn Skeeter returned from her job as an editor at *Essence*, and we headed over to The Cookery on University Place for dinner and some fine jazz. That night we walked around the Village. Next morning Clarence urged me to return from my midtown hotel and meet someone I'd be sure to like: Burt Britton, who often stopped by for coffee before opening up the Strand Bookstore several blocks north. Burt was a delight, and at this first meeting pulled out a binder, opened it to a blank sheet, and without any explanation asked me to draw my self-portrait. He'd been asking writers to do this for years, and had quite a collection. When he learned I'd be heading up to Boston to meet Dan Wakefield and Mark Vonnegut, he asked me to get their self-portraits for him—cautioning that I was not to let them know anything about the project until they'd done their sketch. The charm of these portraits was not just their originality but their spontaneity as well. Once published, of course, there could be no more such surprises, and so over the years Burt had always told folks that he was holding off until the book was complete. When would that be? "When I get Chekhov," he'd insist.

That evening Clarence and Sharyn and I joined Burt and his wife Corby at their apartment up in the West Eighties. Before settling down Burt took me on a tour of the neighborhood, showing me with equal solemnity where Isaac Bashevis Singer lived and the spot where saxophonist King Curtis had been shot (in an argument with one of his tenants). It was pleasant spending time here, not just because Burt was so interesting but because, as one of Clarence's closest friends in New York, he gave me an idea of my new associate's personality. As I'd eventually learn regarding Clarence, Burt could be exceptional about things; not as cranky as Gil Sorrentino, but a bit extreme in some of his habits. Take the matter of books. What had started as the joy of reading turned into a mania of collecting; the tall bookcases lining his living room walls were stocked neatly with complete sets of first editions of every current writer he admired, each volume immaculate, virtually in mint condition with not even the slightest mark on jacket or binding. Nearly all of them were inscribed to Burt by their authors, and as I was handed examples to admire did not need to be cautioned, so sacred was the whole atmosphere about them. Corby, meanwhile, was laughing, telling me from her seat on the couch that whenever she'd try to show some interest in Burt's work by asking to read one of his favorites, he'd make a great fuss of seeking out a shopworn copy from the Strand, for he dared not let anyone *read* one of these precious relics. In time, I'd note that Clarence could be equally fussy about things. What I accepted as an idiosyncrasy in Burt, he admired as a trait of character. It probably accounted for the distance Clarence kept from other black writers just now; he didn't want to be identified as a member of any social movement. He was himself, an original, which is the only way I can describe Burt.

The manner in which Clarence got involved with Sukenick, Federman, and others in the innovative fiction crowd—a gathering that led to the Fiction Collective, a proprietorship of the Coordinating Council of Literary Magazines, the *American Book Review*, and a writing program centered at the University of Colorado—fits this manner. To the best of my knowledge, Clarence was the only black writer involved. Ishmael Reed could have been, but was too caught up in his own network of affairs that comprised a parallel but independent set of activities such as magazines, a publishing house, and what Richard Kostelanetz decried as personal "grants hustling." Unlike Jonathan Baumbach, a cofounder of the collective who feasted on the organizational details, Clarence always kept off to the side, suiting his quiet nature. But on occasion he could bristle with hostility, as he surprised us one evening in the Village. This was a few years later, when a bunch of us, all by now fast friends, were sitting around a big table off Washington Square, finishing a great meal and pushing back for a few hours of drinks and chatter.

Ray Federman was there, and he was telling for the umpteenth time his story about playing sax with Charlie Parker. Raymond was indeed an accomplished tenor man, and when I asked if he'd ever sat in with John Barth when that writer and hobbyist drummer was his colleague at Buffalo Federman rekindled everyone's attention with a story about that. Then, around the table, people chimed in with their own stories of being amateurs at jazz. Baumbach had played something or other, and so had another guest, Thomas Pynchon's sister (whose face we were all studying because insiders confided how it resembled her reclusive brother's). Finally the turn came to Clarence, who hadn't seemed much interested. And so Ron Sukenick began to prompt him.

"Come on, Clarence," Ron chided, "what did you play? You must have played something!"

Clarence had already shaken his head to indicate *no*, but now, under pressure, became visibly angry. "I didn't play anything," he said, quietly but firmly, and then withdrew from the conversation. For the next hour he kept to himself, but afterwards, as he drove me back to my hotel (he was living in Stamford, Connecticut, now, and had brought his car down for the day) he revealed what had been on his mind.

"I really didn't like Ron's comment," he said, and when I asked why replied that he thought it was "racially motivated." In all the years I'd known Clarence, this was the first time the subject had come up; but even as I tried to argue against Ron's intention, I could feel Clarence stiffening further. Then I realized that he'd been the only black person there. That was almost always the case; but then again, all the subjects discussed in this crowd were white, or at least nonracial. Jazz had racial overtones, tones Ron Sukenick had elected to stress. And for that Clarence could not forgive him.

How different this was from Federman's Frenchness, a style Ray exploited and invited us to tease about. And there was the difference, for Raymond's minority status, his uniqueness in our group, was not part of a system that had included slavery for the country's first ninety years and legislated segregation for another ninety afterwards. What was unforgivable in Federman's past, the Holocaust, was of course never joked about. Indeed, Raymond never mentioned or even wrote about it, using just the typographical XXXX to indicate the loss and continuing absence of his parents and two sisters killed in the camps.

For all its unpleasantness (for Clarence and for Ron), the episode let me see an important feature of Clarence Major's work. Just as Federman's fiction could include the Holocaust without ever making direct references to it, Clarence's novels involved the black American experience without ever being *about* it. I recalled Samuel Beckett's famous statement, that the ideal fiction is not about something but is that thing itself. Then there was Sukenick's own addendum, that fiction isn't about experience but is more experience. Just as Federman took those four X's of his family's unspeakable absence and from them generated a systematic infinity of alphabetic possibilities (his first novel, *Double or Nothing*, published in typescript form so readers could see the actual letters having struck the page and resisted being Xed out), Clarence was creating his own life of fiction by dealing with the reality of being black in America not as a subject but as a technique. This was how *All-Night Visitors* functioned, letting his protagonist Eli Bolton not so much experience the ghetto and Vietnam as conceive them through his perception and then generate their existence as linguistic rather than simply social entities. The social alone is a given, but rather lifelessly so; by going to the force that makes it live, the language by which we express our perceptions and cultural formations, Clarence could tap into the generating force, which made his novels such vitalistic affairs.

The life in those books matched the liveliness of sharing times with him. He was quiet but never dull, soft-spoken but always with something interesting to say. During the years he lived in New York and then Stamford I'd see him half a dozen times annually; in summer we'd walk around the Village, enjoying all the sights, smells, and sounds. Wintertime would bring me in for professional meetings; Clarence and I would hit all the parties, then look for more action afterwards. I remember one cold night—actually more like four in the morning—driving Clarence's car down Broadway, being urged by him to race taxi-cabs from light to light as we searched for someplace to eat. Amazingly, we couldn't find anything open, though we'd toured the island from uptown to Canal Street. "You know," Clarence advised, "this is a very Christian city." At times like these he'd be cracking funny lines left and right, always seeming in control. A few years later, after he'd remarried, his new wife cautioned me about the danger of being out like this. "When Clarence drinks too much," she warned me, "he doesn't act like others. He doesn't get loud or silly, just even more quietly serious." Here indeed was a danger, I was told. "When Clarence seems totally reliable," she said, "that's when you have to watch out."

Would race ever be a factor in our friendship? Like comedian Bill Cosby in his earliest days, Clarence seemed determined to keep such matters out of the way. Just when I thought he might be

approaching the topic, he'd turn away from it. One night in particular stands out. It was in New York during the Modern Language
Association convention, and Clarence had an invitation to something he said was special. We piled into his old Dodge and he
began to joke about it in ghetto terms, running through all sorts of
names for such a sorry heap. The one I remember is "struggle
buggy," Clarence laughing as he warned the car would indeed
have to struggle the distance up north of town, on the Hudson,
where the party was taking place. Once there, however, all references to black American life ceased. The affair was being hosted by
Walter Lowenfels, one of Clarence's friends from his first days in
New York and probably the influence that helped his books be
acquired by that Marxist outfit, International Publishers. The party
was a big one, with New Yorkers and other profs and critics in from
around the country. But Clarence was the only black person there,
and I had to wonder if we in the innovative fiction crowd were
using him for our own purposes as obviously as had the Communist Party embraced black writers in the 1930s.

We could tease Clarence easily enough; everyone had sense
enough to stay away from race. His home town, for example, was
ok. Even were references to other minorities. One of our better
laughs happened a few years later out in Fort Collins, Colorado,
where Clarence had driven us up from his new place in Boulder to
meet some friends. As we sat around and emptied several jugs of
wine the topic turned to some Hispanic acquaintances of his about
whom I was confused.

"Was this Victor Cruz and his colleagues?" I asked.

"No," Clarence said, making a brush-away gesture, "just a
bunch of Mexicans. . . ."

At this point one of Clarence's friends along from Boulder
burst into laughter.

"'Just a bunch of Mexicans,'" he roared, and repeated the line.
"There you go with your marvelous Chicago sense of fine discrim-
ination: 'No, just a bunch of Mexicans!'" For several minutes afterwards we were all laughing, Clarence the hardest. And late into the
night that hilarity could be reignited by answering any question, on
no matter what subject, with that same dismissive statement.

In the later 1970s began my closest affinity with Clarence. First
there was the matter of his education. He was a tenure-track professor at the University of Colorado, but like many writers

expected to be delayed in promotions and held down in salary because he did not have a Ph.D. In fact, he didn't have an M.A. or even an undergraduate college degree. This could be remedied by getting the B.A. through some external work by correspondence with the State University of New York system. Then his doctorate could be earned in a similar "university without walls" program administered out of Athens, Ohio. Certain credits could be given for his published works, not without precedent as the University of Chicago, after rejecting their then unknown graduate student's M.A. thesis in anthropology back in 1947, came through in 1971 with an earned degree based on accepting *Cat's Cradle* as valid anthropological work; hence Kurt Vonnegut finally got the credentials whose lack had cost him dearly when he had to work as the University of Iowa's lowest-paid teacher in 1965 and 1966. Now Clarence could receive a doctorate by planning, discussing, and writing a new novel. Its title would be *Emergency Exit*, and as such it was published in 1979 by the Fiction Collective as his fourth such work.

In working toward that point, I served as Clarence Major's doctoral dissertation director. This meant personal conferences (in Cedar Falls and in Boulder) plus a couple committee meetings in New York (once at a friend's loft in SoHo, then at the Royalton Hotel on West Forty-fourth across the street from the Algonquin where we celebrated Clarence's degree afterwards). *Emergency Exit's* success as an innovative novel bore directly on the thoughtfulness Clarence put into it. An idea of its intellectual range comes from its first page, which is in fact a list of copyright acknowledgments for sources used in the book. There are literary references to be sure—Hemingway's *The Sun Also Rises*, Pound's *Guide to Kulchur*, Gertrude Stein's *How to Write*—but also materials from George Harriman's *Krazy Kat* (anticipating Michael Stephens's mention of one of Gil Sorrentino's models), Senator Eugene McCarthy's *Dictionary of American Politics*, and Marjorie Tallman's *Dictionary of American Folklore*. Plus paintings by de Kooning, music by Eric Dolphy, and art history from Thomas B. Hess. Most impressive was the way Clarence melded these materials to form a ground from which true fiction could spring: a protoanthropological situation in which a modern suburban community is required by law to live by a ritual threshold ceremony that throws its otherwise typically sociological doings into high artistic relief. It reminded me of the way Kurt Vonnegut used anthropology for a similar viewpoint, but here the results were immensely more personal. Clarence's marriage with Sharyn had broken up; indeed, his previous novel with the Collective, *Reflex and Bone Structure* (1975), had been generated by imagining what losing her might be like. Now she was gone, and in her absence Clarence reimagined what their situation had been: he, from a lower-middle-class neighborhood on Chicago's south side, having been involved with a glamorous young woman from the black haute-bourgeoisie. Yet if the novel had been just that, it would have remained indistinguishable from any piece of common realism. Clarence knew it, and in his narratives there are occasional references to how differently a scene would proceed "if this were a realistic novel" or "if this were a book by Richard Wright." Instead, he uses the anthropological frame to emphasize the arbitrary, artistically cultured nature of everything, in the process creating a most innovative work of fiction that transcends rather than violates realism.

Working this close with a writer made for a close colleagueship, but what strengthened us as friends were our respective remarriages and the remarkable parallels those marriages formed. In 1978 my first wife and I, having drifted apart over the previous years, divorced, and I married Julie Huffman. For our wedding, Clarence drove in from Colorado to be my best man; his present to us was one of his paintings, a wonderfully expressive oil in which a figure can just be discerned—a model for his way of writing itself. Julie and I left my children with my mother and headed off for a month in France, a honeymoon that changed my travel habits and geographic interests ever after. Then, in 1980, Clarence came through with his new wife, Pamela Ritter. Like Julie, she was quite a bit younger than her husband; but even more coincidental was the fact that her home town had been, like Julie's, Cedar Falls; moreover her parents, just like my new wife's, were in the business of commercial property development. As a final match-up, Clarence and Pamela were on their way to France, where my own frequent visits of the past two years had spread news of his work among the eager young Americanists.

As we sat on that warm September morning, enjoying the woodsy view from our screen porch where Clarence and Pamela were framed by an abundance of hanging plants and bushes flowering out on the lawn, I thought of how Clarence and Sharyn had looked in that photo I'd taken of them before their similarly lush picture window overlooking Waverly Place in Greenwich Village six years before. Like myself, Clarence was unbelievably lucky, turning misfortune into something positive and coming out the better every time. That scene in New York had looked so happy, and was, he and Sharyn seeming like two young lovers on the terrace of a Mediterranean villa. Now, with Pamela, Clarence was off to a real villa overlooking Nice. When our friends returned there for a full year in 1981–82, Julie and I visited them in early spring. The home, to which we followed the old Roman road on the hilltops across the harbor, was the essence of what had been hinted at on Waverly Place and on our porch back in Cedar Falls—but this was the real thing. That first afternoon Clarence gathered deadwood from his estate's olive trees and built an open fire over which he broiled freshly slaughtered lamb. There was wine more delicious than I thought I ever might enjoy. The atmosphere and scenery were ideal.

An hour after the meal, Clarence and I were still standing on the terrace, sipping wine and marveling at the view. Not having spoken for some time, we turned to each other with the same thought. Here I was, this skinny kid from Milwaukee, whose greatest thrill in his first twelve years of life had probably been trips to Comiskey Park in Chicago, where from the elevated train heading through the South Side could be seen the rows of dingy flats and cinder alleys where a slightly older kid named Clarence Major was sketching scenes and writing poems. Could our eyes have met for a half-second back then? As our glances joined now, almost a quarter century later, they laughed with the same thought. In a moment we were chuckling out loud, and soon were giving joyful whoops and shrieks so manic our wives came out to see what was the matter.

What they saw must have been perplexing: a distinguished visiting professor at the Université de Nice and a critic flown over to address a literary festival, horsing around like two teenagers. Later on, when Julie and Pamela seemed patient enough to hear our explanation, we recounted how this fabulous identity we shared was constructed entirely on the basis of words. And not even words about something physically real—just Clarence's imagined constructions and my commentary on them. It was all so totally made up: his novels, my criticism, and this life we were sharing in this virtual wonderland, two pampered princes betrothed to young women who might well have been princesses. And all from just our words.

The words had kept us so happy that day, but in coming years they made us sad and drove us apart. For a while I didn't catch the drift, and continued on with Clarence's writing, reviewing it when I could and recommending it to others. But by the late 1980s I found myself having less and less contact with Clarence. His extended stays in Europe were part of it, as every other year had him off in France or Italy. He seemed drawn to the Mediterranean as if a life force, and soon he was crossing the sea to Africa. His novel *My Amputations* (Fiction Collective, 1986) uses this progress to chart a narrative that begins as the novelist-protagonist disappears to reemerge among terrorists anticipating a new historical Europe (shades of Don DeLillo's *Mao II* five years later!), then to be taken up by a primitive African tribe where history, along with time itself, has not yet happened.

After this, two things happened: his novels became more socially realistic and I was dropped from the list of those to receive them. I could guess that Clarence no longer needed my help, for he was now getting featured coverage in *The New York Times* regularly. At the time it struck me as corny that the reviewers were always black writers themselves, especially since Clarence had shunned them for so long. But now he was writing more in their style and seemed to be welcoming such praise. Which made me happy, for in *Such Was the Season* (San Francisco: Mercury House, 1987) Clarence was handling realism with no real compromises of his innovative talent. I should have paid more attention to the dust jacket, though, for where adulatory critical comments had usually been gathered from Sukenick, Federman, Jack O'Brien, and myself, now the endorsers listed were Toni Morrison, Ntozake Shange, and Al Young.

In early 1989, however, after I'd struggled to find copies to buy of Clarence's subsequent books, the truth came out. There's an oversized reference book published each year by Gale Research in Detroit called *Contemporary Authors Autobiography Series* in which current writers are given between ten thousand and twenty thousand words and acres of space for pictures to fulfill an invitation to tell the stories of their lives. In 1989, Clarence was one of those selected, and I began reading his chapter with great eagerness.

It was all there: his childhood in Chicago, his early interest in art, his work as a crane operator and aspiring writer and publisher. But then followed an immense gap, with absolutely nothing about his work with Jack O'Brien or any other of the critics who'd advocated his career, including myself. There was a passage about something Clarence told me years before: how when he was newly arrived in New York and struggling to make ends meet a letter had arrived from Norman Holmes Pearson, the eminent scholar of American literature at Yale. Tucked into the appreciative note was a $100 bill. Now Clarence retold that story at length; paternalistic as it was, it served as the sole reference to any white critics being interested in his work. The balance of the lengthy essay was devoted to his activities of the past few years, all of which involved the black community and how its writing was received abroad.

I felt crushed, and rather stupidly phoned Clarence in Boulder. He expressed surprise that none of his recent books had been sent, and blamed it on an inefficient publicist. He said he was sorry my part in his career hadn't been covered in the essay, but that there were "space limitations." That was all. I asked how was Pamela; he said fine, but didn't inquire after Julie. And that was that.

Still a cognizant-enough critic to know that innovative fiction was no longer fashionable, I nevertheless felt rejected and betrayed. Looking over the boxes and boxes of Clarence Major material still in my archives made me feel worse, and so in time I sent it off to a book dealer who said he could place the material where it belonged, in a library collection. And what a location the dealer found: a place that impressed me as not only a good home for the material but as one of the very best repositories for papers of leading authors.

But here came another astounding surprise, for after a few weeks the dealer was on the phone, telling me Clarence's agent had heard of the sale and was upset he wasn't getting a commission. This, we both agreed, was preposterous, since as the letters were addressed to me they were my physical property. But even worse was the fact that Clarence himself was furious, not wanting this material on show for anyone to see. It could not have been for any of the letters' contents, for all were strictly limited to professional matters about writing. And as owner of the words (if not of the paper), he could have restricted access as he wished. But for whatever reason, he didn't want them saved. On this he won out, and so the library people sent everything back to the dealer and the dealer offered to send it back to me.

I didn't want it, and so it is probably sitting now in some warehouse, isolated from the stream of literary history. Which matters less than the wounded feelings on both sides. But even those feelings aren't the end of things, for Clarence's fiction had taught me that reality exists in words—and that there is no end to language.

Today, Clarence as a person seems lost to me. Yet there are still words that can summon his presence where it is most important, in one's mind. I think of the passage in *Reflex and Bone Structure* where the narrator ponders his own lost love, Cora. She herself is gone, but returns in memory and can be kept there by the act of writing. It is, I think, the finest paragraph Clarence ever wrote:

> I am standing behind Cora. She is wearing a thin black nightgown. The backs of her legs are lovely. I love her. The word standing allows me to watch like this. The word nightgown is what she is wearing. The nightgown itself is in her drawer with her panties. The word Cora is wearing the word nightgown. I watch the sentence: the backs of her legs are lovely. (p. 74)

6

Others, and a Few Words After

In literary history, keeping ahead of the game isn't something critics continue for very long. Richard Kostelanetz has a theory about it: that no commentators stay actively involved with current fiction much beyond age forty. His basic explanation is that understanding and sympathizing with the new developments of a literary era can be sustained only so long as the critic is growing with it. Whether because of maturity or burn-out, the comforts of tenure and promotion or a simple lack of new ideas, scholars of the contemporary inevitably drift off to other interests as they settle into middle age.

Scanning my bookshelf on contemporary American fiction, I can see how Kostelanetz is right. After his groundbreaking study *Radical Innocence: The Contemporary American Novel*, Ihab Hassan stepped back to broaden his perspectives to include the interface of modernism and the postmodern in the works of Samuel Beckett and Henry Miller, then sped off into nether worlds of intellectualization and pure thought in such works as *Paracriticisms* and *The Right Promethean Fire*. He left the next group of innovators—Kurt Vonnegut, John Barth, John Hawkes—to Robert Scholes. Scholes continued with these writers a bit longer, from *The Fabulators* in 1967 to *Fabulation and Metafiction* in 1979, but afterwards departed for new fascinations with science fiction and the semiotics of reading. This same pattern persists with other students of what, when they started, was current fiction: Marcus Klein, Tony Tanner, Malcolm Bradbury, and so forth. In all cases their subsequent work is brilliant. But it isn't on contemporary fiction.

Looking over my own curriculum vita, it seems I stayed with current fiction only a little bit longer than did Bob Scholes, from *Literary Disruptions* in 1975 to *Structuring the Void*, published in 1992 but written mostly in 1988. By the late eighties I had regressed, some would say, into childhood interests, the things that had fascinated me at ages ten and eleven: baseball, airplanes, and jazz.

But despite everything Kostelanetz might say about professorial laziness and even dotage, there is no way a critic can regress and keep on being a critic. Writing about RAF and Luftwaffe narratives from World War II was something I could do only from having learned to appreciate the artistry of literary language in the fiction writers I'd been studying before. Likewise for baseball: what got me going on the game was that like innovative fiction it asks no suspension of disbelief but plays itself out before spectators who know what everyone's fabricated role must be. As for my book on Gerry Mulligan, it was subtitled as "An Aural Narrative in Jazz," the analysis making sense only as it comprehended the story being told by this master's musical development.

Life goes on, and I've kept in touch with plenty of writers my own age and younger. Michael Stephens, Susan Quist, Kenneth Gangemi, Gerald Rosen, Rob Swigart—a pretty varied sampling of styles. Rosen is actually a few years older, and I fancy him as the big brother I always wanted but never had. We met thanks to his counterargument to *Literary Disruptions,* that fiction could still care about people and their human concerns. I found that concern in his *Blues for a Dying Nation, The Carmen Miranda Memorial Flagpole, Dr. Ebenezer's Book and Liquor Store, Growing Up Bronx*—and it led me to consider a whole style of writing that was news to me but an important part of most other people's reading. I began looking over not just Dan Wakefield's journalism but his fiction, and together with the work of Thomas McGuane and Richard Yates could see there a reinvention of the novel of manners, something possible in the aftermath of not just innovative fiction, which revealed how pliably artificial such conventions could be, but of semiotics, the study of how signs function in our society. There was an entire generation of such writers from Yates to Rosen and to Swigart and McGuane—the latter two, my research revealed, having dated the same young woman in high school, a rivalry still potent enough to have them parody each other as characters in their fiction. From here I looked back over the fiction I'd missed during innovation's great heyday, an oddly male club that had almost totally overlooked what women writers were doing. Now my books would have chapters on Grace Paley, for example, an author whose commitment to politics and social causes did not prevent her from writing a style of fiction no less devoted to innovative ideals than anything else I'd been promoting. It struck me what a limited education I'd had, and how the curriculum had been so wonderfully expanded since those days at Marquette when the last word was Robert Penn Warren (where was Eudora Welty?) and at Wisconsin where the rage remained John Barth, John Hawkes, Thomas Pynchon, and other male writers.

Plus there were still innovators, some of them doing quite well. Stephen Dixon, whom I once rejected as a "slick realist," had become the most prolific serious short fictionist in American history, publishing upwards of four hundred stories (collected in such volumes as *14 Stories, Time to Go,* and *All Gone,* these three coincidentally with the Johns Hopkins University Press) and teaching me how even realism could be used opaquely and self-apparently; in any of his stories one can see the action being generated not simply by references to the outside world but by compositional elements present from the beginning, with the result that his narratives have the same perfect form as a master's painting or musical composer's perfectly structured work. Steve became a close friend. Another ally was found abroad: Peter Handke, in whose work language itself was both protagonist and narrative ground. Walter Abish's *How German Is It?* (1980) matched Handke's prose in brilliant effect, all of which comes from a loving attention to the semiotic surface of our lives, a surface where human invention is the motivating force. And so on, through a library of fiction that has kept my study bookshelves from being taken over completely by interests of the last several years: RAF memoirs, baseball, and jazz.

Spending time with these writers is still an important part of my work, surely something rehearsed in my imagination of scenes where Duyckinck visits Hawthorne and Melville in the Berkshires. There have been times like that at Steve Dixon's summer rental in Maine, and also lively walks amid the bustle of upper Broadway with Michael Stephens as we seek out the best Cuban restaurant. Plus encounters that in my mind have become the stuff of legend and no small influence on my own conduct. Such as the evening Julie and I spent in Boston with Richard Yates.

Yates's reputation for behavior was not the best, and we were warned he could lose his temper easily. Plus too much drinking was, at this time in 1982, still a problem. But the evening before Dan Wakefield had assured me that, with Julie along, Yates would be quite the gentleman. "Dick dotes on young women," Dan insisted, "he'll turn on the charm and be just fine."

Which he would have been and probably thought he was, had not some bad news from the doctor earlier that day taken him down to the Crossroads Bar and prompted a head start on our social evening. He wasn't discourteous, but all these worries made him vociferous and combative in expressing his literary opinions. For three hours we sat in this college tavern and listened to him rant and watched him pound the table as he railed against the failings of his age. Then he'd tire out, lean back, and be mellowly reminiscent for a time, speaking with great fondness of mutual acquaintances (Vonnegut, Loree Rackstraw). A few times he taught me some truly masterful lessons, such as how to transfer point of view from one character to another as they pass on the street (I dutifully used it in a passage in *Short Season* that worked well). But overall it was a devastating evening, for physically Yates was in such poor shape that we felt like we were sharing company with a person who except for the mightiness of his willpower and devotion to writing would surely be dead.

Afterwards, on our drive out to Concord where we were staying, Julie cried for him and for herself, having seen, as a vibrant young person in her mid-twenties, such a physically aged and wearied man. Later, reading his work, she saw what was to be admired in his spirit that produced such flawless books. But for now the reality of his presence was too much to bear.

For my part, I'd been just as deeply impressed—not by Yates's unintended conduct but by something he conveyed as a crucial message. It happened while Julie had excused herself, less for a restroom visit than to simply get away from the spectacle of Dick's presence. And what an awesome presence it was, bent over in his tallness from years of writer's slump aggravated by recurrent TB and a hacking smoker's cough. Everything about him was worn and gray, the sole brightness being in his mind, an intelligence that in the morning he'd address to writing but now was directing toward myself.

"Jerry," he said, almost croaking the invocation. "You're a fine young man, and you've got a wonderful young wife." He smiled, but it came across as a leer, which I think he realized as he shook the expression off and tried for something different. "Well," he continued, "you've got to listen!" To make it clear that listening had a physical dimension, he reached across the beery table and seized my forearm with a yellowed, boney hand. "You've got it fine now," he rasped, "but don't kid yourself—it doesn't always have to be like this!"

One lives to learn, and by learning lives that much better. From their books and from what moments of their lives they've been willing to share with me, I've benefited much from these writers. Some are gone, yet others are still with us, often when we least expect them. Midway through this book the person with whom it all started, Kurt Vonnegut, came through town—not for a lecture or other literary visit, but just to see his friends. Loree Rackstraw phoned to ask Julie and me over, and at her door we were welcomed by Kurt himself. "Come on out on my patio," he said, and ushered us through the kitchen and porch to Loree's back terrace which on previous trips had been one of his favorite spots: a typical small-town Iowa back yard where even now the gathering dusk was a bit deeper thanks to the presence of a huge, hundred-year-old cottonwood tree that promised shelter from New York and anything else Kurt wanted out of his mind. He'd been back in the Midwest to receive some literary awards, but getting a chance to relax in his homeland seemed his goal. And relaxed he was, so comfortable sitting out here in his open shirt, baggy pants, and loose suspenders that he could have been any other old guy on Walnut Street.

We couldn't make it a late evening, for he was flying back to the city tomorrow and wanted a good night's sleep at his hotel. But for two hours we sat with Loree and enjoyed the warm Iowa night.

Kurt's first words were about this book—for Bob Weide, the documentary producer who I'd fancied as the ideal reader for Kurt's work, had seen the initial chapter and told Kurt all about it. Kurt was glad I treated Bob so prominently, and agreed that such treatment was due; he respected Bob's work and liked him a great deal. Then Kurt asked if I was doing a chapter on Jerzy Kosinski, and I told how I'd started it almost at the hour Jerzy must have died. There was lots to say about this mutual friend Vonnegut still held in high regard. Had Jerzy been still bothered, years afterwards, by *The Village Voice*'s claims of plagiarism? Yes, it had killed him. Had it interfered with his writing? Yes, it had, but so did other, more general perceptions that were equally limiting: Jerzy had always felt emphasis on the Holocaust was misplaced, that more should be said about an entire culture's next generation of writers, artists, and musicians working to overcome a half-century gap in the history of such endeavors. He'd written an essay about this, Kurt said, that proved almost impossible to publish. Then there were items of small talk by which we tried to bring our old friend back to life in our minds. I told Kurt how my getting a job here at Northern Iowa might have been due to Jerzy's intervention; Kurt told me about how the day after Jerzy's death he'd chanced upon a present Kosinski had made for him long ago, an exquisitely modeled bird made from clarinet reeds and, of course, painted. Clarinet, Jerzy must have known, had been Kurt's instrument in high school band.

Then on to another casualty, Donald Barthelme. "You know," Kurt began, "he made the center of his life the neighborhood, among his friends downstairs and across the street, which strikes me as an utterly sensible way to live." He then added some comments on Don's writing, something I'd never heard him do with regard to work of another living writer, much less a friend. "Barthelme was a good example of how a magazine like *The New Yorker* confines one's growth," he advised. Then, speaking like the trained anthropologist Vonnegut was, he explained how and why. "Once you have such membership in a group, it's like you'll do anything not to be excluded. And the group itself of course has a very narrow definition of what fits." As an example, Kurt gave the case of S. J. Perelman, a writer "who could do almost anything with words and could have developed into one of the world's great writers." The problem was, he came to *The New Yorker* as a college humorist and was never allowed to write much beyond that style.

By now it was dark, and the soft but ever-present sounds of a college neighborhood could be heard. Across the alley I thought I heard a student musician warming up on trumpet, noodling through a few low scales. "Did you hear that?" I asked, just as the louder sound of the university's campanile began to chime. "Those are bells, Jerry," Loree said, but I insisted that there'd been a trumpet. Now the chimes were louder, ringing out an unmistakable tune, and Kurt spoke up. "I'm not going to read your book on Gerry Mulligan!" he scoffed, and we all collapsed into laughter. Minutes later we were all still chortling, and even the now audible trumpeter's ascent into the upper register couldn't spoil the fun.

Listen: Gerry Mulligan/An Aural Narrative in Jazz was one of my new books I'd given Kurt that night, together with *Donald*

Barthelme: An Exhibition. The former was an example of what had been taking me away from Kurt's generation of fiction, while the latter was an example of what had been drawing me back. Now I realized how Kurt was with me, not just physically but as part of my fabric of values and beliefs—and also part of our joy in a common laugh pealing out through this calm Midwestern night. He asked if there was anything else forthcoming, and I mentioned *Writing Baseball* and *Structuring the Void,* two more works of litcrit. "I can't believe how much you write," he laughed, and I made some joke in return.

As always, though, Kurt would have the last laugh and the final word. As ten o'clock came we gathered up our empty glasses and what was left of the peanuts and crackers to carry inside. Then, in the kitchen, we shook hands and said goodbye. "This is remarkable," Kurt said, "we're seeing each other just about every eighteen months!" Though he hadn't lived in the Midwest for nearly half a century, it occurred to us, he still wasn't that far away after all. And he seemed so happy to be here that we trusted he'd be back soon.

All this said, Julie and I turned to leave. But as we headed out the door, Kurt had some words of farewell. "Listen," he urged, "try to get some work done!" As we headed down the walk to our car, Julie and I could hear him laughing at his own joke still.

Bibliography

Abish, Walter. *How German Is It?* New York: New Directions, 1980.

Aldridge, John W. *The American Novel and the Way We Live Now.* New York: Oxford University Press, 1983.

Alexander, Marguerite. *Flights from Realism: Themes and Strategies in Post-modernist British and American Fiction.* London: Edward Arnold, 1990.

Allen, Mary. *The Necessary Blankness: Women in Major American Fiction of the Sixties.* Urbana: University of Illinois Press, 1976.

Allen, William Rodney. *Understanding Kurt Vonnegut.* Columbia: University of South Carolina Press, 1991.

Baker, Houston A., Jr. *Blues, Ideology, and Afro-American Literature: A Vernacular Theory.* Chicago: University of Chicago Press, 1984.

———. *The Journey Back: Issues in Black Literature and Criticism.* Chicago: University of Chicago Press, 1980.

Barthelme, Donald. *Amateurs.* New York: Farrar, Straus and Giroux, 1976.

———. *City Life.* New York: Farrar, Straus and Giroux, 1970.

———. *Come Back, Dr. Caligari.* Boston: Little, Brown and Co., 1964.

———. *The Dead Father.* New York: Farrar, Straus and Giroux, 1975.

———. *The Emerald.* Los Angeles: Sylvester and Orphanos, 1980.

———. *Forty Stories.* New York: Putnam's, 1987.

———. *Great Days.* New York: Farrar, Straus and Giroux, 1979.

———. *Guilty Pleasures.* New York: Farrar, Straus and Giroux, 1974.

———. *Here in the Village.* Northridge, Calif.: Lord John Press, 1978.

———. *The King.* New York: Harper and Row, 1990.

———. *Overnight to Many Distant Cities.* New York: Putnam's, 1983.

———. *Paradise.* New York: Putnam's, 1986.

——. *Presents*. Dallas: Pressworks, 1980.

——. *Sadness*. New York: Farrar, Straus and Giroux, 1972.

——. *Sixty Stories*. New York: Putnam's, 1981.

——. *The Slightly Irregular Fire Engine*. New York: Farrar, Straus and Giroux, 1971 (for children).

——. *Snow White*. New York: Atheneum, 1967.

——. *Unspeakable Practices, Unnatural Acts*. New York: Farrar, Straus and Giroux, 1968.

Barthelme, Donald and Seymour Chwast. *Sam's Bar*. New York: Doubleday, 1987.

Bellamy, Joe David, ed. *The New Fiction: Interviews with Innovative American Writers*. Urbana: University of Illinois Press, 1974.

Boyers, Robert. "The Avant-Garde," in *The Columbia History of the American Novel*, ed. Emory Elliott, pp. 726–51. New York: Columbia University Press, 1991.

Bradbury, Malcolm and Sigmund Ro, eds. *Contemporary American Fiction*. London: Edward Arnold, 1987.

Britton, Burt. *Self-Portrait: Book People Picture Themselves*. New York: Random House, 1976.

Broer, Lawrence. *Sanity Plea: Schizophrenia in the Novels of Kurt Vonnegut*. Ann Arbor: UMI Research Press, 1989.

Bruss, Paul. *Victims: Textual Strategies in Recent American Fiction*. Lewisburg, Pa.: Bucknell University Press, 1981.

Cahill, Daniel J., and Jerome Klinkowitz. "The Great Kosinski Press War: A Bibliography," *Missouri Review* 6, no. 3 (summer 1983): 171–75.

Caramello, Charles. *Silverless Mirrors: Book, Self, and Postmodern American Fiction*. Tallahassee: Florida State University Press, 1983.

Chénetier, Marc. *Au-delà du soupçon: La nouvelle fiction américaine de 1960 à nos jours*. Paris: Seuil, 1989.

Couturier, Maurice, ed. *Representation and Performance in Postmodern Fiction*. Montpellier: Presses de l'Imprimerie de Recherche—Université Paul Valéry, 1983.

Couturier, Maurice and Régis Durand. *Donald Barthelme*. London: Methuen, 1982.

Dewey, Joseph. *In a Dark Time: The Apocalyptic Temper in the American Novel of the Nuclear Age*. West Lafayette, Ind.: Purdue University Press, 1990.

D'haen, Theo and Hans Bertens, eds. *History and Post-war Writing*. Amsterdam: Rodopi, 1990.

Dickstein, Morris. *Gates of Eden: American Culture in the Sixties*. New York: Basic Books, 1977.

Everman, Welch. *Jerzy Kosinski: The Literature of Violation*. San Bernardino, Calif.: R. Reginald/Borgo Press, 1991.

————. *Who Says This? The Authority of the Author, the Discourse, and the Reader*. Carbondale: Southern Illinois University Press, 1988.

Federman, Raymond. *Amer Eldorado*. Paris: Stock, 1974.

————. *Double or Nothing*. Chicago: Swallow, 1971.

————. *Journey to Chaos: Samuel Beckett's Early Fiction*. Berkeley: University of California Press, 1965.

————. *Play Texts/Spieltexte*. Berlin: Literarisches Colloquium Berlin/Berliner Künstlerprogramm des DAAD, 1990.

————. *Smiles on Washington Square*. New York: Thunder's Mouth Press, 1985.

————. *Take It Or Leave It*. New York: Fiction Collective, 1976.

————. *To Whom It May Concern*. Boulder, Colo.: Fiction Collective Two, 1990.

————. *The Twofold Vibration*. Bloomington: Indiana University Press, 1982.

————. *The Voice in the Closet*. Madison, Wis.: Coda Press, 1979.

————, ed. *Cinq Nouvelles Nouvelles: Beckett, Vian, Pinget, Le Clézio*. New York: Appleton-Century-Crofts, 1970.

————. *Surfiction: Fiction Now and Tomorrow*. Chicago: Swallow Press, 1975.

Federman, Raymond and John Fletcher, eds. *Samuel Beckett: His Works & His Critics*. Berkeley: University of California Press, 1970.

Federman, Raymond and Lawrence Graver, eds. *Samuel Beckett: The Critical Heritage*. London: Routledge and Kegan Paul, 1979.

Fokkema, Douwe and Hans Bertens, eds. *Approaching Postmodernism*. Amsterdam: John Benjamins, 1986.

Friedman, Ellen and Miriam Fuchs. *Breaking the Sequence: Women's Experimental Fiction*. Princeton: Princeton University Press, 1989.

Gallop, Jane. *Around 1981: Academic Feminist Literary Theory*. London: Routledge, 1992.

Gardner, John. *On Moral Fiction*. New York: Basic Books, 1978.

Gates, Henry Louis, Jr. *Black Literature and Literary Theory*. London: Methuen, 1984.

———. "Ishmael Reed," in *African American Writers*, ed. Valerie Smith, pp. 361–77. New York: Scribners, 1991.

Giannone, Richard. *Vonnegut: A Preface to His Novels*. Port Washington, N.Y.: Kennikat, 1977.

Goldsmith, David H. *Kurt Vonnegut: Fantasist of Fire and Ice*. Bowling Green, Ohio: Bowling Green State University Popular Press, 1972.

Gorak, Jan. *God and the Artist: American Novelists in a Post-Realist Age*. Urbana: University of Illinois Press, 1987.

Gordon, Lois. *Donald Barthelme*. Boston: Twayne, 1981.

Graff, Gerald. *Literature against Itself*. Chicago: University of Chicago Press, 1979.

Handke, Peter. *The Weight of the World*. New York: Farrar, Straus and Giroux, 1984. Translated by Ralph Mannheim from *Das Gewicht der Welt*. Salzburg: Residenz Verlag, 1977.

Harris, Charles B. *Contemporary American Novelists of the Absurd*. New Haven: College and University Press, 1971.

———. *Passionate Virtuosity: The Fiction of John Barth*. Urbana: University of Illinois Press, 1983.

Hassan, Ihab. *Paracriticisms: Seven Speculations of the Times*. Urbana: University of Illinois Press, 1975.

———. *The Postmodern Turn: Essays in Postmodern Theory and Culture*. Columbus: Ohio State University Press, 1987.

———. *Radical Innocence: The Contemporary American Novel*. Princeton: Princeton University Press, 1961.

———. *Selves at Risk: Patterns of Quest in Contemporary American Letters*. Madison: University of Wisconsin Press, 1990.

Hendin, Josephine. *Vulnerable People: A View of American Fiction Since 1945.* New York: Oxford University Press, 1978.

Hicks, Jack. *In the Singer's Temple: Prose Fictions of Barthelme, Gaines, Brautigan, Piercy, Kesey, and Kosinski.* Chapel Hill: University of North Carolina Press, 1981.

Hulley, Kathleen, ed. *Grace Paley.* Montpellier: Presses de l'Imprimerie de Recherche—Université Paul Valéry, 1982.

Hume, Kathryn. *Fantasy and Mimesis: Responses to Reality in Western Literature.* London: Methuen, 1984.

Hutcheon, Linda. *Narcissistic Narrative: The Metafictional Paradox.* Waterloo, Ontario: Wilfrid Laurier University Press, 1980.

———. *A Poetics of Postmodernism.* London: Routledge, 1988.

———. *The Politics of Postmodernism.* London: Routledge, 1989.

Kennard, Jean E. *Number and Nightmare: Forms of Fantasy in Contemporary Literature.* Hamden, Conn.: Archon Books/Shoe String Press, 1975.

Klinkowitz, Jerome. *The American 1960s.* Ames: Iowa State University Press, 1980.

———. *Basepaths.* Baltimore: Johns Hopkins University Press, 1995.

———. *Donald Barthelme: An Exhibition.* Durham, N.C.: Duke University Press, 1991.

———. *Here at Ogallala State U.* Madison, Wis.: White Hawk Press, 1997.

———. *Kurt Vonnegut.* London: Methuen, 1982.

———. *Listen: Gerry Mulligan/An Aural Narrative in Jazz.* New York: Schirmer Books/Macmillan Publishing, 1991.

———. *Literary Disruptions: The Making of a Post-Contemporary American Fiction.* Urbana: University of Illinois Press, 1975.

———. *Literary Subversions: New American Fiction and the Practice of Criticism.* Carbondale: Southern Illinois University Press, 1985.

———. *The New American Novel of Manners: The Fiction of Richard Yates, Dan Wakefield, and Thomas McGuane.* Athens: University of Georgia Press, 1986.

———. *The Practice of Fiction in America: Writers from Hawthorne to the Present.* Ames: Iowa State University Press, 1980.

———. *Rosenberg/Barthes/Hassan: The Postmodern Habit of Thought.* Athens: University of Georgia Press, 1988.

———. *The Self-Apparent Word: Fiction as Language/Language as Fiction.* Carbondale: Southern Illinois University Press, 1984.

———. *Short Season and Other Stories.* Baltimore: Johns Hopkins University Press, 1988.

———. *Slaughterhouse-Five: Reinventing the Novel and the World.* Boston: Twayne, 1990.

———. *Structuring the Void: The Struggle for Subject in Contemporary American Fiction.* Durham, N.C.: Duke University Press, 1992.

———. *Their Finest Hours: Narratives of the RAF and Luftwaffe in World War II.* Ames: Iowa State University Press, 1989.

———. *Yanks Over Europe.* Lexington: University Press of Kentucky, 1996.

Klinkowitz, Jerome and Roy R. Behrens. *The Life of Fiction.* Urbana: University of Illinois Press, 1977.

Klinkowitz, Jerome and James Knowlton. *Peter Handke and the Postmodern Transformation.* Columbia: University of Missouri Press, 1983.

Klinkowitz, Jerome, Ed. *The Diaries of Willard Motley.* Ames: Iowa State University Press, 1979.

———. *Nathaniel Hawthorne.* Cáceres, Spain: Ediciones Universidad de Extramadura, 1984.

———. *Writing Baseball.* Urbana: University of Illinois Press, 1991.

Klinkowitz, Jerome and Donald L. Lawler, eds. *Vonnegut in America.* New York: Delacorte Press/Seymour Lawrence, 1977.

Klinkowitz, Jerome, Asa B. Pieratt, Jr., and Robert Murray Davis, eds. *Donald Barthelme: A Comprehensive Bibliography.* Hamden, Conn.: Archon Books/Shoe String Press, 1977.

Klinkowitz, Jerome, Asa B. Pieratt, Jr., and Julie Huffman-klinkowitz, eds. *Kurt Vonnegut: A Comprehensive Bibliography.* Hamden, Conn.: Archon Books/Shoe String Press, 1987.

Klinkowitz, Jerome and John Somer, eds. *Innovative Fiction.* New York: Dell, 1972.

———. *The Vonnegut Statement.* New York: Delacorte Press/Seymour Lawrence, 1973.

————. *Writing Under Fire: Stories of the Vietnam War.* New York: Dell, 1978.

Kosinski, Jerzy. *The Art of the Self: Essays à propos Steps.* New York: Scientia-Factum, 1968.

————. *Being There.* New York: Harcourt Brace Jovanovich, 1971.

————. *Blind Date.* Boston: Houghton Mifflin, 1977.

————. *Cockpit.* Boston: Houghton Mifflin, 1975.

————. *The Devil Tree.* New York: Harcourt Brace Jovanovich, 1973.

————. *The Future Is Ours, Comrade.* Garden City, N.Y.: Doubleday, 1960 (as "Joseph Novak").

————. *The Hermit of 69th Street.* New York: Henry Holt/Seaver Books, 1988.

————. "Hosanna to What?", in *Passing By*, pp. 165–69. New York: Random House, 1992, first published as "The Second Holocaust," Boston *Globe*, November 4, 1990, *Focus* section, pp. A1, A19.

————. *Notes of the Author on The Painted Bird.* New York: Scientia-Factum, 1965.

————. *No Third Path.* Garden City, N.Y.: Doubleday, 1962 (as "Joseph Novak").

————. *Passion Play.* New York: St. Martin's Press, 1979.

————. *Pinball.* New York: Bantam Books, 1982.

————. *Steps.* New York: Random House, 1968.

————, ed. *Socjologia Ameriykánska.* New York: Polski Instytut Naukowy w Amercye, 1962.

Kostelanetz, Richard. *American Writing Today.* Troy, N.Y.: Whitston, 1991.

————. *The Old Fictions and the New.* Jefferson, N.C.: McFarland, 1987.

Kuehl, John. *Alternative Worlds: A Study of Antirealistic American Fiction.* New York: New York University Press, 1989.

Kunen. James S. *"How Can You Defend Those People?": The Making of a Trial Lawyer.* New York: Random House, 1983.

————. *Standard Operating Procedure: Notes of a Draft-Age American.* New York: Avon, 1971.

————. *The Strawberry Statement: Notes of a College Revolutionary.* New York: Random House, 1969.

Kutnik, Jerzy. *The Novel as Performance: The Fiction of Ronald Sukenick and Raymond Federman.* Carbondale: Southern Illinois University Press, 1986.

Lavers, Norman. *Jerzy Kosinski.* Boston: Twayne, 1982.

LeClair. Tom. *The Art of Excess: Mastery in Contemporary American Fiction.* Urbana: University of Illinois Press, 1989.

LeClair, Tom and Larry McCaffery, eds. *Anything Can Happen: Interviews with Contemporary American Novelists.* Urbana: University of Illinois Press, 1983.

Lilly, Paul R., Jr. *Words in Search of Victims: The Achievement of Jerzy Kosinski.* Kent, Ohio: Kent State University Press, 1988.

Lish, Gordon. *All Our Secrets Are the Same.* New York: Norton, 1976.

Lupack, Barbara Tepa. *Plays of Passion, Games of Chance: Jerzy Kosinski and his Fiction.* Bristol, Ind.: Wyndham Hall Press, 1988.

Major, Clarence. *All-Night Visitors.* New York: Olympia Press, 1969.

————. *The Dark and Feeling: Black American Writers and Their Work.* New York: The Third Press/Joseph Okpaku, 1974.

————. *Dictionary of Afro-American Slang.* New York: International Publishers, 1970.

————. *Emergency Exit.* New York: Fiction Collective, 1979.

————. *Fun and Games: Short Fictions.* Duluth, Minn.: Holy Cow! Press, 1990.

————. *My Amputations.* New York: Fiction Collective, 1986.

————. *No.* New York: Emerson Hall, 1973.

————. *Painted Turtle: Woman with Guitar.* Los Angeles: Sun and Moon, 1988.

————. *Reflex and Bone Structure.* New York: Fiction Collective, 1975.

————. *Such Was the Season.* San Francisco: Mercury House, 1987.

————, ed. *The New Black Poetry.* New York: International Publishers, 1969.

Maltby, Paul. *Dissident Postmodernism: Barthelme, Coover, Pynchon.* Philadelphia: University of Pennsylvania Press, 1991.

Marshall, Brenda K. *Teaching the Postmodern: Fiction and Theory*. London: Routledge, 1992.

Martin, Stephen-Paul. *Open Form and the Feminine Imagination: The Politics of Reading in Twentieth-Century Innovative Writing*. Washington, D.C.: Maisonneuve Press, 1988.

Mayo, Clark. *Kurt Vonnegut: The Gospel From Outer Space*. San Bernardino: R. Reginald/Borgo Press, 1977.

McCaffery, Larry. *The Metafictional Muse: The Works of Robert Coover, Donald Barthelme, and William H. Gass*. Pittsburgh: University of Pittsburgh Press, 1982.

————. *Storming the Reality Studio: A Casebook of Cyberpunk and Postmodern Fiction*. Durham, N.C.: Duke University Press, 1991.

McCaffery, Larry and Sinda Gregory. *Alive and Writing: Interviews with American Authors of the 1980s*. Urbana: University of Illinois Press, 1987.

McCaffery, Larry, ed. *Postmodern Fiction*. Westport, Conn.: Greenwood Press, 1986.

McHale, Brian. *Postmodern Fiction*. London: Methuen, 1987.

McPheron, William. *Gilbert Sorrentino: A Descriptive Bibliography*. Elmwood Park, Ill.: Dalkey Archive Press, 1991.

Mellard, James M. *The Exploded Form: The Modernist Novel in America*. Urbana: University of Illinois Press, 1980.

Merrill, Robert, ed. *Critical Essays on Kurt Vonnegut*. Boston: G. K. Hall, 1990.

Molesworth, Charles. *Donald Barthelme's Fiction: The Ironist Saved from Drowning*. Columbia: University of Missouri Press, 1982.

Monod, Jacques. *Chance and Necessity*. New York: Knopf, 1971.

Mustazza, Leonard. *Forever Pursuing Genesis: The Myth of Eden in the Novels of Kurt Vonnegut*. Lewisburg, Penn.: Bucknell University Press, 1990.

Newman, Charles. *The Post-modern Aura: The Act of Fiction in an Age of Inflation*. Evanston, Ill.: Northwestern University Press, 1985.

O'Brien, John. *Interviews with Black Writers*. New York: Liveright, 1973.

O'Donnell, Patrick. *Passionate Doubts: Designs of Interpretation in Contemporary American Fiction*. Iowa City: University of Iowa Press, 1986.

Olderman, Raymond M. *Beyond the Waste Land: The American Novel in the Nineteen-Sixties*. New Haven: Yale University Press, 1972.

Olsen, Lance. *Circus of the Mind in Motion: Postmodernism and the Comic Vision*. Detroit: Wayne State University Press, 1990.

Olster, Stacey. *Reminiscence and Re-Creation in Contemporary American Fiction*. New York: Cambridge University Press, 1989.

Paley, Grace. *Enormous Changes at the Last Minute*. New York: Farrar, Straus and Giroux, 1974.

———. *Later the Same Day*. New York: Farrar, Straus and Giroux, 1985.

———. *The Little Disturbances of Man*. Garden City, N.Y.: Doubleday, 1959.

———. *Long Walks and Intimate Talks*. New York: The Feminist Press, 1991.

Patteson, Richard F., ed. *Critical Essays on Donald Barthelme*. New York: G. K. Hall, 1992.

Pearce, Richard. *The Novel in Motion: An Approach to Modern Fiction*. Columbus: Ohio State University Press, 1983.

Porush, David. *The Soft Machine: Cybernetic Fiction*. London: Methuen, 1985.

Pütz, Manfred. *The Story of Identity: American Fiction of the Sixties*. Stuttgart: Metzler, 1979.

Quist, Susan. *Indecent Exposure*. New York: Walker, 1974.

Rackstraw, Loree. "The Vonnegut Cosmos." *North American Review* 267, iv (December 1982): 63–67.

———. "Vonnegut the Diviner, and Other Auguries." *North American Review* 264, iv (December 1979): 74–76.

Rackstraw, Loree and Jerome Klinkowitz. "The American 1970s: Recent Intellectual Trends." *Revue Française d'Etudes Américaines* (Sorbonne Nouvelle), no. 8 (October 1979): 243–54.

Reed, Peter J. *Kurt Vonnegut, Jr*. New York: Warner, 1972.

Renner, Rolf Günter. *Die Postmoderne Konstellation: Theorie, Text und Kunst im Ausgang der Moderne*. Freiburg: Rombach, 1988.

Roe, Barbara L. *Donald Barthelme: A Study of the Short Fiction*. New York: Twayne, 1992.

Rosen, Gerald. *Blues for a Dying Nation*. New York: Dial, 1972.

——. *The Carmen Miranda Memorial Flagpole*. San Rafael, Calif.: Presidio, 1977.

——. *Dr. Ebenezer's Book and Liquor Store*. New York: St. Martin's Press, 1980.

——. *Growing Up Bronx*. Berkeley: North Atlantic Books, 1984.

——. "Post-Modernism." *Exquisite Corpse* 7, nos. 1–5 (January–May 1989): 1.

——. *Zen in the Art of J. D. Salinger*. Berkeley: Creative Arts, 1977.

Russell, Charles. *Poets, Prophets, and Revolutionaries: The Literary Avant-garde from Rimbaud through Postmodernism*. New York: Oxford University Press, 1985.

Saltzman, Arthur M. *Designs of Darkness in Contemporary American Fiction*. Philadelphia: University of Pennsylvania Press, 1990.

Schatt, Stanley. *Kurt Vonnegut, Jr.* Boston: Twayne, 1976.

Scholes, Robert. *Fabulation and Metafiction*. Urbana: University of Illinois Press, 1979.

——. *The Fabulators*. New York: Oxford University Press, 1967.

Schulz, Marx. *Black Humor Fiction of the Sixties*. Athens: Ohio University Press, 1973.

——. *The Muses of John Barth*. Baltimore: Johns Hopkins University Press, 1990.

Sherwin, Byron L. *Jerzy Kosinski: Literary Alarm Clock*. Chicago: Cabala Press, 1981.

Showalter, Elaine. *Sister's Choice: Tradition and Change in American Women's Writing*. Oxford: Clarendon, 1991.

Siegle, Robert. *Suburban Ambush: Downtown Writing and the Fiction of Insurgency*. Baltimore: Johns Hopkins University Press, 1989.

Sorrentino, Gilbert. *Aberration of Starlight*. New York: Random House, 1980.

————. *Blue Pastoral*. San Francisco: North Point, 1983.

————. *Crystal Vision*. San Francisco: North Point, 1981.

————. *The Darkness Surrounds Us*. Highlands, N.C.: Jonathan Williams, 1960.

————. *Flawless Play Restored*. Los Angeles: Black Sparrow, 1974.

————. *Imaginative Qualities of Actual Things*. New York: Pantheon, 1971.

————. *Misterioso*. Elmwood Park, Ill.: Dalkey Archive Press, 1989.

————. *Mulligan Stew*. New York: Grove Press, 1979.

————. *Odd Number*. San Francisco: North Point, 1985.

————. *Rose Theatre*. Elmwood Park, Ill.: Dalkey Archive Press, 1987.

————. *The Sky Changes*. New York: Hill and Wang, 1966.

————. *Something Said*. San Francisco: North Point, 1984.

————. *Splendide-Hôtel*. New York: New Directions, 1973.

————. *Steelwork*. New York: Pantheon, 1970.

————. *Under the Shadow*. Elmwood Park, Ill.: Dalkey Archive Press, 1991.

Stengel, Wayne B. *The Shape of Art in the Short Stories of Donald Barthelme*. Baton Rouge: Louisiana State University Press, 1985.

Stephens, Michael. *The Dramaturgy of Style*. Carbondale: Southern Illinois University Press, 1986.

————. *Jigs and Reels*. Brooklyn: Hanging Loose Press, 1992.

————. *Lost in Seoul*. New York: Random House, 1990.

————. *Season at Coole*. New York: Dutton, 1972.

————. "Why I Hate Baseball," in *Writing Baseball*, ed. Jerry Klinkowitz, pp. 70–77. Urbana: University of Illinois Press, 1991.

Stevick, Philip. *Alternative Pleasures: Postrealist Fiction and the Tradition*. Urbana: University of Illinois Press, 1981.

Sukenick, Ronald. *Blown Away*. Los Angeles: Sun and Moon Press, 1986.

————. *The Death of the Novel and Other Stories*. New York: Dial, 1969.

————. *Down and In: Life in the Underground*. New York: William Morrow, 1987.

——. *The Endless Short Story*. New York: Fiction Collective, 1986.

——. *In Form: Digressions on the Act of Fiction*. Carbondale: Southern Illinois University Press, 1985.

——. *Long Talking Bad Conditions Blues*. New York: Fiction Collective, 1979.

——. *98.6*. New York: Fiction Collective, 1975.

——. *Out*. Chicago: Swallow Press, 1973.

——. *Up*. New York: Dial, 1968.

——. *Wallace Stevens: Musing the Obscure*. New York: New York University Press, 1967.

Tanner, Tony. *City of Words: American Fiction 1950–1970*. New York: Harper and Row, 1971.

Thiher, Allen. *Words in Reflection: Modern Language Theory and Postmodern Fiction*. Chicago: University of Chicago Press, 1984.

Tobin, Patricia. *John Barth and the Anxiety of Continuance*. Philadelphia: University of Pennsylvania Press, 1992.

Trachtenberg, Stanley. *Understanding Donald Barthelme*. Columbia: University of South Carolina Press, 1990.

Varsava, Jerry A. *Contingent Meanings: Postmodern Fiction, Mimesis, and the Reader*. Tallahassee: Florida State University Press, 1990.

Vonnegut, Kurt. *Between Time and Timbuktu*. New York: Delacorte Press/Seymour Lawrence, 1972.

——. *Bluebeard*. New York: Delacorte Press, 1987.

——. *Breakfast of Champions*. New York: Delacorte Press/Seymour Lawrence, 1973.

——. *Cat's Cradle*. New York: Holt, Rinehart and Winston, 1963.

——. *Canary in a Cat House*. Greenwich, Conn.: Fawcett, 1961.

——. *Deadeye Dick*. New York: Delacorte Press/Seymour Lawrence, 1982.

——. *Fates Worse than Death: An Autobiographical Collage of the 1980s*. New York: Putnam's, 1991.

——. *Galápagos*. New York: Delacorte Press/Seymour Lawrence, 1985.

———. *God Bless You, Mr. Rosewater*. New York: Holt, Rinehart and Winston, 1965.

———. *Happy Birthday, Wanda June*. New York: Delacorte Press/Seymour Lawrence, 1971.

———. *Hocus Pocus*. New York: Putnam's, 1990.

———. *Jailbird*. New York: Delacorte Press/Seymour Lawrence, 1979.

———. *Mother Night*. Greenwich, Conn.: Fawcett, 1962.

———. *Palm Sunday: An Autobiographical Collage*. New York: Delacorte Press, 1981.

———. *Player Piano*. New York: Scribners, 1952.

———. *The Sirens of Titan*. New York: Dell, 1959.

———. *Slapstick*. New York: Delacorte Press/Seymour Lawrence, 1976.

———. *Slaughterhouse-Five*. New York: Delacorte Press/Seymour Lawrence, 1969.

———. *Wampeters, Foma, and Granfalloons: Opinions*. New York: Delacorte Press/Seymour Lawrence, 1974.

———. *Welcome to the Monkey House*. New York: Delacorte Press/Seymour Lawrence, 1968.

Vonnegut, Kurt and Ivan Chermayeff. *Sun Moon Star*. New York: Harper and Row, 1980 (for children).

Waugh, Patricia. *Feminine Fictions: Revisiting the Postmodern*. London: Routledge, 1989.

———. *Metafiction: The Theory and Practice of Self-Conscious Fiction*. London: Methuen, 1984.

Werner, Craig Hansen. *Paradoxical Resolutions: American Fiction since James Joyce*. Urbana: University of Illinois Press, 1982.

Wilde, Alan. *Horizons of Assent: Modernism, Postmodernism, and the Ironic Imagination*. Baltimore: Johns Hopkins University Press, 1981.

———. *Middle Grounds: Studies in Contemporary American Fiction*. Philadelphia: University of Pennsylvania Press, 1987.

Yates, Richard. *Cold Spring Harbor*. New York: Delacorte Press/Seymour Lawrence, 1986.

———. *Disturbing the Peace.* New York: Delacorte Press/Seymour Lawrence, 1975.

———. *The Easter Parade.* New York: Delacorte Press/Seymour Lawrence, 1976.

———. *Eleven Kinds of Loneliness.* Boston: Atlantic Monthly Press/Seymour Lawrence, 1976.

———. *A Good School.* New York: Delacorte Press/Seymour Lawrence, 1978.

———. *Liars in Love.* New York: Delacorte Press/Seymour Lawrence, 1981.

———. *Revolutionary Road.* Boston: Atlantic Monthly Press/Little, Brown and Co., 1961.

———. *A Special Providence.* New York: Knopf, 1969.

———. *Young Hearts Crying.* New York: Delacorte Press/Seymour Lawrence, 1984.

Ziegler, Heide, ed. *Facing Texts: Encounters between Contemporary Writers.* Durham, N.C.: Duke University Press, 1988.

Ziegler, Heide and Christopher Bigsby. *The Radical Imagination and the Liberal Tradition: Interviews with Novelists.* London: Junction Books, 1982.

Index

ADO-5904

PS
3561
L515
Z469
1998

9/10/98
App